SKILLED SUCCESS

OTHER WORK BY BOGDAN JUNCEWICZ

ACCELERATED ACHIEVEMENT

6 DAY PUBLISH

SKILLED SUCCESS

LEARN FASTER, TRAIN LIKE THE BEST & BECOME EXTRAORDINARY AT ANYTHING

BOGDAN JUNCEWICZ

www.BogdanJuncewicz.com
ISBN-10: 1986202062
ISBN-13: 978-1986202060

CONTENTS

INTRODUCTION:

1 | UNDERSTANDING:
DEMYSTIFYING LEARNING

2 | FOUNDATIONS:
THE PATH TO GREATNESS

3 | ACCELERATION:
TRAIN LIKE THE BEST

3. Immersion
How the power of immersion (sustained focus over a longer period of time) can be applied to accelerate skill development.

4. Train Hard To Ease Execution
Why you should train with more difficulty than it may seem logical to do so - how Brazil creates so many football stars - how pressure affects results - easing execution.

5. Rest & Recovery
How the world's highest achievers rest (& recover) to ensure sustained progress.

5 hurdles - killers - of learning speed, as well as how you can remove each one for faster learning.

1. Low Teachability Level
Those who lack a willingness to learn will not learn, no matter how great the conditions may be - boosting teachability.

2. A 'Fixed Mindset'
We explore Carol Dweck's research & talk about how a 'fixed mindset' kills learning.

3. Slow Feedback Speed
Why slow feedback speed slows down learning speed & simple tweaks to make.

4. Distraction
In today's distracted world, how does this affect learning - keys for greater focus.

5. Lack Of Clear Strategy
How to remove this & be more intentional.

4 | INTEGRATION:
BECOME EXTRAORDINARY

INTRODUCTION

THE GREATEST POWER: THE SIMPLE SECRET BEHIND THE WORLD'S HIGHEST ACHIEVERS

"Success is a science; if you have the conditions, you get the result"

- OSCAR WILDE

The world's highest achieving people all tap into a specific source of power. And it's this power that enables them to experience success beyond most people's wildest dreams.

In society, the highest achievers - the wealthiest, smartest, healthiest, most influential - all tap into a form of mental & physical intelligence that few ever truly tap into.

And it's what drives their ambition, their confidence & their extraordinary levels of achievement.

This simple secret correlates to higher levels of influence, wealth, fame, power, abundance & overall success.

This book is about this simple secret.

Throughout history, it's those who have tapped into this great power who have received back the greatest results. People like *Gandhi, Nikola Tesla, Leonardo da Vinci,*

Michael Jordan, Pelé, Sócrates, J.D. Rockefeller, Van Gogh, Julius Caesar, Mother Teresa, just to name a few.

We must not be confused though; this simple secret isn't complicated, it's not some big mystery, and it's definitely not some big conspiracy theory.

Identifying it is actually pretty damn easy. What's harder though - much harder - is actually tapping into it. And that, again, is where this book comes in.

This secret has little-to-nothing to do with IQ, DNA or how genetically superior you or I may believe we are.

And it's something that anyone - regardless of age, race, gender, occupation or upbringing - can tap into.

This simple secret is *the power of skill.*

Skill; it's the single biggest reason why athletes win gold medals (or not), why wars are won (or lost), why world records are broken, why social change occurs and why some people can achieve things, others only dream about.

Skill is the reason some can achieve extreme wealth, while others just live paycheck to paycheck. It's why certain people can reach super-fame and have millions of raving fans hanging on their every word, while others struggle to get a room of a 5 people to listen to them.

Skill is what we admire most, what people envy most, and what inspires us most. It's what drives new innovations, revolutions and moments of human inspiration.

| Skill is the biggest differentiator between success or failure at anything

Everyone wants more from life. Yet, few really understand that achievement is a process. To get any result, we must take the right steps to get there. And that process of achievement starts with skill.

The world's highest achievers are - not so coincidentally - also, the world's most knowledgeable & skilled people.

It's because success requires that we develop the right skills. And no amount of luck, good intention or positive thinking can replace the skill it takes to achieve the things you want to achieve in your life. It all starts with skill.

In the great words of H. Jackson Brown, Jr,

"When a man with money meets a man with experience, the man with experience ends up with the money and the man with the money ends up with experience."

People don't rise to the occasion & suddenly become skilled as soon as fame, opportunity or success comes along. It doesn't work that way. It's a journey. It's a process.

Too many people chase financial success, fame, influence, power & abundance without realizing that skill comes first.

Behind every Olympic Gold Medal, is an athlete (or team of athletes) with massive skill. And behind that skill, are years of tireless, day-in, day-out, training.

Behind every successful IPO is a company of massively skilled individuals, lead by, very often, an even more knowledgeable & skilled leader.

Behind every Nobel, Pulitzer Peace Prize or Oscar Nomination is a massive level of skill, built up through intentional & strategic learning & skill development.

Whatever your ambitions are, if you have the skills & you deploy them effectively, you can achieve those ambitions. Hence, developing your skills - and becoming truly extraordinary at what you do - is the surest, most proven, most predictable, path to achievement at anything.

And when you do become extraordinary at your craft - when you can do what others only wish they could - and when you become so good that others can't ignore you, that's when you achieve things others simply dream about. That's when you become truly unstoppable.

Important to understand, when we talk about *'skill,'* I'm referring to both the 1) intellectual ability to learn, absorb & utilize previously learned knowledge *(labelled 'learning')* and, 2) the ability to develop & perform trained actions, repeatedly, with competence *(labelled 'skill development').*

Personally, I've been blessed to travel all around the world, speaking & teaching from stages & platforms across 3 different continents, teaching & coaching thousands & thousands of people, ranging from multi-millionaires to teachers, from authors to TV producers, from TEDx speakers to Reiki Masters. As well as entrepreneurs, CEOs, doctors & almost every profession & life path in between.

And having taught people of almost all ages, races, & nationalities, combined with 5 years of my in-depth research in the fields of neuroscience, human psychology & human behavior, the above consistently rings true; *skill is the biggest differentiator between success or failure.*

Most importantly, think of learning & skill development this way: *it's controllable.* Contrary to media brainwashing and the implanted beliefs from the education system:

| You control your skill level

Skill doesn't discriminate. It's not racist, sexist or ageist. It doesn't care if you're 15 years old, or 84 years young. It doesn't care who you are, where you're from or how rich your parents are.

It only cares that you put in the work to develop it. And when you do, it opens up the floodgates to endless new opportunities for greater abundance in all areas of life.

Skill isn't something you're either born with (or not), or something you either have (or lack); it's more than that.

Studies in the fields of neuroscience & human behavior now show that factors like IQ, DNA, genetics & even so-called 'innate talent' have little-to-no correlation with someone's level of skill or success.

IQ, genetics or talent don't control your skill or success. You control that. Skill is controllable. You're in charge.

Now, this secret - skill - may be simple to identify, however, realizing it is only 1% of the way to tapping into it.

1% IDENTIFICATION, 99% IMPLEMENTATION

Identifying the path you want to take is only 1% of the process. And it's only once you've taken that first step, that the journey truly begins. That's when it's time to dig into the 99% *(what you may not initially see)*, learn it & apply to reach the destination you want to reach.

After we've identified this - the power of skill - how do you bridge the gap between where you are & where you want to be? How do you learn anything faster, train like the best & become extraordinary at what you do?

I believe we all have incredible potential to become extraordinary at what we do & achieve whatever we want. And that's what this book will help you unlock.

HARNESSING THE POWER OF SKILL

"The more you learn, the more you'll earn"

- *WARREN BUFFETT*

It all starts with this understanding; *the higher your skill level is, the greater your income & impact potential is.*

THE SKILL PYRAMID

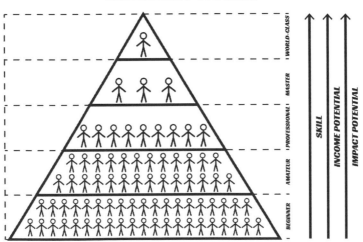

Skill: *How skilled are you (both 'knowledge' & 'skill')*

Income Potential: *If effectively monetized, to what extent could you be compensated for what you do.*

Impact Potential: *If effectively shared, what impact could your skill have on other people's lives.*

Let's say that I just completed my first ever piano lesson...

Right now, my level of skill would be very low and as a result, my odds of creating a musical masterpiece people would listen to for generations (impact) are very slim.

Comparatively, if I was a masterful pianist like Mozart - who played the piano & composed music since age 4 - now, my chances of creating massive income and impact from my piano ability would look pretty damn promising.

| The greater the skill, the greater the upside

In sports, Roger Federer, Michael Jordan, Bobby Fischer or Usain Bolt have far greater potential to create massive income & impact than someone who began a new sport.

In entertainment, David Copperfield, Steven Spielberg, Ellen DeGeneres or George Lucas, have far greater potential for massive income & impact than most other movie producers, illusionists, actors or entertainers.

Greater skill leads to greater upside. But, it starts with skill.

In many ways, the world's best are like magicians. At first glance, what they do seems like magic, but when you peel back the curtain & deconstruct how they do it, their skill, like magic - loses its elusive nature. It loses its mystery.

What you gain instead though, is something far more valuable; a path to becoming extraordinary yourself.

You can't become a great magician believing that magic is just magic and that the magician has no control over it.

In the same way, you can't become extraordinary believing that the worlds best are extraordinary simply because of innate talent, IQ, DNA, genetics or plain luck.

This book peels back that curtain of learning, skill development & extraordinary achievement.

In which case, I apologize upfront for taking away the elusive nature of 'genius', 'mastery' & 'talent.'

What I promise to give you back in return though is far greater; a complete set of proven, research-backed, learning & skill development, strategies, tactics, habits & practices that you can use to move to the next level.

ACCELERATION OVER FOUNDATION

> *"Life is like a ten speed bicycle. Most of us have gears we never use"*
>
> - *CHARLES M. SCHULZ*

We are all born in a similar way; naked, bare and incapable of pretty much anything. Yet, at the same time, we are born with a massive gift; the ability to learn anything we choose.

We may not be born with driving ability or coding skills, but we are all born with the gift of learning itself.

And, we learn our entire lives. We learn to walk, to talk, to read, to write, to run. We - as human beings on this incredible planet - are gifted with this incredible ability. We have the potential to learn anything & develop any skill if we put in the work & take the right steps.

With that said, this book is not about *'how to learn,'* or *'how to train skills,'* rather, this book is about acceleration.

We are all born with the ability to learn, however, what doesn't come naturally to us at birth is the ability to 'learn faster' or 'develop skill more effectively' - and that's what truly separates the world's highest achievers from the rest.

We all know how to learn. But what makes people extraordinary, isn't this natural born learning ability, rather, it's the enhanced methodologies they use to learn anything faster & develop their skill more effectively.

The world's highest achievers are far more strategic & intentional in their learning & skill development. And that's what allows them to become extraordinary.

The world's highest performing people - athletes, artists, presenters, business owners, media personalities - don't learn like the majority. They think & act differently.

They have very different learning habits & skill acquisition methods that allow them to get ahead faster.

They don't just read some information & hope that they remember it. They don't simply 'repeat' something over & over and hope they get good. They don't run and hope that they'll win Olympic gold; they're more strategic than that.

They have different understandings, practices & strategies. And that's what makes the difference. They are far more intentional, purposeful, & strategic in their approach.

And throughout the chapters in this book, you'll learn those same methodologies, frameworks & strategies, so that, you too, can become more strategic in your skill development and, as a result, achieve anything, faster.

WHO THE HECK AM I & HOW YOU CAN GET THE MOST OUT OF THIS BOOK

> *"The great aim of education is not knowledge, but action"*
>
> - *HERBERT SPENCER*

When I was 14 years old, I made, probably, the smartest decision I've ever made; I dropped out of high school.

It was the end of the school year, and I left school that day knowing that I would never step into a school, as a student, ever again. I dropped out, never to return.

I made this decision for one simple reason. I was sick of the impracticality of the whole education system.

At that time, I had already been involved in self-help & alternative learning. I was already aware that there was a better way to learn & move forward. Hence, I take this leap.

I was excited to leave school, start my own businesses, do what I was truly passionate about & craft my legacy *(rather than spend 8 hours a day, bored to death, disengaged, learning things I knew wouldn't help me in life)*.

Despite this dream-driven outlook, a part of me was terrified (which I had too much pride to admit at the time). By choosing to drop out, I was cutting off my backup. If my entrepreneurial dreams didn't work out, I had no plan B. I wouldn't be able to just go back, get a job & continue living a normal, ordinary, cookie-cut life because nobody would hire me; I was a high school dropout.

But, the excitement & prospects for the future far outweighed the fear. I knew if I didn't do this, I would regret it. Big time. With that, I started this journey.

And many years later, that journey lead me right here. And this journey of discovery forms the backbone of this book.

After dropping out, I became obsessed with figuring out what separates the world's highest achievers from the rest. I started to research the fields of neuroscience, human psychology & human behavior to gain insights on how I could join the best (instead of watching them from afar).

At first, I never actually intended on sharing these learning with anyone. It was just a way of quenching my curiosity. But, soon after, it became more than that. It became my mission; the life purpose that I wake up to fulfill every day.

Over the last 5 years, I've traveled all around the world, spoken on stages & platforms - across 3 different continents - and have helped thousands & thousands of people move to higher levels of awareness, skill & success.

This journey led me to start & run 2 businesses, serving fans, readers, customers & clients, spanning across 4 different continents, with clients now paying me many thousands of dollars for one to one coaching & consulting.

This book is packed with 5 years of in-depth research & testing. It also shares real-world case studies of how these specific concepts, strategies & tactics are being applied by the highest achievers today. All mixed with the latest studies in neuroscience, psychology & human behavior.

This book levels the playing field by laying out a proven path anyone can follow to become extraordinary.

It's divided into 4 core sections, 1) *Understanding*, 2) *Foundations*, 3) *Acceleration* & 4) *Integration*.

In the first section, *Understanding*, you'll discover a new approach to learning, skill development & achievement. We'll demystify things like 'genius', 'talent' or 'mastery' & you'll learn what it takes to go from beginner, to amateur, to pro, to master, to one of the best, at what you do.

In the second section, *Foundations*, you'll learn the habits, mindsets & practices of the world's highest achievers. *How do they deal with failure? How do they predictably create improvement? How do they become extraordinary?*

You'll also learn a 9 step learning process that you apply, to learn anything faster & dominate in the information age.

Inside section 3, *Acceleration*, you'll discover the 5 things that kill learning speed (so you can avoid them), as well as in-depth look at 7 proven growth strategies of masters.

We wrap up with section 4, *Integration*. *What are the actionable steps you can take, after reading this book, to implement & become extraordinary at what you do?*

This book is different to many others out there (as you'll see). You may have already realized, it's written, formatted & laid out a little differently than most other books.

This is on purpose. This book is structured for maximum benefit for the reader (you), based on the very principles & concepts within it. This book isn't crafted to make an English teacher happy, rather, to give you the most value.

With that, here are 3 simple steps that will help you get the most out of this book:

1. Don't dabble, commit.

A lot of people dabble in a lot of things but rarely commit to truly following through something.

If what you've read inside this Introduction makes sense, and you can begin to picture the positive impact it could have on your life, I implore you to trust the process & commit to following through.

Don't dabble. Don't read 2 pages today, 12 more next month & 8 more next year - that's dabbling. Be committed. Make time, read & implement.

2. Complete the exercises & processes

This book is filled with exercises & processes that will help you execute & get the best results.

This isn't a book you passively read. It's a book you do. Because the greatest value comes from combining learning with effective integration.

3. Implement

Awareness gives you the possibility for growth, but implementation is what makes the difference. Go into this book with an implementation mindset. Constantly filter for things you can implement.

I believe we all have potential to become extraordinary, achieve whatever we want & move the human race forward.

And with that, let's begin this journey together...

1.

UNDERSTANDING:
DEMYSTIFYING LEARNING

"An investment in knowledge pays the best interest"

BENJAMIN FRANKLIN

It's only once we truly & deeply understand something - the mechanics of it, how it works, how it operates, how it functions - that we can really tap into the power of innovation to improve it, accelerate the process & achieve the result we are after with a new, more powerful, sense of clarity & confidence.

1 | RE-DEFINING GENIUS: THE POWER OF LEARNING

"The capacity to learn is a gift; The ability to learn is a skill; The willingness to learn is a choice"

- BRIAN HERBERT

Every day, we see the extraordinary. We see people with extraordinary abilities, extraordinary skills, & now, more than ever, we see the incredible results that those skills enable those people to create in their lives.

We see athletes with extraordinary athletic abilities, celebrities with incredible abilities to influence & business icons with outstanding abilities to accumulate wealth.

We see actors, performers & illusionists who can perform, express & entertain so skillfully. We see sales pros with incredible charisma, writers with inspiring writing abilities & leaders with seemingly magical abilities to inspire.

Assuming you want to see it, it's pretty easy to realize that the extraordinary is all around us.

Between the internet, social media, TV, the news, word of mouth & the people we meet in person, we are - physically or virtually - surrounded by extraordinarily skilled people.

But, the best part, not only do we see the extraordinary levels of skill these people have, we also see their results. Every day, we see the riches, the influence, the fame, the legacy, the confidence & the happiness that high achievers are able to create as a result of their extraordinary skills.

That's what this book is about. Now, more than ever, we can see the correlation between skill & success.

In fact, failing to realize that the train routed for 'success' must first pass through the stations of learning & skill development is one of the biggest mistakes people make.

Like a plant, success is a result. It's the result of the right seeds being planted & nurtured.

Of course, there are many factors that create success, but the main one - the one most correlated to success - is *skill*.

However, as you read these words, deep down, at some level, you already know that. You know that to get to the next level, you need to develop a new, higher level of skill. You know that; what comes next is the *know-how* & *how-to*. And that's where this book really comes in.

Inside it, you'll discover the mindsets, strategies, practices, habits & routines of the world's highest achievers, so you can learn faster, dominate in today's information age, develop your skill most effectively (like the world's best) & reach new higher levels of success in all areas of your life.

And although on the surface, this may appear as a book about learning or skill development, it's far more than that.

From the greatest philosophers, such as Socrates, Plato or Aristotle, to some of history's great thinkers like Albert Einstein or Isaac Newton, through to business icons, such as Warren Buffett or Bill Gates, they've all talked about the importance & value of ongoing learning & self-mastery.

.

Beyond even that, as we talked about in the *Introduction*, skill is the biggest differentiator between success or failure. Which makes this book, not only about skill development, but rather, a book about success in all areas.

It's may not technically be a 'financial' book, the contents have the potential to make you more money than any investment, pay raise or Christmas bonus ever could.

And although it's not categorized as a book about 'influence,' 'power,' or 'fame,' we know the influence is a trainable skill & this book will help you develop that skill.

It's also, on paper, not a 'happiness' book, yet the strategies within it have the potential to bring you more happiness, joy &, straight up, ecstasy, than any Hawaiian vacation, TV show or shopping spree ever could hope to.

Why? The reason is simple. People who do what they love experience greater levels of happiness in their lives. When you learn the contents inside - combined with deploying *The Specialization Model* you'll learn about in Section #2 - you'll be able to spend far more time doing what you love.

Lastly, this book is not about 'confidence' or 'self-esteem', yet again, the strategies within these pages will give you more self-confidence than you could have ever imagined.

With this one, it's because with greater skill comes greater confidence. Psychologists refer to this phenomenon as the *'Confidence-Competence Loop'* (& we'll talk about it later).

Massive power comes with the ability to, learn fast, adapt to change in the fast-moving world we live in, develop your skill effectively & become extraordinary at what you do.

It's why, at the core, what this book will *really* give you is a new, higher level of power & control of your own destiny.

And that's the journey we're going on...

A JOURNEY OF DISCOVERY

> *"The best scientist is open to experience and begins with romance - the idea that anything is possible"*
>
> - *RAY BRADBURY*

If there's anything I've learned from my work with customers, clients & fans worldwide, it's that people *do not* - by any stretch of the imagination - want the same things.

And, that this *extraordinary quality* we're talking is also different for different people. That there's a certain uniqueness to every person - a certain nuance - that few people ever explore, let alone understand.

For one person, seeing a masterful musician perform is near hypnotic & they too aspire to become a magician like that. For others, seeing how easily & elegantly some people accumulate wealth inspires them. For others, it's the fame & influence that draws them in.

For some people, their ambition is to become extraordinary in the sport of tennis. For others, basketball is their game. For others, their passion is in music, or philosophy, or poetry, or entrepreneurship, or marketing, or web design.

As we both know, *different people want different things.*

The key here though is not the differences, but rather, the similarities. Although the ambitions are always different, the underlying principles of learning, skill development & achievement stay very similar, & borderline, *the same.*

Meaning, there are proven strategies that you can apply, irrelevant of whether you want to become a MasterChef, a golfing pro, a business icon or a street dancer, that will help you learn & achieve what you want, faster.

That's where the true leverage is. That's what we want to - & will - focus on: *the universal learning, skill development & achievement principles that work, irrelevant of topic, profession, age, current skill level or the ambition itself.*

EXERCISE: BE INTENTIONAL
If you want to get the most out of this book - or any other book for that matter - you don't want to just *hope* you'll learn *some stuff* that will help you achieve *some stuff.*

You want to be more *intentional & specific.* A pattern of high achievers is that they're simply more intentional.

What do you want to learn from this book? What do you want this book to help you achieve? You may have a vague idea, but it's time to go deep. *What specifically?*

When you do this before you learn, it will help you...

1) heighten your awareness of what you're reading

2) raise your 'pre-learning state' *(more on this later)*

3) subconsciously support your brain to 'zero-in' (focus) on the information that will help you most

Take 2 minutes right now & think - or journal - on those questions. Then, continue reading.

There are many factors that make the difference between wanting something & actually achieving it. In the same way, there are many factors that will enable you to learn faster, develop skill effectively & become extraordinary.

However, it starts in the same place: *new understandings*.

The straightest path to becoming extraordinary starts with understanding what *already* makes people extraordinary...

WHAT CREATES THE EXTRAORDINARY?

"Heroes are ordinary people who make themselves extraordinary"

- GERARD WAY

We all want more skill & achievement in our lives. We all want something more. We want to reach that higher level.

And, we know that in order to do that, just like the world's highest achievers, we must become extraordinary at what we do *(which, we know, is different for different people)*.

However, how do you do that? How does somebody become extraordinary at what they do? What's the secret?

So often, we go through life observing those who are extraordinary but rarely do we actually dive deeper & learn what *really* makes them extraordinary at what they do.

And worse, because of this lack of in-depth research, we - human beings - often pass off other people's extraordinary skills to innate talent, superior genetics, better upbringing, higher IQ or, worse of all, plain luck & good fortune.

And, a few decades ago, this was as much as one could do; pawn off the answer to factors like genetics, talent or luck.

Back then, we - as human beings on this incredible planet - didn't have much solid, proven, research to show us that anything correlates to - or creates - extraordinary skill.

Today though, things are vastly different. The world is different. And over those last few decades, we - humanity - have spent thousands, tens of thousands & millions of hours (collectively) discovering what really correlates to extraordinary levels of skill & results in people's lives.

We don't know everything. And, chances are we never will. If we look at the history of humanity, we will always continue to learn new things & make things better.

But, decades of research have given us a far more in-depth, more accurate answer to questions like...

Why is it that 2 siblings - born with similar genetics, and raised by the same parents, same schooling & in the same environment - can have such vastly different skills?

How come, 2 students, with the same schooling, teachers & curriculum can have such varied levels of skill?

How come, 2 aspiring athletes, with similar opportunities coaching & resources can achieve such different results?

Why is it that one person gets remembers by millions of people, many decades after they pass away - legacy - while another is only remembered by family & friends?

Why do some people go on to learn faster, acquire greater levels of skill & achieve greater results than others?

At the end of the day, we were all born with the same limited abilities. No baby was born singing perfectly the moment it was first born in the hospital. No child was born with the ability to do Calculus or know the capitals of every country on the planet. *It was all learned.*

Really think about that for a moment. Everything that you know intellectually, every skill that you've developed, every ability you've worked to attain, you *weren't* capable of at birth. You learned it all. You trained those skills. You developed those abilities. You stepped into that potential.

| Almost everything you're capable of today, you weren't capable of at birth. You learned it.

It important because, when we truly realize that we're natural learners - that the capacity to learn is a gift - it may just change how you approach learning forever.

But, beyond that, although the *capacity* to learn may be a gift, the *ability* to learn *effectively* is a *skill*. Something we must develop. And, something that gives us a huge advantage & allows us to become extraordinary.

So, what is it that makes the difference? Why is it that some people are able to achieve such extraordinary results, that others only dream of achieving one day?

If ambition alone was the secret then everybody would be extraordinary at everything & would be walking around with loaded bank accounts, ripped bodies & never-ending levels of happiness & ecstasy in their lives.

Learning, skill development or success may start with ambition (frankly, if you don't know what you want or which direct you're heading in, you're going to get lost), but ambition alone isn't enough. There's more to it.

If DNA or genetics were the secret than 2 siblings would always have the same - or at least very, very, similar - levels of skill & results in their lives. Yet, they don't. And often, their results aren't a little different, but wildly varied.

If upbringing was the secret, than those who had rich parents & gifted childhood's would achieve the best results & those who came from extreme scarcity & hardship would never amount to anything. Yet, we know that's not the case.

If skill (or success) was dependant on pure 'experience,' then it would be the 24-years-of-experience accountant that would get the promotion, rather than the new, hotshot accountant who has already gotten 2 promotions this year.

If pure ambition, IQ, genetics, upbringing or even years of experience were the secret, we would never see people who seem to have everything going against them become extraordinary. *Yet, we do.*

We consistently see - or hear stories - of people who go on achieve extraordinary levels of skill at what they do who come from very rough childhoods, have had low levels of IQ, no innate advantages, little experience. *But, why?*

I have spent the last 5 years of my life seeking the answers. And this obsession that with the extraordinary, that in big parts, has fueled the answer you'll find in this book.

In this first section of this book, we are going to dive deep into what makes someone masterful at what they do. We are going to challenge many of the misconceptions about learning, skill development & skill. And, we are also going to deconstruct learning & dissect it into parts, so we have a greater awareness of how to learn, develop skills & become extraordinary, faster & with greater predictability.

Unquestionably, we all have the potential to become extraordinary at what we choose and as a result, live a life of joy, prosperity and fulfilment. Potential to change the world in our own way. To live life how we choose to live it.

Yet, too often, people don't. Too often, they settle.

They don't go and reach for the things they really aspire to achieve because they never believe they are good enough to get there. They don't believe feel that they are in control, and ownership, over their skills and their results in life.

When in actuality, based on what we now know, learning, skill development & achievement is far more controllable & possible that we were misled to believe.

And there *is*, in fact, a path to learning faster, becoming extraordinary & achieving what you want.

The path is there, but we must first realize that...

SKILL MATTERS (NOW, MORE THAN EVER)

> *"It is not the strongest of the species that survives, nor the most intelligent that survives. It is the one that is most adaptable to change"*
>
> - *CHARLES DARWIN*

Skill has always been critical, & will forever continue to be.

It's the foundation behind every Olympic Gold medal, every Nobel nomination, and on a more day-to-day level, the key behind every promotion, career success, business success, sporting success & achievement - in our lives.

Frankly, nobody has ever achieved anything significant without having a matching or higher level of skill.

However, beyond just this, in the day & age, we live in...

| Skill is more important than ever before

There are many reasons for this. But, one of the first (& biggest) is that, while a few decades ago being good at what you did would get you good results, today, it doesn't. Today, being good gets you *less-than-good* results.

In the past, being average at what you did would give you average results. Today, it doesn't. Today that same level of skill gives you back *less-than-average* results.

In the 20th century, a graphic designer was competing against over graphic designers in the same city or country. A lawyer was competing against other lawyers in the same city or country. Same applies to the accounting firm, the marketing agency & the sales rep. They were competing on a local, regional, or worse case, national, scale.

| Today, we compete on a global scale

Innovation has given us greater interconnectedness & opportunity than ever before. Distance has become astronomically less significant for the consumer than ever before. And competition has become more widespread.

Today, thanks to modern innovation, with a few clicks, you could have someone on the other side of the world doing your accounting, handling your marketing or writing a song for your niece's 5th birthday party.

It's why a musician is no longer just competing against another musician in the same region, but rather against all musician in the world. The accounting firm is competing against, not just other local firms, but other firms nationally & even globally. And, the consultant is competing against others consultants all around the world.

And with new competition, being mediocre (average) isn't enough to get average, 'ok,' results anymore. The same skill level that would have allowed your parents or grandparents to live a good, comfortable life, will leave you struggling.

Competition has changed. Standards have heightened.

Another reason is the widespread availability of information. Today, anybody you can find tutorials, guides & how-to information on virtually anything they choose.

It doesn't matter whether you live in a penthouse in New York City & went to a private school, or you're a teenager in a 3rd world country with just a phone & an internet connection, you both have a similar access to information.

Over the last few decades, this interconnectedness & widespread availability of information has toughened the competition, making *skill more important than ever*.

But, as competition heightened, so has the upside.

MORE PAIN. MORE GAIN.

> *"It's supposed to be hard. If it were easy, everyone would do it"*
>
> - *TOM HANKS*

This interconnectedness that innovation has created over the last few decades has made it *harder* for people to break out the extraordinary, but, at the same time, it has given those who do, far greater upside than ever before.

Thanks to modern media capabilities, those who do become extraordinary at what they do, have greater income & impact potential than ever before. They can reach more people, more easily. They can create & seize opportunities for greater wealth, fame, influence & power, more easily.

Just one example: 50 years ago, if you did something good *(value-adding, insightful, entertaining, funny)* someone might tell 5 people. Today, that people can share something & reach hundreds & thousands of people - if not millions - with just a few clicks.

It's harder to break out, stand out & become extraordinary *(comparatively to those around you)*, but when you do, the upside is greater than it's ever been before.

And, no matter whether your ambition is to become one of the world's best, or just to get good enough to live comfortably, with great work-life balance - no matter where you are or where you want to be - now, more than ever before, it's critical for you to level up your skills.

The world has changed. And, will continue to do so.

Deep down, we all know that, yet few realize that the important of skill has followed that change.

There has never been more opportunity for success, growth & innovation. Which, once again, causes a widening gap between the successful (the skilled) and the unsuccessful.

Skill is more important than ever. And, we all have greater potential to tap into that & live out our ambitions.

DOMINATE IN TODAY'S INFORMATION AGE

"It is possible to fly without motors, but not without knowledge and skill"

- *WILBUR WRIGHT*

Beyond the importance of skill, in the information age, we are in, your ability to learn & adapt to change is crucial.

If you work & operate in any industry - especially in high growth industries - chances are you are faced with change on an going basis: *new tools to learn, new software to figure out, new machinery to operate, new procedures to follow, new updates to master*. It's because...

| Change is a constant in life

Almost everybody on the planet is confronted with this constant need to learn & adapt to ongoing change. And, it's why, those that are able to learn faster than others - and adapt better - that thrive *(while others, sadly, fall behind)*.

If a web designer stops learning the new in-&-outs of web design - updates, software, integrations - they'll fall behind.

If an athlete fails to embrace new technologies for speeding up training, other, more intentional athletes will beat them.

If a business owner fails to learn, understand & adapt to, new, arising opportunities, they will, inevitably, fall behind.

Hence, it's those that can learn fast & adapt quickly that have a massive competitive advantage over the rest.

It's the techie that can learn a new software in 2 days - instead of in 7 days - that has the advantage.

It's the engineer that can figure out a new piece of machinery in 2 hours (instead of 6) that has the advantage.

It's the entrepreneur that can deeply understand a new emerging industry within a few weeks (rather than a few months) that has the greatest competitive advantage.

The same pattern repeats over & over again. Those who have the ability to learn fast & adapt to ongoing change out-achieve those who don't (over the long term)

The reason a lot of people miss this is because 1) the education system doesn't support us to think like that, & 2) just like many things in life, this ability to learn quickly will not showcase immediate advantages, but rather, will play out to your advantage over the long term.

It's like going to the gym. If you workout for 1 day & your friend doesn't, you won't see much of a difference. But, if you consistently workout (while that friend doesn't), now, that difference - the results - become very visible.

The same applies to learning. Learning a new industry update in 3 hours instead of 7 hours may not seem like a big, success-altering difference, but over time, if you consistently out-learn & out-adapt others, the results show.

It's about realizing the long-term, accumulated benefit that matters *(something high achievers are great at doing)*.

And, unlike in the industrial age, in which those who know how to follow instructions succeeded, in the information age, it's those who can be creative, learn effectively, adapt & influence that reap the biggest reward.

This is how we should approach learning & change if we want the best results. More strategically & intentionally. Beyond that, as you learn new topics & train new skills, you now put yourself in a position to add more value to those around you *(your customers, clients, fans, your boss, your employer, your friends, family, community, etc)*.

And when you do that, of course, just as great thought leaders throughout history have told us...

| The more value you add, the more value you will receive back

This value you receive can come back in many forms *(wealth, fame, influence, legacy, power, appreciation, etc)*, but the key here is simple: you want to become more valuable to others in society. You do that, of course, by becoming more knowledgeable & developing your skills.

It's the law of *cause-and-effect*. You get what you put in. *You reap that which you have sown.*

This may seem basic, but it's critically important. And I'm banging on about this only because most people don't get it. Not because it's their fault, but because the education system has failed to teach these critical understandings.

And it has lead to people finishing schooling & *never* focusing on learning or self-improvement *ever again.* They have somehow been misled to believe that by finishing their schooling, their education is completed.

Meanwhile, the world's most successful people view learning as a never-ending process of improvement, growth & self-mastery. And they know that it's what they learn *after* school that will really make the difference.

In the words of Jim Rohn,

"Formal education will make you a living; self-education will make you a fortune."

Now, the very fact that you're reading this book shows me that you're already far further ahead of most people & you're already thinking like a high achiever (constantly looking to learn & get better), but, what I really implore you to do is challenge yourself to step up more.

Become even more adamant about constant learning. Because as well as you may be following the path of the world's highest achievers, you & I both know they're more for you. There's an even higher level & its time to get there.

| Learning is an ongoing process from birth until death. Those who embrace that, thrive.

You may have heard that *'leaders are readers'*, that an investment in knowledge pays back the best returns & that self-education is what's really to help you succeed. Some research goes as far as to say that the average CEO reads 60 books per year. Despite this all, few really live these understandings in their lives. While, those who do, thrive.

| Successful people are constant learners

Those who do, are those who experience greater levels of confidence & control in life. Which creates the question...

How do you create amazing results & achievements in your life, in a way in which those achievements last & your success is in your control - & not controlled by the government, economy or current trends? How do you thrive - no matter what is going on around you?

It's this approach that truly forms the answer...

BECOME UNSTOPPABLE: PEACE IN CHAOS

"The best way to predict your future is to create it"

- ABRAHAM LINCOLN

A great meditation teacher once shared that there shouldn't be any difference between, meditating in a cave, or meditating in the centre of a city, because peace is *inside* us and not dependent on what's going on around us.

In the same way, an effective approach to learning - or life - shouldn't depend on external circumstance.

If you want to create success - *and sustain it despite the unquestionable chaos that will occur in life* - you can't rely on a good economy, a loophole or a good opportunity.

That doesn't last. And it puts you at the mercy of others.

Fortunately, there's an alternative. It's what the world's highest achievers have been doing for generations to attain massive personal power. And, it all starts by developing the *intangible* & often, hard to quantify.

Because while knowing that we are doing well now is great, that feeling perishes in comparison to the feeling of 1) knowing you are doing well now *and, at the same time,* 2) knowing you will continue to do well & thrive *in the future.*

We all some level of variety, surprise & unknown in our lives. Frankly, if you knew exactly what was going to happen every moment of our future, we'd get bored (like watching the same movie over & over again, on loop).

However, while we may need that, that's not the challenge that most people are faced with.

For most people, it's the contrary. Most people already have too much unknowns & uncertainties in their lives. It's what gives them fear & takes away their confidence.

To be really straight up, for many people, success feels like a complete mystery. They trek blindly *hoping* one day they'll achieve something; they're confused & lack clarity. And, it's very dangerous for multiple reasons:

1. Research shows *too much uncertainty & unknown* correlates to higher levels of stress & lower levels of happiness. We know this based on extensive research into human wellbeing & happiness. But it's also very logical. If someone has very little certainty & control over their future & success feels like a gamble, it causes much more emotional struggle.

2. If you, I or anybody, wants to achieve anything, it's an ineffective way to get there *(more on this later)*

What a lot of people lack is a sense of personal power & a feeling of being unstoppable. Because, at the end of the day, we all want to know that in 10 years we'll still be thriving physically, economically, emotionally & mentally.

We all want a sense of being unstoppable & unshakable no matter happens. We want to have a sense of peace & control over our destiny - even in the midst of chaos.

THE GAME OF LIFE

"Smooth seas do not make skillful sailors"

- *AFRICAN PROVERB*

In this game we all play called life, things happen. People change. Situations change. Circumstances change.

Which should never come as a surprise. Of course, things are going to change when you put billions of different people - with different beliefs, ambitions, viewpoints, opinions & values - together on 1 planet. It's inevitable.

Making life, in some ways, like a big, 7+ billion person game of Monopoly. But, not the ordinary version. Rather, a version in which everybody is playing with their own rules.

Some believe they are moving clockwise around the board. Other's, anti-clockwise. Some are rolling 1 dice. Others are rolling 3. Some pass 'go' & collect $200. Some collect $750. Different people are playing for different objectives and with different actions because of their varied beliefs.

And if you've ever played any board game with anybody, you'll know that there is going to be some sense of unpredictability along the way.

In the same way, when you have billions of people playing the game of life - with different ambitions, values & beliefs - of course, there's going to be change along the way.

Worse part, even the greatest control freak won't be able to control the chaos & unpredictability of life. Doing that would mean aligning billions of people to think, believe & behavior in the exact same, predictable ways, every single moment of every single day. Which, plain & simple, isn't going to happen.

Plus, we shouldn't even want that to happen. We should value the uniqueness of various people, organizations & groups. But, at the same time, we should learn to work together, & personally, thrive within the chaos.

So if we can't remove, ignore or control the chaos around us, what should we do to thrive? And, how do we sustain high levels of success - no matter what?

Imagine this scenario for a moment.

Imagine if you lost everything. Imagine you just lost your job, career, business or investments. You lose your house, your car & everything else you may own. All gone.

What would you do? How could you recoup everything & continue to thrive - despite losing everything?

It's this higher level of thinking that allows us to realize that most valuable thing we have is not the businesses we own, the possessions we have or the investments we make.

Rather, it's the *'mental assets'* we have acquired. The knowledge we've accumulated & skills we have developed.

These intangible aspects are astronomically more valuable than any material possession you could ever possess. And, these are the things that can make you feel unshakable, where you can continue to thrive - no matter what.

The economy may crash. The value of your possessions may depreciate. Things may change. But, nobody can take away the knowledge & skills you've acquired & developed.

In the words of B.B. King, *"The beautiful thing about learning is that nobody can take it away from you."*

Skill is the ultimate controllable. You may not be able to control the economy, the competition, consumer trends or opportunities, but you have control over your skills.

And, just like in the sport of sailing, the greatest confidence doesn't come from knowing the weather is going to be good today, but rather, from knowing you have the skills to weather any storm or situation that may come up.

As you develop your skills, you begin to remove worry & focus on creating a better future. It boils down to this...

The greatest power comes from knowing that, even if you lost everything today, what you know & the skills you've acquired, would allow you to rebuild bigger & better.

That's how we create greater confidence in our lives. That's how we stand strong, knowing that we can weather any storm. And that's how we take control of our destiny.

EXERCISE: STEP INTO THE FEAR
If you lost everything today, how would you rebuild? *What intangible knowledge, skills & resources do you have that would make you certain of a positive future?*

Take a few minutes & journal on this. Step into the fear & emerge on the other side with greater confidence.

And, if skill gives you power, becoming truly extraordinary & masterful gives you the *greatest* power. In other words...

MASTERY IS POWER

> *"Only one who devotes himself to a cause with his whole strength and soul can be a true master. For this reason mastery demands all of a person"*
>
> - *ALBERT EINSTEIN*

Not only do masters tap into higher level thinking, but they also have the highest levels of income & impact.

The top 10%, in any industry, generates approximately 90% of the revenue within that industry.

And while the exact numbers depend on what the industry, or profession, it is, the principle remains; *a small percent of highest performers reap the majority of the upside.*

If becoming good or great at what you do gives you confidence for the future, become truly masterful at what you do will give you more power & control over your destiny (& legacy) than most people can even quantify.

It's all a *mindset* game. If you go and study high achievers, you'll clearly see that they *do* things differently. That's easy to spot. But, when you dig a bit deeper, you'll discover that those *different actions* are driven by *different thinking.*

Those that learn fast, adapt to ongoing change, effectively develop their skills & become extraordinary at what they do think about skill & achievement very differently.

And, arguably, the biggest difference is how *strategically* they think about achievement. They *don't* look at success as a massive guessing game in which they are *hoping* to win the game that they're playing, but rather, they approach success with far greater clarity. They know that...

ACHIEVEMENT IS A SCIENCE

"Whatever you reap, is what you have sown"

- *JIM ROHN*

The world's highest achievers know that there are practices *(customary, habitual, or expected procedure or ways of doing something)* that will give them certain results. And, other practices, that won't give them the results they want.

They know that a lot of the game of success comes down to the right strategies. And they know that if they deploy those right strategies, they will get the results.

They know that if somebody else (a coach, role model, mentor or guide) did A, B & C to achieve a particular goal, they too can achieve a lot by also doing A, B & C.

They think about achievement like a science (rather than a guessing game), knowing that, just like a lab experiment, all they have to do is find the right combinations of ingredients, put them in in the right quantities & at the right times & they will get the result they're after.

There are strategies that will make you extraordinary at whatever skill you want to become great at, & there are other strategies, habits, practices & actions that will make you mediocre. It's all about finding those right strategies.

How do we know this? We - humanity - didn't before. Achievement used to be a massive guessing game.

But, unlike what you grandparents may have been aware of, today, we have far greater understanding of what creates skill & success than we've ever had before.

Decades of data tracking, data analysis, brain scans, & pattern recognition, combined with research in fields such as *neuroscience* (study of the nervous system), *human psychology* (study of behavior and mind) *performance psychology* (human behavior in sport & performance), *positive psychology* (study of strengths that allow people & groups to succeed), *human behavior* (subcategory of broader topics, such as sociology & economics) & more, has *turned* skill, performance & *achievement into a science.*

And it's these understandings - knowing the sweet science of achievement - that allows some people to get far better results than those simply wondering around, guessing & stumbling, attempting to get to where they want to go.

Great power comes from predictability & understanding.

And beyond understanding that *achievement is a science,* it's also important for us to understand that we are...

AN ACCUMULATIVE SPECIES

"If I have seen further than others, it is by standing upon the shoulders of giants"

- ISAAC NEWTON

When a scientist starts studying a topic, he doesn't get rid of all existing research within that field & start from scratch, no - that would be stupid - instead he takes that existing accumulation of knowledge & builds on it through this own study, research, experimentation & testing.

In the same way, a cook doesn't go and attempt to figure out a new recipe on his own, no, instead, he picks up existing cookbooks, uses them & improves on the recipes, over time, if he finds new, better ways to cook those dishes.

Rather than starting from scratch, a great scientist, cook, marketer, entrepreneur - or whoever, the profession is irrelevant - will build on the existing research, testing, failures & successes of those that have come before them.

And this causes an *'accumulation'* effect that, over time, leads to greater & greater results.

And it's this - the fact that we're *an accumulative species* - that gives us one of the greatest advantages that we all have. It's what allows us to achieve such incredible things.

A field of study doesn't refresh back to zero after 1 person's work. Instead, it accumulates from one person to another.

It's with this understanding that we must adapt our approach & look to model from - & learn from - the best, instead of figuring everything out on our own.

ACHIEVEMENT HACKING: MODEL SUCCESS

"Success is a science; if you have the conditions, you get the result"
- *OSCAR WILDE*

Almost anything you could ever dream about achieving has been achieved by somebody else throughout history.

Want to become a great musician? People have done that. *Want to become a top-class basketball player?* People have done that too. *Want a great relationship? A successful business? Huge, global reach & influence?* People have achieved all of those things.

And even if your ambitions haven't been achieved before, if you're really committed, you can still find people who've achieved *similar* things from who you can learn.

The key here is to go & model their success, instead of attempting to figure it all out on their owns. It's because...

| Success has been figured out

Success isn't as mystical as it's made out to be. It's a science. And the key to that science is figuring out what already works for those who have achieved what you want & to model (not copy, but model) their success.

This is also why, throughout history, many of the world's highest achievers (across most professions) had mentors who taught them. It's because they understood that the mentor had *'been there, done that'* & could provide insights that could save them years of figuring it out themselves.

This master-apprentice dynamic is really fascinating to study throughout history *(& we'll talk more about it later)*, but it's important for us to understand that the many of the world's most successful people become successful by standing on the shoulders of giants, modelling their success & accelerating the learning curve that way.

Yet, how often in today's society are we compelled to follow the age-old, yet, in most cases, wildly ineffectively, guidance of *'if you want it done right, do it yourself'*.

I know this, not only by observing & teaching thousands of people, worldwide, but also, because I used to be like that.

I used to be a person who would turn away help because I always had to do it myself. Looking back, it limited my success because I was repeating all the same mistakes that I could've easily learned to avoid by studying others.

This book is designed to model the mindsets, patterns & methods of top athletes (such as Michael Jordan, Kobe Bryant, Roger Bannister, Cristiano Ronaldo & others), musicians (such as Mozart & The Beatles), business leaders (such as Elon Musk, Sara Blakely, Bill Gates) and others.

And, beyond that, it mixes in decades of research in the fields of neuroscience, psychology & human behavior &

rounds off with my personal nuances teaching thousands & thousands of people all around the world.

The goal here, once again, is to model what works, but also to learn *how* & *why* each principle works so you can tailor these 'success principles' to our own preferences, interests, situations, priorities & ways of living.

EXERCISE: 'ACHIEVEMENT HACKING' INDEX
Let's talk about you & put this all into practice.

1. *What's one area of your life that you've done a great job modelling - & learning - from others?*

2. *What are 3 of the greatest lessons you've learned from others (from a parent, a mentor, a coach, a friend, a teacher, etc) & what impact has it had?*

3. *What's 1 area of your life in which you could do a better job modelling the success of others?*

4. *Who are 3 people - current or historical - who's success you could model & how could you do it (e.g. read their biographies, watch interviews, watch documentaries, study their work, etc)*

Take 5 minutes to answer these 4 questions in depth.

IT'S NOT BORN. IT'S DEVELOPED.

"Every artist was first an amateur"

- *RALPH WALDO EMERSON*

If you ask the majority of people what makes someone a 'genius', 'master' or 'extraordinary' at their craft, in most cases, the answer you'll receive, won't be pretty.

In one particular poll, researchers found that more than 75% of people believed that things, like singing or composing, requires an innate gift or god given talent.

Other polls have been done, and consistently people believe that things like innate talent or genetics correlate to skill & success, when in fact, research now shows us these elements have little-to-zero correlation to skill or success.

If you ask, many people will attempt to tell you that people like Shakespeare, Warren Buffett, Henry Ford, Abraham Lincoln, Richard Branson, or Beethoven, are special. That they have natural gifts that the rest of us just weren't fortunate enough to be born with.

They'll tell you that skill, mastery or genius is outside your control. And if you weren't born with some kind of innate abilities of natural born gifts, well then, you're screwed.

Yet, research just doesn't back any of this up.

Studies & experiments in the fields of neuroscience, human psychology & human behavior - as well as the pattern recognition of the world's highest achievers - consistently shows us that we all have far more control over our skill & achievement - than we have been misled to believe.

Just like *achievement is a science*, become extraordinary is far more controllable & predictable than people think.

But, please don't misread that to say 'easy' & 'simple'. It's still not easy. It never was and never will be.

Frankly, it shouldn't be. If it was easy, everyone would have it. And if everybody has it, it's not a success, it's a standard.

The idea that *everybody* can be *above average* at the *same thing* is very paradoxical & irrational if we really think about it. If *everybody* was an extraordinary chess player, then *nobody* would be an *extraordinary* chess player. That new heightened level would now be a new standard.

If everybody was *above average*, nobody would be *above average*. Everybody would be, by definition, *average*.

With that said, while not everybody can become extraordinary at the *same thing*, everybody can absolutely become extraordinary at *something* because there are hundreds - even thousands - of different skills, professions, & industries one can choose from. And, as we know, not everybody wants the same things.

But, in order to do, we must become aware of the truth behind skill (& the myths that derail so many others)...

DNA, IQ, TALENT & TRUTH ABOUT SKILL

> *"I have no special talent. I am only passionately curious"*
>
> - *ALBERT EINSTEIN*

At age 5, he was already composing music for the piano and the violin.

By age 6, he was already impressing his peers with this piano abilities.

Age 8, he wasn't just playing the compositions of others, but rather, he was already composing his own music.

Wolfgang Amadeus Mozart, from an external perspective, seemed like he was born with some kind of innate abilities.

Yet, when you look behind the curtain, just like Michael Howe did in his book, *Genius Explained*, you'll find a very different outlook on this innate musical ability.

You'll find that his ability wasn't innate or god gifted at all, but rather, it was developed.

Michael Howe researched *Mozart's* life & estimates that *Mozart* had already clocked up upwards of *3500 hours* of musical training before his 6th birthday *(which is more hours of training that some musicians put in throughout their lifelong careers - he did that before he turned 6)*

And when you compare his ability, not to those of a similar age, but to a similar amount of hours of training, you'll find that his ability wasn't all that impressive after all.

What he was able to do was compress 3500 hours of training into the first 6 years of his life, making it seem like he was born with musical gifts, when in fact, he wasn't.

3 PHASES OF THE GENIUS ILLUSION

> *"Genius is one percent inspiration and ninety-nine percent perspiration"*
> - *THOMAS EDISON*

The illusion of 'natural born genius' or 'child prodigies' always goes through the same 3 phases. It starts with...

PHASE #1: 'GENIUS'

A new star explodes onto the scene with extraordinary ability. People are shocked & begin to label their genius.

With no other justification for their extraordinary ability, people simplify justify it with 'it must be god given talent,' 'it must be natural born gifts' that created this prodigy.

And sometimes they go even further to justify, *'I could never be as good as that because I just wasn't born with the same superior talent that this person was born with'*.

Now, you've probably seen this play out yourself on the news, the internet, on social media, or throughout history & you've probably heard about so-called 'prodigies' before.

That's the first phase, *'the genius phase'*. Where people are in complete, disillusioned awe of this so-called *'genius'*.

However, just like in the metaphor from the *Introduction*, this phase is an illusion. Like a magician doing a magic trick, it may seem magical at first, but once you learn the trick *(dive behind the scenes)* it loses its elusive nature.

PHASE #2: 'STUDIED'

Over time, people (like myself) go & research these people who are seemingly born with natural born talents or gifts, & attempt to gain greater insight into what really creates their extraordinary achievement.

This starts when certain people become dissatisfied with the justification that these people were just born special.

And once again, just like in the 'magician metaphor,' they go behind the scenes and see what *really* creates their skill.

It's that curiosity, & the discoveries that come of it, that form the basis of pretty much all education we have today.

Every topic we can learn nowadays, at some point, didn't exist. That's until somebody got curious, asked better questions, sought better answers & discovered something.

The topic of *gardening* never existed until somebody found a way to predictably grow crops & passed on that wisdom.

The topic of *psychology* didn't exist until someone decided to research how people think & how the brain works.

It's in that same way that, the topic of *'achievement'* never existed until some people become dissatisfied with the justification that luck (or some other uncontrollable factor) created success & decided to dive deeper into it.

That's how new topics of study are born. People begin to question the socially-accepted norms & discover new things that change our understanding of the world.

And as the 'star's' path to greatness gets researched & analyzed, they discover that it wasn't natural born talent or superior genetics that created their success, but rather other factors that you'll learn in this book. At which point, the illusion of genius fades away.

PHASE #3: 'UNDERSTANDING'

The new discoveries form new understandings about what created this person's success.

After the research, Mozart stops being considered a 'child prodigy,' but rather, became considered an incredibly disciplined, passionate, dedicated child *(with over 3500 hours of training before age 6)* with incredible support around him. Leopold Mozart - Mozart's father - was was already a famous composer & performer himself, and started teaching young Mozart the piano from age 3. It's uncovered research like this that moves us into this 3rd phase of 'Understanding,' where we now have deeper insights into what *really* creates a genius or mastery.

However, Mozart isn't the only example. Far from it. Tiger Woods was considered a genius. So was Van Gogh. So was Beethoven. And while this list may go on & on, what's important, is that today, these icons are no longer considered 'genius' because of 'superior talent' or 'innate gifts,' but rather for their hard work & skill development.

Furthermore, if we're really looking for the best example, few compare to the example of the Italian sculptor, painter & poet, *Michelangelo*, who painted the ceiling of the Sistine Chapel & was once considered the greatest artist of all time. He too was considered a genius.

What's surprising is that while others may have pawed off this extraordinary ability to talent or 'genius,' here are some of Michelangelo's famous quotes throughout history:

"If people knew how hard I had to work to gain my mastery, it would not seem so wonderful at all."

"If you knew how much work went into it, you wouldn't call it genius."

Others couldn't see the thousands of hours of learning & skill development that Michelangelo had put into his craft, hence for them, it's 'genius,' but for Michelangelo himself, he knew how much happened behind the scenes, hence, his approach was very different about this skill.

It's amazing to think that we - human beings - can actually get *so incredibly good* at something that people are in such awe that they prefer to justify it as god given talent, rather than the effect of hard work & dedication.

And when it comes to the debate about 'child prodigies,' too often we look at their innocent, naive, young faces & we are deluded to believe that it was a god gifted gift that lead to their ability, forgetting that these extraordinary young performers have put in hundreds & thousands of hours of hard work to get to where they are at a very young age.

These 3 phases of genius repeat over & over again. Just like magic, it starts of with an elusive appearance of god given talents, but end up, as expected, as nothing more than hard work & strategic skill development that creates their skill.

Hence, we must stop putting so much emphasis on talent & rather re-allocate that focus over to this new perspective.

Studies actually show us now that having an *'I control my results'* mindset - not only makes you feel better because you're in charge - but also enhances your performance.

We have research to support that, but it's really just common sense. If someone believes they control their fitness results, they are far more likely to go the gym & exercise than if they believe they are 'genetically fat' & no matter what they do they're still going to remain fat.

Which is why, even though it's sometimes scary to be fully & completely responsible for all our successes & failures, we must step into this responsibility because it will help us, not only achieve more but be more fulfilled in the process.

Beyond 'talent,' another myth people often accept about skill is the importance of IQ.

IQ *(which stands for 'intelligence quotient')* is the metric measure of intelligence. And we've been told that those who higher IQ are more skilled & achieve more.

However, since then, lots of research has been done to test this correlation & once again, it turns out this too has little-to-no correlation to skill & real-world success.

In fact, in 1921, a man by the name of *Lewis Terman*, decided to study the so-called 'gifted,' *which he assessed based on IQ exclusively.*

Over the next years, he had sorted through the records of over 250,000 students (elementary & high school students) with the goal of finding the top 1000 most gifted students.

He eventually ended up with 1,528 students (856 males & 672 females) with the *highest IQ* (which averaged at over 140 & ranged up to 200). He labelled this group *'Termites.'*

Over the next few decades he - & members of his team - went on to perform the longest psychological, longitudinal study to date around this group of high IQ students. The study today is known as the *'Genetic Studies of Genius.'*

Terman was driven to do this because he believed - as he once said - *"There is nothing about an individual as important as IQ, except possibly his morals."*

During this study, he went on to follow & study the lives of this 'gifted' group. They were all tracked, tested, analyzed & studied. He tracked everything. Every job. Every promotion. Every marriage. Every illness. He collected everything he could get his hands regarding the lives of his *'Termites;'* news articles, letters, documents - you name it.

When he began to report his finding, at first, they seemed promising. A large group of his 'gifted' students went to good school & got good grades. In fact, final schooling results from the study show that over 50% of *'Termites'* finished college, compared to 8% of the general population at that time. A massive difference. And, a big win for the importance - & value - of high IQ.

But, over time, his discoveries didn't match his ideas about the importance of IQ & its correlation to skill (& success).

Although some of *'Termites'* did reach great levels prominence, skill & achievement in their respected fields, the majority of their lives were more mundane. By the 4th volume of *'Genetic Studies of Genius,'* *Terman* had noted that as adults, his subjects pursued common occupations "as humble as those of policeman, seaman, typist and filing clerk" & concluded his multi-decade study by saying:

"At any rate, we have seen that intellect and achievement are far from perfectly correlated."

Which is simply a nice way of saying *'There is little correlation between intellect (IQ) & achievement"*

During the study, Terman went as far as to meddle in the 'Termites' lives, giving them letters of recommendation for jobs and colleges, which makes the study tainted & biased.

But, even despite the fact that *Terman* went *this* far to give his 'gifted' children an advantage, despite that, the results still don't show what he was attempting to prove.

In the book, *Fads and foibles in modern sociology & related sciences*, sociologist, *Pitirim Sorokin* expands on the findings by showing that Terman's selected group of high IQ children *performed no better* than a random group of children selected from similar family backgrounds.

Since about 90% of the high IQ children in his study were white, & the majority came from upper or middle-class families, it's a fair criticism, which only continues to reaffirm how *little* IQ matters in the game of success.

Now, it may seem sad to hear about a man who spent his entire life studying the importance of high IQ only to find that there was *little correlation between IQ & success*, but his work did actually bring a huge amount of value.

He may have set out to prove that those who were born with high IQ *(estimates place the heritability of IQ between 55% & 77%)* go on to achieve more, but instead, he proved the opposite, which, if we really think about it, is a far more empowering conclusion that gives us far greater control over our skill & success.

His study went on to show us that IQ *doesn't* have much of a correlation to skill (or success) at all. And, no matter whether you have incredibly high IQ or very low IQ, it doesn't really affect your ability to become extraordinary.

In another study, a group of researchers studied the IQ of chessmasters & found that their IQ was, statistically, no higher than the IQ of other, less successful, chess players.

And other studies have been done to show this same trend across other industries, topics & skills, continuing to re-confirm that higher IQ does not lead to higher skill.

Which all means, if you were born with low IQ, you are *not* - by any means - genetically screwed, suck at impotence.

And, if you've believed that it's been your *high IQ* that's been giving you the edge in life, it's hasn't. Something else is responsible for that; not IQ.

However, as you may have realized in Terman's study, there is 1 thing that high IQ does correlate & link to.

Because of how top universities & colleges assess applicants, IQ *does* correlate - strongly - to your odds of getting into to a top school. And, as you saw in Terman's study, a staggering 50% of his high IQ children went to college (compared to the national average at the time of 8%). This may change in the future as colleges catch up to current research, but for now, IQ matters in this situation.

Meaning, if you want to get into a good college, then, yes, IQ *does* matter for that, but if you believe is that IQ correlates to skill, business success, relationship success, life satisfaction, or happiness, then, just like *Terman*, you may just go your whole life believing something that 1) latest research shows as a very inaccurate assumption & 2) may just be holding you back from taking full control of your life & achieving that which you really want to achieve.

IQ correlates to your odds of getting into a great college but doesn't correlate to skill, or success itself. It's why some of the most skilled & successful people in the world don't have high IQ, yet become extraordinary.

Furthermore, people have been debating the importance of, not just IQ, but genetics - or DNA - in general.

And, since then, research teams have been looking to find specific DNA combinations that link to specific skills.

Simply put, they've been looking for 'the chess gene,' 'the musical gene' or 'the entrepreneur gene.' They are seeking genetical advantages that link to success in certain areas.

Yet, after decades of seeking, they are yet to find any specific DNA combinations that link to superior level of ability at particular topics or skills.

Plus, if genetics or DNA *really* correlated with higher levels of skill, then all families, siblings & twins would have *similar* talents & abilities. Yet, they don't.

You can take 2 twins, & 30 years later, they'll be vastly different. One may be an incredible artist, the other may suck at art. One may be an amazing creative mind, the other very analytic. *Similar genetics. Different results.*

It's because hard work, passion, training, preference, mindset, deliberate practice, deliberate experimentation *(& other factors you'll learn in this book)* have a far greater effect on *skill* than DNA, genetics or IQ ever could.

And, this doesn't just apply to skill development; it applies to other areas of life as well. For example; health.

Particular studies show that your future health is only about 10% controlled by your genetics, with the other 90% coming from controllable factors like nutrition & lifestyle.

In essence, saying that illnesses & health problem are only about 10% shaped by genetics. Which is pretty shocking baring in mind that most people believe that their illnesses or health problems stem from their genetics.

For now this research - & these findings - have remained very niched, but, based on past behavior, odds are, they'll hit far more mainstream attention over the next few years.

Also important to understand, the numbers vary based on context. 10% is very generic. And, researchers are still testing a lot of this stuff to get increasingly accurate data. It may be 12%, or 9%, or 4%, but the underlying premise stands for health, just like for skill development; *you have far more control of your destiny than we think.*

Back to skill development; please understand there are a lot of nuances to this. For example, in some industries or professions, there are genetic advantages like height, foot size, race, or body composition that affect success.

A great example is the physical attribute of *height* in basketball. Of course, if you're genetically taller, your odds of succeeding in the sport of basketball go up dramatically.

But, the premise still stands, because height is not a skill. Foot size is not a skill. Body composition is not a skill, but rather a physical attribute.

Genetics may correlate with height, foot size or other physical attributes, but they don't correlate with *skill*.

In basketball, 3-point shooting is a skill, defence is a skill, & genetics have little-to-no correlation to these skills.

Someone may be genetically taller, but there are no findings of DNA combinations that make somebody a genetically superior at 3-point shooting or any other *'skill'*.

What you're reading here may seem like a contradiction to everything you're read in this chapter so far, but, it's not. It's the opposite; it's the nuance that will further deepen your understanding of mastery, genius & the extraordinary.

Beyond height (or other physical attributes), often we hear the term *'strengths,'* being passed around in this industry. The idea that some people are naturally stronger at art (or other creative tasks) than at analytical tasks. Or have a 'strength' of being great with people. Or great in competitive environments. And yes, these also do play a difference, but, often, these *'strengths'* are *not* 'innate' - you're *not* born with them - but rather, you've learned them at a young age, making them seem innate.

For example, if a child is born into family of artists & creative-minded people, that child is far more likely to become great artistically. And while some will say that child was 'genetically gifted' with creative, artistic abilities, the more accurate explanation is that that child's environment *(the families influence) made* that child more artistic. It's not born, it's developed. In this scenario, just *developed at a very young age.*

Most of all, I implore you to really understand that even these factors (physical attributes like height, or 'strengths' developed young) aren't restrictions, but simply challenges.

Just because you may not have the physical advantages or strengths to become great at what you do, *these* factors have little correlation to skill or success compared to factors like hard work or intentional skill development.

Height doesn't always link to basketball success. There are plenty of tall people who suck at basketball. It gives an advantage, but only as long as the basketball 'skills' are in place. And, that's all trainable.

Which all means 1 of 2 things...

1. If you believe you were genetically gifted with particular innate gifts, please note that you weren't. You simply worked hard, trained smart & strategically developed your skills. Congratulations.

2. And if you believe that you were born with natural *disadvantages*, you weren't. And, it's time for you to take control, figure out what you really want, reverse-engineer it, develop your skills & get it.

As you read this all, I implore you to pontificate on what you're reading - & even, at times, begin to questions, whether you've been buying into some of these misconceptions in the past & how they've affected your life.

This takes a lot of courage. I get that. But the difference new ways of thinking can make for you are incomparable.

EDUCATION SYSTEM & EXPERIENCE MYTH

"If you judge a fish by its ability to climb a tree, it will live its whole life believing that it is stupid"

-   ALBERT EINSTEIN

Anyone passionate about human potential knows that the education system is, in many ways, broken.

If it's purpose is to help people succeed during adulthood than, in today's day and age, the education system has fallen behind innovation & doesn't fulfil that purpose.

We've been sold the idea that to go well in life, you must do well in school, but it's just not true anymore.

The data, once again, shows there is little-to-no correlation between success in the education system & success in life.

Meaning, doing well in school doesn't necessarily mean you will do well in the real world & doing badly in school doesn't mean you'll do badly in the real world.

At the end of the day, we've all heard countless stories of people who dropped out or failed at school, yet went on to become wildly successful at what they do.

People like Richard Branson, founder of *Virgin*, Lord Alan Sugar, founder of *Amstrad*, David Karp, founder of *Tumblr*, and countless others success stories.

If a link between success in school & success in the real world existed, these examples wouldn't. Yet, they do.

What's best is that these examples are not anomalies, but rather, many times, the norm. We continually see D & F students doing well, while A* students, at times, struggle.

The only research that shows the slightest hint that the schooling system leads to better real-world results is the research that shows those who go to college, on average, earn more than those who do not.

But, of course, if we really think about it, we easily find that this statistic is based on a very flawed premise because those who can afford - or whose families can afford - a college education in the first place start with more money, more connections, more opportunities & greater economic status than those who can't afford college. Which, really taints this statistic & massively undermines its premise.

Which all leads us back to where we started. If there was an actual correlation between test results & life results, A* students would live great lives & F students wouldn't achieve anything. Yet, that's not the case.

Which makes it all the more surprising, how many people limit themselves with *'Of course I failed, I don't have the education,'* or *'I'm not an A* student, I can't do well'*.

They use excuses like *'I'm uneducated,' 'I'm not smart', 'I didn't go to a fancy university or college,'* or *'I didn't have the right teachers'* to justify their lack of skill or success.

Firstly, as you know, those excuses are unjustified because schooling success doesn't correlate to real-world success.

Secondly, the problem is that these beliefs are, often, not even there own, but rather, at the deepest levels, beliefs that the education system that ingrained into them.

It's shocking to see that the education system has actually managed to get people to believe that, without it, they can't achieve any significant success. That without success in the schooling system, people will fail in life. It's ludicrous.

It why, for me personally, I pride myself on the words *'high school dropout.'* For me, it's a status symbol. It makes me living, breathing proof to everyone around me what is truly possible without a fancy, traditional education.

And I believe it's time for all to collectively wake up, realize the data & lack of correlation between the two & step up into new, higher levels of ownership, knowing that...

| The education system doesn't control your results. You control your results.

But, please understand that I'm not against the education system. And I don't, by any regard, believe that *every single person* should do what I did & drop out of school.

In many ways, the education system is very important. And, it really does to do a good job at teaching the basics at a large scale *(hundreds of millions of students worldwide)*.

What I've found is that the education system is, in many ways, flawed. And this opinion has grown rapidly in popularity (particularly over the last few years).

It's why we must step into higher levels of thinking & know that, nowadays, there are *multiple ways* to educate ourselves, acquire skills & gain insights for success.

Jack Ma, founder of *Alibaba*, shares how he recommends people should *intentionally* avoid focusing on getting the best grades in school. He says that if somebody is getting the best grades, they're often spending too much time on the school curriculum & not enough time learning what they actually want to learn to succeed in the real world.

In the information age we're in, in which, with a few clicks, we can get an answer to any question, a lack of traditional education is no longer an excuse; *it's an opportunity.*

So, if talent, DNA, genetics or success in the education system don't create skill or success, then what does?

One of the next big things people turn to is *experience.*

If you go to job interview, you'll most likely find that the company is looking for *experience,* asking questions like, *'How many years of experience do you have in this field?*

At first, this makes sense. *'Surely people get better over time? Experience must correlate to skill, right?'* Not quite.

Data shows that *experience* - how long someone has been involved in a topic, profession or industry - is yet another *inaccurate* predictor of skill or success.

Shockingly, we also now know that, in some cases, *more* experience actually causes *lower* levels of skill.

Early research shows that, often, experienced doctors & fraud investigators are no better at their job than when they first started many years ago.

In fact, doctors with *lots of experience* will regularly score *lower* on medical tests than *less experienced* doctors.

Although at first, this may seem bizarre, when you analyze human behaviour, you'll find it's actually very logical.

And that reason is simple; *people settle.*

Too many people get 'good enough' to make a decent living & settle. They get comfortable & stop seeking to get better.

And it's why, although the clock is ticking & technically, they're still accumulating *experience* at what they do, they're actually not getting any better.

There are plenty of people who have been doing something for 5, 10, 15 + years, yet they are still only 'ok' at it.

And, on the contrary, we all know people who are very skilled at something, yet haven't been doing it as long.

Like an athlete that goes to training every day with the *intentional purpose* of getting better; that's what creates skill. Simply doing something for a long time *('experience')*, is not the same as *intentional skill development*. And that's why experience doesn't correlate to skill (or success).

And worse, because of *skill degradation*, over time, their skill doesn't just stay the same, but rather, their competencies degrade & they sometimes get *worse.*

In the words of Lou Holtz, *"In this world you're either growing or you're dying so get in motion and grow."*

Now, as you read this - & especially so, if what you're reading is contrary to your existing beliefs about IQ, talent, genetics, schooling, experience or skill - your survival instincts may kick in attempting to protect you.

And, as you read particular research & understandings in this book, you may even be compelled to search the internet in search of examples to contradict this research.

That's what I wanted to do when I first learned this. At the time, I believed in the importance of IQ, I trusted experience & thought that talent was innate. And, when I first started studying this all, it felt a little like a punch in the face. Not physically, but psychologically.

It's because, based on what we also know from human psychology studies, often, we tie our beliefs & ideas about how the world works into our own identity & self-worth.

And, when those beliefs are challenged, it's easy to let our survival instincts (our old, reptilian brain) to kick in & fight the new information. Which, may make us feel good for a moment (because it saves us from feeling 'wrong'), over time, the effects of fighting new awareness are detrimental.

And, in those moments - perhaps even now - we must remember, it's radically more beneficial for us to overcome this temptation than fighting the new evidence presented.

And, beyond that, we must remember that our beliefs are, so often, not even our own. What we believe, so often, is simply passed down to us from our parents, grandparents, friends, teachers & others. Odds are, there are certain things you believed 10 years ago, that today, you don't. It's because you are learning, growing & getting better. And, that's what I implore you to do here.

I challenge you, to adapt, rather than closing yourself off from this new way of thinking about skill & success. Because although going to the internet & finding examples of Nobel Prize winners with high IQ, or people who *seem* to have 'innate talent,' may support our existing beliefs, so often these individual examples are not complete. They are just 1 piece of the puzzle, not the whole puzzle.

The information in this book is not just my own. It's, in many parts, based on the backbone of decades of in-depth, scientific research, & it's only the most accurate, most recurring findings about success that are shared here.

Lastly, these finding, at the end of the day, are actually incredibly supportive. They consistently conclude that we are in far greater control of our own skills, success & achievements than we have been misled to believe. An understanding that pushes us to consistently be our very best. Which, at first, may feel tough at the time, but over time, is incredibly freeing to know we are in control of your future & can shape it how we choose.

YOU ARE IN CONTROL

> *"When we set about accounting for a Napoleon or a Shakespeare or a Raphael or a Wagner or an Edison or other extraordinary person, we understand that the measure of his talent will not explain the whole result, nor even the largest part of it; no, it is the atmosphere in which the talent was cradled that explains; it is the training it received while it grew, the nurture it got from reading, study, example, the encouragement it gathered from self-recognition and recognition from the outside at each stage of its development: when we know all these details, then we know why the man was ready when his opportunity came"*
>
> *- MARK TWAIN*

Back in 1990, Anders Ericsson went and studied many of the world's highest performers; chess champions, violin virtuosos, star athletes, and others, and he identified that it took them 10,000 hours of 'deliberate practice' (focused, intentional, skill development) to become masterful.

This research was then deepened, expanded on & shared by people like Malcolm Gladwell in his book, *Outliers*, Geoff Colvin, in his book, *Talent Is Overrated*, and Daniel Coyle and his book, *The Talent Code*. As well as many others.

This research coined the *'10,000-hour rule'*. The rule that states that it takes 10,000 hours of intentional & focused skill development to become a master at what you do.

And, in many ways, this rule has skyrocketed in popularity & consumer adoption over the years. Mainly because it adds a specific benchmark for people to aim for.

By putting a number on it, in many ways, this rule moved people away from myths like DNA, IQ or genetics, and, it gave people back control over their own skill.

And, this rule, does, in many ways, correlate to skill & success. But, even better, the rule is far from flawless.

The problem with the *'10,000-hour rule'* is that it fails to account many important factors, like...

1) not all 'deliberate practice' is equal

2) not everybody learns the same way

3) learning speed *(if you learn faster, you can actually accelerate the '10,000 hours')*

Hence, we must understand the nuance. And that nuance is that, yes, 10,000 hours is a great benchmark, but, also, you can absolutely accelerate that process.

If someone is a fast learner *(& they develop their skill using the most up-to-date, cutting-edge, strategies)* they can absolutely be better after just 7,000 hours than somebody else is after 11,000 hours of training.

And this is why learning faster & developing skill effectively is so important. It can shave off hundreds & thousands of hours off the growth curve it takes to reach mastery.

And while that may sound appealing, another outlook is that 2 people can put in the same number of training hours, yet one person can become 20%, 30%, 40% or 50% better because they are a greater learner.

| Learning speed is a crucial metric

Learning speed matters. It matters more than most people ever realize. And, once again, it's controllable & trainable.

And, in future sections, you'll discover exactly how to increase your learning speed to achieve far more, far faster.

But, for know, it's important that we're on the same page. The purpose of this first chapter was obvious; to help people understand how truly controllable skill is.

| Extraordinary skill isn't something you're born with. It's something you develop.

And while it may be easy to stay in doubt & remain a victim of some of the factors we've discussed in this chapter, I hope this chapter inspires people to step out, move past the misconceptions & step up into higher levels of potential.

I believe that human potential is near boundless. And, both, research & historical analysis, shows us it really is.

The research is there to back it, but we need to be open to seeing it. Which takes courage. It takes courage to rethink beliefs. It takes courage to take full control of our destiny.

But, I know if you picked up that book, you either already understand this *(hence, use this chapter as reinforcement & strengthening of those beliefs)* or you now have new understandings - & mixed with courage - new beliefs that will support you to become even more extraordinary.

With that, we must take control & proceed courageously...

2 | THE SKILL TRIANGLE:
DECONSTRUCTING GREATNESS

"Learning is not attained by chance, it must be sought for with ardor and attended to with diligence"

- *ABIGAIL ADAMS*

So often we look at the world's highest skilled & highest achieving people, as they are *today*, and we somehow let ourselves believe that this who they always were.

We see Oprah Winfrey, Michael Jordan, Roger Federer, David Copperfield or Elon Musk with their extraordinary levels of skill today, yet we often forget to realize that they too went through a process of strategic skill development.

We fail to re-calibrate our perspective & realize that they too were beginners - newbies - at one point in time. That they too had to start somewhere.

And they didn't start at the peak of the mountain, no, just like everybody else, they started the bottom, with low levels of skill, success or impact. And, over the years, they climb up to the lofty heights they are at now.

And, not just them, but everybody. Nobody that is extraordinary - or masterful - at what they do, started there. Nobody. They started just like everybody else.

I implore you to go & read their biographies, study their backstory & you'll find it's the same pattern on repeat.

At first, they sucked. Which is hard to picture sometimes.

It's hard to imagine a world in which Michael Jordan is a basketball newbie or a world in which David Copperfield isn't yet mesmerizing audiences with magic & illusion.

However, in the wise words of Ralph Waldo Emerson...

"Every artist was first an amateur."

And, that's where their skill development journey - just like everybody else's - began. At the bottom. It's because...

| Skill doesn't discriminate

Skill doesn't care how rich your parents are, how famous your grandad is or, even, how much you dream about it.

It doesn't respond to good vibes, but, rather, to hard work & *strategic* skill development.

It doesn't care how much money you have or how good looking you are. More money may buy you better equipment or hire you a better coach, but it doesn't buy you skills. It still takes purposeful & intentional training.

Nobody starts of extraordinarily skilled at what they do. It's a process. Which asks the question...

How does somebody go from a complete newbie at something, to an amateur, to a pro, to master, to world-class at that same skill that they once sucked at?

The answer is that extraordinary levels of skill are simply the result of an accumulation of *'distinctions'*.

And, skill development - the process of getting increasingly skilled at what you do - is simply the process of *'accumulating distinctions'* within your field of expertise.

This is so important that this entire chapter is dedicated to the understanding of distinctions & how they create skill.

And, once you get this, it will truly change how you view, & approach, skill development.

UNDERSTANDING 'DISTINCTIONS'

"Great things are done by a series of small things brought together"

-   *VINCENT VAN GOGH*

What separates people with lower levels of skill - newbies, beginners, amateurs - from those with high levels of skill - professionals & masters - is a *depth of distinctions*.

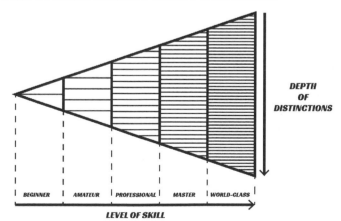

THE SKILL DEVELOPMENT TRIANGLE

Distinction: a piece of stored & trained information, data or muscle memory that gives someone a specific insight, understanding or nuance into a topic or skill.

A beginner has some basic distinctions about their field of craft. Hence, they know how to do the basics. But lack deeper, richer insights (distinctions) into their craft. They lack nuance. They lack detail. They lack precision. They lack the finer distinction (insights) that masters have accumulated through their training.

Meanwhile, as you can also see in *The Skill Development Triangle*, someone who's a master (or world class) at what they do has a far greater *depth of distinction* in their field.

They have deeper, richer insights into the skill they've mastered. They know the in's & out's. They know the rules, best practices, exceptions, details & nuances. They know what tactics works best, at which time, to get best results.

They have a *'depth of distinctions'* that they have accumulated over years of training, that they can *pull on* to make the right decision that brings back the best results.

Skill is simply a game of *'distinctions.'*

| Distinctions separate the best, from the rest

IQ, genetics or innate talent may not correlate to high levels of skill, but, what does, is an accumulation of 'distinctions'. *The more distinctions you accumulate - & train - the more skilled you become at what you do.*

| The more distinction you accumulate, the more skilled you become at something.

What makes an extraordinary artist is the accumulation of thousands & thousands of little distinctions about art, painting & design that most other artists just don't possess.

In the same way, a great scientist understands thousands & thousands of little details about science that most people just don't have the *'distinctions'* to understand.

Mozart was not a genius because he was born with some type of 'innate musical gifts,' but rather, because he had spent over 3500 hours accumulating *'distinctions'* in the areas of music & composition, before his 6th birthday.

| Those that are extraordinary at what they do have accumulated far more distinctions - a depth of distinctions - in their area of craft

A 'distinction' is a little like a cooking ingredient. And, in this metaphor, a 'master' or 'genius' is like a great chef.

They have a kitchen (their brain), in which they've accumulated thousands of *'distinctions'* (insights) into what works, what doesn't, what order, which sequence, which intensity or many other nuances. And they know which particular 'distinctions' must be combined to create a result (in this example, an incredible meal).

While, most people (newbies, beginners, amateurs) are cooking with a lack of ingredients (distinctions), masters are making the best dishes (putting on the greatest performances) because they have a much wider range of ingredients (distinctions) to pull from when they need to.

For a master chef, an example of a *'distinction'* is how much salt to add to a dish, how much pepper (another distinction), how long to let it sit (another distinction).

For a designer, a *'distinction'* is knowing which background image will best show off the brand (a set of distinctions), which font will work best (another set of distinctions) or how transparency it should be (another distinction).

In the sport of tennis, a *'distinction'* is knowing how to hold the racket correctly (a set of distinctions), when to use a forehand swing (a distinction), when to use the backhand (another distinction) or how much power is too much in a serve (another distinction).

Think of 'distinctions' as images on a camera. A beginner has a blank camera with no images on it. They have zero insight or understanding - no accumulated distinctions - within a topic or skill. Meanwhile, a master has thousands & thousands of images they've taken & stored on the camera (distinctions & insights stored in the main) that their brain can refer back to at any time to make a better, more effective decision.

EXPANDED AWARENESS

"The key to growth is the introduction of higher dimensions of consciousness into our awareness"

- *LAO TZU*

If you've ever seen someone extraordinary at what they do demonstrate their skill - whatever it is - you'll know almost everything they do, in *your* mind, leaves you thinking...

'How did they do that?' 'How did they know?' 'How is that even possible?'

It leaves you amazed, yet confused & curious.

How did that basketball player know the ball would bounce off the hoop exactly like that?

How did that masterful photographer know that it's this exact angle that would give that best camera shot?

How did they know that adding oregano to that dish was going to make it taste better?

How did they know that paintbrush was going to give them a better brushstroke that the other brushes?

That's a little what it's like when you see someone of high levels of skill do what they do. It's amazing, but confusing at the same time. It's a little like watching a magic show.

However, what we now know about skill development (& success) allows us to explain this phenomenon.

What's going on is that the master is demonstrating *'distinctions,'* that we, the spectators, do not yet possess.

It's a little like you downloading a file onto a computer, but not having the right software to open that file. Your mind is downloading it - by visually processing what you're seeing the master do - but it can't understand how it's possible because it lacks the software *('stored distinctions')* to understand it. Leaving you confused, but curious.

Meanwhile, if a fellow magician would watch that same magic show, their response would be very different.

They wouldn't be confused or shocked by what they were seeing, but rather, they would think something along the lines of, *'I know how they did that,'* or *'That's so basic.'*

This is because the fellow magician has already acquired the *'distinctions'* (the software) required to read the files (distinctions) that are being downloaded.

They've already put in the learning before to accumulate those *same* distinctions, hence, they can process that information & understand how the magician is doing that.

While others, who haven't learned magic *(accumulated distinctions in the skill of magic & illusion) don't* have the distinctions to understand what the magician is doing, causing that feeling of confusion, wonder & amazement.

It's almost like me talking in a new language to someone. Their brain wouldn't have the distinctions (insights) into this new language to interpret what I would be saying.

However, as soon as they learn (accumulate distinctions) in this new language, understanding what I'm saying would be easy because you have the distinctions to interpret it.

Every distinction you accumulate gives you an *expanded awareness* of your craft & a higher level of skill within it.

But, that's not it. This new, higher level of skill then gives you new, higher levels of decision-making potential. And...

MORE SKILL LEADS TO BETTER DECISIONS

> *"A good decision is based on knowledge and not on numbers"*
>
> -   *PLATO*

As you become better at what you do (increased skill), you're able to make better, more effective, decisions, and it's what helps you achieve more. It comes down to this...

| 'Skill' is simply the ability to make - & execute on - the best, most effective, decisions.

The more skilled somebody is, the more effective their decision making - within that area of craft - is.

A masterful tennis player is able to make - & execute on - far better decisions during a tennis match than a newbie.

Why? It's because when you become more skilled, you now have accumulated more distinctions, which your brain uses as data & information to base your decision on.

And, when you have more data & information to base your decision on, you'll make better, more effective, decisions.

A master is leveraging thousands & thousands of distinctions - accumulated through year & years of experiences, learning & training - to make decisions, while a newbie is making decisions based on just a few piece of information it has available. And that makes the difference.

Hence, with very rare exception, someone with higher levels of skill will consistently make better, more effective decisions - within that area of craft - that someone of a lower level of skill.

It's almost like watching 2 detectives both attempting to solve a mystery. The first detective only has a few pieces of data (evidence) to base his/her decisions on. Meanwhile, the second detective has hundreds - even thousands - pieces of data, information & insight (evidence, in this case) to base his/her decisions on.

Who do you think is going to make more informed, more strategic, more effective decisions in this mystery?

Of course, it's going to be the detective with more data & insights to pull from. And, that's how it works with skill.

Somebody skilled has thousands & thousands of pieces of data (distinctions), accumulated through years of training, stored inside their brain, that they can base their decision upon. Meanwhile, a newbie has very limited information (a small number of accumulated distinctions) to act on.

Which all, in turn, allows a skilled person to make better decisions & be classified, by definition, as *'more skilled'*.

And it's also what allows them to, more often, be in the *'right place at the right time.'* You've probably heard the phrase before, right? (*'right place at the right time'*) It often used to justify a success or victory.

Whether its a sports player in the right place at the right time to get that game-winning point, a business leader at in right place in the right time, seizing the opportunity of an emerging industry, or a team of skilled reporters who seem to always be a few steps ahead in providing the latest news headlines, the justification seems to be the same, *'I was just in the right place at the right time.'*

Now, if that happened just a few times, we could put it off to luck, or good fortune. But, it doesn't. So often, it's the *same people* who always seem to be in that magical, *'right place at the right time.'* Which begs the questions...

Why do the same sports players & athletes always seem to be in the 'right place at the right time?'

Why do top business leaders seem to always be in the 'right place at the right time' when new business opportunities & industries emerge?

Why do top investors always seem to be ahead to the market - like they're always a few steps ahead - & constantly are in the 'right place in the right time' to accumulate the greatest wealth?

It's because, once again, those with *high levels of skill* have more distinctions that they've accumulated, which, in turn, allows them to judge situations more accurately.

It's like a top-rated sports scout (someone's whose job is to find up-&-coming talent). They can see potential more clearly than others.

They have more data (distinctions) to judge a situation or circumstance with greater accuracy.

While other people may only see that player for who they are today, - current skill level - a top rated scout can see potential more clearly, because, once again, they've got more distinctions that allow them to assess a player's future with more accuracy.

But, it's only possible for the top-rated scout to do that because he's spent years - & often decades - consistently watching & observing player, learning (accumulating distinctions) within his area of expertise.

In that same way, top investors that always seem to make the right investment decisions, are able to do that because they've developed a much greater *depth of distinctions* about investing, consumer trends & reading the market than the average investor.

Higher skill lets you see the full puzzle while others are only seeing part of it, which leads to the correlation - between skill & success - that we've been diving deeply into in this book.

THE POWER OF 'NUANCE'

"Life is about the gray areas. Things are seldom black and white, even when we wish they were and think they should be, and I like exploring this nuanced terrain"

- *EMILY GIFFIN*

With greater skill comes greater nuance. And with greater nuance comes even greater decision making & skill.

Because, you can do all the right things, but if you do them with the wrong timing, or in the wrong order, or with the wrong intensity, you won't get the result you want.

Doing the right things is only the first step. What comes beyond that is what we call, *nuance.*

Nuances are still distinctions, but they are the smaller, finer, distinctions that really separate the good from the great. The details, inches & small elements that make all the difference & move you up to that mastery level.

But, you don't start there. You start with the basics. You start by learning the rules, the guiding principles & the best practices. Only later, when then you move into higher levels of skill - when you move into 'incremental growth' - is when you start focusing on the *nuances.*

If you're learning chess, you start by learning all the rules, as well as the guiding principles that create victory in chess. However, as you learn more, you begin to realize that the rules & guiding principles you learned previously begin to get challenged.

You begin to see successful people doing the opposite of what you learned & succeeding at massive levels. It, once again, caused confusion, because it goes against the initial best practices.

And, it's only then that you begin to realize that every rule has its exception. You realize that even the best practices, at certain times, aren't the best. You begin to realize the impact of, not just doing the right thing, but doing it with the right nuances, like timing, intensity & intent.

A beginner may learn a principle, but a mastery may break that rule and get better result. *Why?* Because with greater skill, you gain greater nuance of your craft.

Now, for most people, nuances are never a discussion. Everything is black & white. Right & wrong. Good & bad. That's where everybody starts within a new topic or skill, but, it's only once they reach a certain level of competence that nuances join the discussion.

And, odds are, unless this is the first self-improvement & self-mastery book you've ever read, you may have experienced this within this industry of self-improvement.

At one time, you may have read a great insight like this...

"There's no reason to have a plan B because it distracts from plan A" - Will Smith

You hear that & begin to approach everything in life with that philosophy. You begin to de-prioritize back up plans & focus even more on what you want.

But, then - maybe next week, or next month - you hear something like this...

"If Plan A isn't working, I have Plan B, Plan C, and even Plan D" - Serena Williams

Or something like this...

"The key is for the audience never to know, so I have a plan B for every illusion" - David Copperfield

3 extremely successful high achievers with such wildly different approaches to planning. Many may hear those two quotes & get confused, asking;

'Which one is right, which one is wrong?' 'Which approach is good, which is bad?

The answer is that they're both right. They're both very effective approaches & clearly, based on results, both of these approaches work very well for different people.

And this is where - in this scenario & in pretty much every other conflicting set of options in any area of your life - *nuances* come in.

And, as you dive deeper, experiment & test, you begin to realize that, at times it's more effective to forget the backup plans & focus only on Plan A, & in other times, it's more effective to have strategic backup plans in place. Nuance.

This is an insight that, frankly, may annoy some people. In fact, it used to annoy me, because I wanted the world to be very binary. Black & white. Right & wrong. But, it's not. And, neither is skill development.

And, as you become increasingly skilled at what you do, you'll begin to discover greater nuance to your craft.

| Beginners know the rule. Masters know the nuances, exceptions & counters to the rule.

And that exactly is the goal & where the greater advantage comes from. Not from knowing the rules, but from understanding the nuances to every rule & best practice.

You begin to, not only know the rules & guiding principles but also understand the exceptions to every rule. You acquire a greater understanding of when it's best to deploy one strategy, & when to deploy another.

Because, if you're really looking for loopholes, you can find an exception to almost every rule. I don't care which book it is, who's the author, what film it is, how foolproof & research-backed the framework is, there are exceptions. Throughout history, anomalies exist.

And as you read some of the information in this book (or any other one for that matter), you may sometimes think...

'Hey, but certain people - anomalies - don't follow all of these rules - principles & best practices - for achievement'

To which, whenever anybody says that to me, my response is simply, *'Exactly. That's the point.'*

It's also why I implore people to stop looking for 'the secret to success,' & instead look for 'correlations.'

Because there is no 1 secret to success. Never has; never will be. There are too many variables. But, we can always identify what best correlates (links to) success.

Once you know the rules of the game, your goal is to push them, challenge them & stretch them. Sometimes, even, to break them & see what happens, in search of effectiveness.

What I can tell you is that, although some people throughout history - a very small fraction - break the frameworks & 'success principles' revealed in this book, it's with method & intention.

They start by learning the rules of success (everything we're covering now) & only once they've gotten to a certain level, they begin to intentionally break rules to see if they can climb even higher. It's not accidental; it's intentional.

The world's highest achievers don't succeed by accident. There's a method to it. There is intention to their actions.

I was recently studying storytelling; the art of telling stories in an engaging and captivating way, and, I was going through a great storytelling program by a brilliant guy by the name of *Michael Hauge*.

Michael works with top Hollywood movie producers, screenwriters & actors to improve their storytelling,

As I was going through the program I remember Michael saying that he often gets asked the same question:

'This movie, this tv show or this story doesn't follow the storytelling structure you're sharing... how come?'

He went on to explain about how he personally works with many of the best Hollywood producers & that they know all of the rules - they know the best practices - & it's only *because* they know them, that they can then go on to break them to see if they can get even better results.

And, the same happens with the learning, skill acquisition & success rules, frameworks & principles inside this book.

The best results come from first learning the rules - & best practices - & then progressing to strategically learn the nuances & exceptions to each rule. But, all in the search for even greater effectiveness.

It all comes back to nuance. And, *nuances* are critically important if you really want to become extraordinary.

A sports star, athlete, chess player or business owner that only has 1 move, disregards the nuance & fails to understand the details to the field they're in, isn't a master.

Nuance is about many things. Here are a few examples:

1. **Timing:** If you do the right thing, at the wrong time, you'll fail.

2. **Intensity:** If you do the right thing with too much (or too little) intensity, you'll fail.

3. **Order & Sequencing:** If you do the right thing, in the wrong order, you'll - you guessed it - fail.

4. **Context & Environment:** If you do the right thing in the wrong context or environment (e.g. say the right thing to the wrong people), you'll fail.

5. **Intention/Motive:** If you do the right thing, with the wrong intention or motivation, you'll fail.

As well as many other elements that make up *nuance*. Doing the right things isn't enough. It will only get you so far. The world's highest achievers thrive because they combine the right actions with the right nuance *(that they've accumulated over year of research, testing, failing, self-improvement & overall, skill development)*.

THE SKILL TRIANGLE: 5 LEVELS OF SKILL

"Mastery is not a function of I.Q. or natural talent or wealthy parents who can send you to the best school, but rather the result of going through a learning process, fueled by the desire to grow and the persistence to push past any obstacles"

- *ROBERT GREENE*

If you go and observe any industry, you will find people at each of these 5 levels of skill.

THE SKILL DEVELOPMENT TRIANGLE

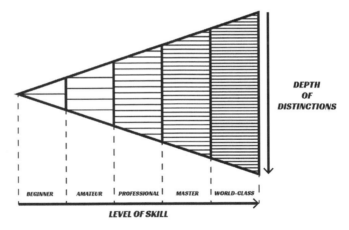

By understanding these 5 levels - & the progressive path between then - you'll be able to level up your skills far more intentionally, strategically & predictably.

BEGINNER:

When we start developing a new skill for the first time, we suck. No need to hide it. We can admit it. At first, we suck.

And of course we do, we've never done it before. It's logical to be bad at it at first. Everybody starts here.

I don't say this to discourage anybody, but rather, the opposite; to encourage people to get started.

I say that because skill is an open game where everybody starts at the same place & only those who put in the hard, strategic training reap the rewards.

A beginner has very few distinctions at what they do.

A beginner may have seen how to play tennis on the TV, but they haven't taken the information they observed & turned it into trained distinctions in their mind & body.

A tennis beginner may be able to hold the racket with the correct hand (that's a distinction), with the right grip (another distinction) and at the right angle (yet another distinction), but that will only get them so far.

Meaning, they've accumulated a handful of distinctions about tennis, but, if they want to progress to the next level, they're going to have to spend a lot more time learning (accumulating distinctions) in the sport.

It's important to understand that we've all been here are some point or another. Me, you, everybody, we've all experienced being a beginner at a particular skill.

Think back to a new skill you've learned in your lifetime. Think back to the very first encounter with that skill; your first lesson, first training session or first time doing it.

Most people would agree that this first stage is a little frustrating, confusing & a little overwhelming sometimes.

It's because learning a new skill is like entering a new world. A new world filled with new etiquette, new language & new ways of moving, talking & doing.

It's in those moments that I want you to remember these 2 things, 1) everyone starts here, it's a journey, & 2...

| 'Confusion,' is your brain's signal that you're about to learn something new

And at this first stage - beginner - there's a lot of confusion because there's a lot that you don't know.

And that's a big reason people quit. They view 'confusion,' as something negative. When, really, confusion is a gift. It's signal you're about to accumulate new distinctions.

I challenge you to make this mental shift & begin to fall in love with confusion because confusion is something great.

Everybody may start as a beginner, but, how do they go to the next level? How do you get good at something?

Plain & simple, you begin to accumulate distinction (insights), by allocating time to learn & train the topic, or skill, you're looking to get better at.

Once again, if you think back to anything you've ever learned in your life, you'll find that, you've been - knowingly or unknowingly - doing this for every topic or skill you've ever learned or trained.

And, as you accumulated more distinctions *(this is how you do this... is is what 'not' to do, this is how to move that... how to make that look...)* within that skill, you've progressed to the next level of skill...

AMATEUR:

An amateur has accumulated more distinctions - a greater *depth* of distinctions - & therefore, has achieved a higher level of skill than a beginner.

A tennis amateur has accumulated a few dozen key distinctions in the sport of tennis. An amateur knows the basics at a decent level.

The accumulated distinctions are slightly smaller, finer distinctions (smaller details in the are of craft), but are still fairly large, obvious distinctions. And, each new accumulated distinction has a huge performance impact.

Comparatively, if Roger Federer - who's already at the world-class level for tennis - wants to improve his tennis ability, he would be focusing on much, much finer distinctions (details) in the sport of tennis. And, each extra distinction that *he* accumulates will only give him a small, tiny, fractional gain in skill & results.

The reason for this is simple. When we first learn something new, we make big progress very quickly - it's because we're accumulating big clearly, visible distinctions. Beyond that, if you've only ever accumulated 20 distinctions (insights) into a skill, 1 extra distinction is a 5% growth toe number of distinctions you've accumulated.

Meanwhile, if you're world-class like Roger Federer, you already have thousands & thousands of distinctions accumulated & 1 extra is only a 0.1% gain in the number of distinctions you have. And, this is why it's easy to make quick progress when you start, but then that progress moves into 'incremental improvements' as you get good.

Day 2 of learning a new skill, you might get 40% better at the skill (a big jump), but day 922 of learning a new skill, a 0.1% improvement on your ability is a big win. The key is...

| Don't get discouraged by incremental growth

When you start learning something new, it's especially exciting because, at first, as you can see in *The Skill Development Triangle*, you're learning big distinctions.

However, later on, once you've learned the big distinction, that's when the learning curve slows down & you begin to make incremental improvement by working on smaller distinctions (finer details, small nuances & tiny tweaks).

The problem is that this 'incremental growth' discourages a lot of people. However, what people fail to realize is that, yes, the learning curve may slow down, but, the upside begins to grow exponentially.

Every incremental improvement, every 'extra mile' you go brings you astronomically greater returns because, 1) a lot of other people settle, 2) you begin to jump the ranks & become one of the best at what you do.

Number 1, earn far more, impact far more people & reaps far greater upside than #4 or #5. Yet, to become the best in the world, you do not need to become 10X or 100X better than 2nd, 3rd, 4th or 5th best, You just need to be a tiny, little bit better. You just need to go that extra mile & pursue that incremental growth, knowing that each increment makes a massive difference to your upside at this level.

And the world's highest achievers have become the world's best, in part, because they simply outlasted those around them. They've been willing to go that extra mile. And that's the challenge for you; stay in the game & go the extra mile.

Beyond an amateur, comes the professional, who has already accumulated hundreds - & thousands - of distinction & has moved into incremental growth.

PROFESSIONAL:

By this level of skill, the world can clearly see that you have put in a lot of hard work to build up your skill.

For many people, this level takes a few solid years of training & skill development.

During the chapters in this book, I will show you how to supercharge your skill development & progress your skill level faster, but, to get to this point - no matter what - it still takes a lot of work & effort.

This level is often, when, first enter *financial competency.*

Financial Competency: a point during your skill development at which you get good enough to get properly financially compensated for your skill.

While somebody is a beginner or amateur, often, that skill is still just a hobby, they're still waiting to get paid for their skill or getting paid very little.

Sometimes people pay for beginners or amateurs, but in most cases, this level, *professional*, is when people really get compensated for their skill.

I'm not talking about getting a job waiting tables at a local restaurant, I'm talking about the point a musician gets paid to perform at concerts, an upcoming sports star gets paid to play the sport full time, or when a painter can earn a full-time living selling their art. In examples like these, it's only usually at this level - *professional* - that the real financial rewards kick in. Financial competency.

And beyond that, the income often just continues to climb with skill. A beginner, or amateur, will often work for free, or get paid very little. A professional will often begin to earn a full-time level exclusively from their skill. A professional approaching mastery will earn a lot more. A master; even more. And world-class, will often, get compensated most (exponentially more than others).

Although, please understand, this financial upside varies wildly between industries & professions & is also, often, the results of a combination of skills working together.

At this level - professional - the person has accumulated hundreds & hundreds - approaching thousands - of distinctions within their area of craft.

Important to understanding, there are a huge amount of beginners (pretty much everybody alive is a beginner at something), there are fewer amateurs. A lot of people drop off, quit or take a different path.

Beyond that, there are even fewer professionals, because only a small fraction of people put in the work to become highly skilled at something.

Beyond that, even fewer - only a very small percentage - ever go on to master their craft. And even fewer, ever become world-class what they do.

MASTERY:

A master has accumulated thousands & thousands of distinctions within their area of expertise.

Michael Jordan has accumulated thousands and thousands of distinctions in the sport of basketball.

Roger Federer has accumulated thousands & thousands of distinctions in the sport of tennis.

Oprah Winfrey has accumulated thousands & thousands of distinctions in the skill of human communication.

David Copperfield has accumulated thousands & thousands of distinctions in the craft of magic & illusion.

And, it what makes them masters (& even world-class) at what they do. It's what allowed them to make better, more effective, decisions, outperform others, be in the 'right place at the right time,' & succeed far beyond the norm.

Masters have accumulated thousands of distinctions including finer, smaller distinctions, nuances & deeper understanding, that together, make a huge difference.

WORLD-CLASS:

The next level beyond mastery is world-class. These are the top few people in the world at that particular skill.

The people that reach this level of skill are the people that get talked about within their industry, and outside of it, and often get talked about *(their legacy continues)* long after they pass away.

Once again, what separates someone at this level from someone at the mastery level is simple, *an ever deeper range & accumulation of distinctions.*

Someone who's world-class can see & do things that even a master can't.

A NEW APPROACH TO SKILL

"Intelligence is the ability to adapt to change"

- *STEPHEN HAWKING*

Learning - or skill development - is simply the process of *accumulating distinctions* (insights, nuances, experiences, pieces of data) within a field of expertise.

And that's how we should approach learning & skill development. Whenever you're *learning*, what you're doing is simply accumulating *new distinctions*.

And with *repetition*, your brain is storing those *distinctions* deeper & deeper into your *subconscious mind (as we'll talk about in the next chapter)*, where execution becomes more & more automatic & increasingly effortless.

However, the best part of this all is that, you knowing *this* - combined with the understanding that *achievement is a science* - gives *you* the potential to become as skilled as, Michael Jordan, Roger Federer, Madonna, Oprah Winfrey, Elon Musk, Cristiano Ronaldo, Martin Luther King Jr, or Albert Einstein - *if you choose to*. But, the *potential* exists.

And just like in the movie, *The Matrix* - in which a skill can simply be *'uploaded'* into a person's brain - it's possible for you to something similar in the real world.

It won't be as easy to do. Far from it. This isn't a movie; this is real life. Let's get serious. However, the potential exists, because, if you're able to decipher & deconstruct the exact distinctions *(insights, nuances, understandings, experiences & points of view)* that a particular world-class achiever has accumulated, & you train those *exact same* distinctions into your mind, often through, years of training, you too, can reach the same level of skill as them.

It's not easy. Rarely, anything really worth doing is easy; however, it's *possible*. As to how, it requires you to, 1) study somebody's skill to discover the exact distinctions they've accumulated, & 2) be willing to put in a lot of work & skill development to develop those *same* distinctions.

The potential exists. You can absolutely become as good - or even, better - than each & every one of those high achievers (or others) - *if you're committed to.*

That doesn't mean everybody will get there. Most people won't. They won't put in the work. They'll choose a different path. They'll have different priorities. But, it's very freeing - & inspiring - to know the possibility is there.

Also, it's important to understand that we're talking about replicating one's *skills*, not about replicating their *success*.

Replicating one's skill is absolutely possible because, it's often, independent of context, environment or timing.

Meanwhile, replicating success is much harder & moves into the realm of the *'near impossible'* because there are many factors - far outside our control - that we can't replicate, yet were crucial to that person's success.

A great example is *Bill Gates* & Microsoft. You can absolutely become as *skilled* as he was in the skills of computing & business, but you wouldn't necessarily be able to replicate his success.

This is because, once again, if you took the same actions as he did, you'd started a software, computer company, & in today's world, 1) you'd be far behind modern innovation &,

2) you'd be facing much greater competition than he did at the forefront of the computing industry. That industry has changed massively since the 1970's & 1980's. Both supply & demand within it has increased massively. Competition has changed. The opportunities have changed.

Which all, as a result, would get you very different results. Same actions. Different timing & context. Different results.

You can replicate his *skill*, which would give you massive potential to succeed in business & tech - & would positively impact your results - but, other factors must be factored in.

It's why, if you go back to *The Skill Pyramid* visual in the *Introduction* of this book, you'll find it talks about higher skill equals higher income & impact *'potential'*.

Which means, higher skill gives you the *potential* for greater income & impact, but the end result is often also controlled by other factors that, unfortunately, are outside our control, such as timing, environment, economics, consumer trends, supply-&-demand, & others.

With that said, skill is, without a doubt, the biggest factor that correlates to success. It doesn't *equal* success. There is no 1 'secret to success'. But, it does, *strongly correlate* to it. And, looking at the highest achievers just re-affirms that.

And, skill, as you know, is very controllable. Which makes your future, in many ways, very controllable. And you can shape it by taking control of your skill development.

3 | FEEDBACK LOOPS: ACCUMULATING DISTINCTIONS

"Live as if you were to die tomorrow. Learn as if you were to live forever"

- *MAHATMA GANDHI*

We learn through *feedback loops*. That's how the process of accumulating distinction (learning) works.

'Feedback loops' are the seeds we plant that grow & turn into *'distinctions,' (as discussed in the last chapter),* which then, in turn, make you more *skilled* at something.

One of the things I've found very strange on my journey is how many lack clarity about how learning *actually* works.

For most of us, we've spent anywhere between 10 & 20 years *'learning'* within the education system. Yet, if after all those years, you ask most people:

'How does learning work?' 'How does your brain actually go from 'not knowing' something to 'knowing' something?

How do your mind process information? What happens - in the brain - to create insights & learnings?

For most people, they'll give you blank stare. Or maybe, a confused look. I find it shocking that we spend so much time learning, yet most people don't understand it.

It's a little like a car mechanic, who has spent 20 years as a mechanic, yet doesn't understand how a car works. You can bet, they're *not* a very good mechanic.

In the same way, if you don't really understand the mechanics of how learning works, your learning ability - & learning speed - is being limited from its greater potential.

In learning, our mind is the equivalent of a car for a mechanic. When you better understand how the car (your mind) works, you'll become a better mechanic (learner).

This is yet another thing that, frankly, in my belief, the education system should have taught us, tet, didn't. It's not your fault, but now, it's your responsibility (if you're willing) to learn this, better understand the powerful asset that is your brain & use it effectively to achieve results.

We learn (acquire distinctions) through *Feedback Loops*.

FEEDBACK LOOPS

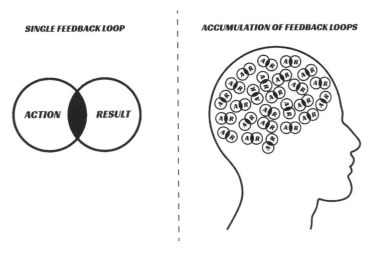

SINGLE FEEDBACK LOOP · ACCUMULATION OF FEEDBACK LOOPS

ACTION · RESULT

This applies to any skill you are developing, any topic you're learning, or any area of expertise you are working on mastering. It's universal & happens on autopilot.

However, when we consciously step back & understand it, we'll, almost automatically, become better, faster learners.

It's because when you understand something, your mind starts paying greater attention to it & taps into greater capacity to optimize that thing for greater effectiveness.

It's a bit like if you were a sales rep & you began to really understand what your customer wants, you'll, almost immediately, become a better salesperson. It's because you now understand what's needed - what's required - & you can, consciously, tailor your approach for the best results.

HOW 'FEEDBACK LOOPS' WORK

"Learning never exhausts the mind"

- *LEONARDO DA VINCI*

A *feedback loop* is a combination of 2 things:

1. **Action:** the cause
2. **Result:** the effect

A child walks up to a hot pan & touches it. *Ouch!*

And, in that moment, mentally, the child links the *'action'* - touching a hot pan - with the *'result'* - physical pain - to form a single *feedback loop* in their brain.

That's called learning. And, thanks to this experience, the child can now use this *feedback loop (a 'distinction' stored in the brain)* to base his future decision upon & make better decisions. Which, by definition, makes that child more knowledgeable & skilled now.

When you receive new information, your brain takes that information & finds both the 1) *action* & 2) *result* of that information & links it together to form a *feedback loop.*

Another example; let's say you're training your basketball skills, by shooting hoops in your backyard.

You shoot a hoop ('action') You narrowly miss ('result'). Then, you adjust your footing slightly (new 'action') It's closer to going in, but narrowly misses (new 'result').

So, you adjust your footing *again* (new 'action'). And, this time, it goes in (new 'result').

Your mind, as you do this, links these *'actions'* with the corresponding 'results' to create insights (distinctions) for better performance - higher skill - next time.

But then, let's say, you got excited & with these new, raised emotions, you forgot to pay attention to your footing (new 'action'), & this time, you missed the shot (new 'result').

This once again creates a new feedback loop (distinction) & reinforces the existing ones.

Every time you *self-correct*, & adjust back to what worked - & it works again - you reinforce that existing feedback loop.

This is also the reason why it's most effective when we...

| Get to a point of 'self-correction' quickly

When we do that, it allows us to radically accelerate our learning (which we'll talk about more later in this chapter).

So, whenever you're learning anything new, find a way to get to a point of 'self-correction' as fast as you can.

Train in front of a mirror, film yourself training or accumulate adequate knowledge to know when something is off; those are 3 ways to get to a point of 'self-correction'.

And, every time we take an action, & get a result, we accumulate feedback loops *(distinctions)* - or reinforce existing ones - which, in turn, raise our level of skill.

Your mind forms a connection (like code on a computer):

> *Footing positioned like 'this' = Worse shot*
> *Footing positioned like 'this' = Better shot*

This process occurs every time you learn or train a skill, no matter whether you're aware of it, or not.

For example, realize how every time I wrote, *'feedback loop,'* it was followed up with *'(distinctions)'.*

This is to help reinforce your understanding that a feedback loop, is in essence, a distinction being acquired.

And, this within itself, is creating a *feedback loop* in your mind that helps you understand this information.

| Feedback Loops = Distinctions

A feedback loop is like a seed that you plant, that, once it's grown, turns into a *'distinction'* (something you know).

And once again, the more distinctions you accumulate - through the power of feedback loops - the more knowledgeable & skilled you become at something.

ACCELERATING FEEDBACK SPEED

"Growth is never by mere chance; it is the result of forces working together"

- *JAMES CASH PENNEY*

The faster the feedback loop links together *(action to result)*, the faster you learn. That's how you, at the most fundamental level, *accelerate* your learning. And although this may sound simple, don't let that misguide you.

FEEDBACK SPEED

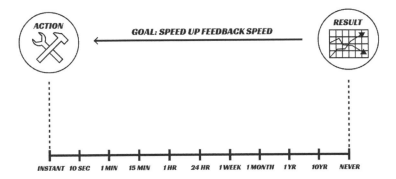

For example, let's say you want to get good at the skill of *marketing & branding*. And, within that skill, you're looking to test a new style of video promotion on a big national branding campaign.

You put the campaign out there. You've taken the *'action'*. But, unless you have some way of accurately tracking the impact of that branding (which, in this example, is rather hard to track effectively), that feedback loop remains incomplete & you don't learn anything few.

You've taken the *'action,'* but you can't see the direct result that new style of video promotion has had. There's no visible 'result'. And, although it has made people like your brand, from the perspective of learning & skill mastery, this is an incredibly ineffective way, because you don't allow your mind to learn (no complete feedback loop).

This may be a great action to take for your business growth, but not if your main objective is skill development.

Your feedback speed, in this example, is 'never'. The feedback loop *never* completes, which doesn't allow you to pick up any new *'distinctions'* in the skill of branding.

Now, compare that to the basketball example we used before. You decide to test how your foot positioning affects your 3-point shooting to become better at the sport.

You alter your footing (new 'action'). You miss ('result').

You alter your footing, *again* (new 'action'). This time, it goes in (new 'result').

You adjust your footing again (new 'action'). An even better shot this time (new 'result).

Each time you shoot, you get *'near-instant'* feedback. From the time you take a new 1) action, to the time you get a new 2) result, the time elapsed is near zero. *'Instant feedback.'*

In this scenario, you're going to be learning very quickly & developing your skills at a quick pace.

Why? Simply because you have a quick *feedback speed.*

From the time of a new 'action' to the time of a new 'result,' close to no time has elapsed. Quick feedback speed.

Our goal of course - if we want to *accelerate learning* - is to accelerate our feedback speed from 'never' (worse for learning), all the way down to 'instant' (best for learning).

Another example; if you want to learn a new topic faster & you're doing that by answering test questions, please be aware that answering all 100 question & checking the 100 answers at the end is a slower way to learn.

A much faster way to learn - & retain the information - is for you to answer 1 question, check that answer, then move onto the 2nd, 3rd or 4th, question. This way you'll learn much faster because of the accelerated feedback speed. The link between 'action' & 'result' is accelerated.

However, beyond just feedback *speed*, the other important part of it is feedback *accuracy*.

The reason we sometimes begin to believe - & do - things that turn out to be ineffective is because we accumulated those distinctions through a lack of *feedback accuracy*.

For example, you go buy a lottery ticket, you win money first time around & your mind may just link the 'action' - buying lottery tickets - to the 'result' - effective money making method - as a linear, straightforward link.

The reason for that being that your mind is creating the feedback loop based on inaccurate, or incomplete, feedback. A lack of *feedback accuracy*.

Our goal shouldn't be just to increase *feedback speed*, but also to increase *feedback accuracy* - by basing our learning on greater volumes of data - so we can create more accurate, more effective, feedback loops (distinctions).

To do this we need to track our progress better, chart our skill development, check our assumptions & focus on only the most accurate metrics we're looking to improve.

EXERCISE: FEEDBACK OPTIMIZATION
Let's get past the philosophical, & let's get practical.

If you want to learn anything faster, start with powerful questions like these:

Within the skill you've currently developing in your life (or planning to develop), how could you improve 'feedback speed' & 'feedback accuracy'?

How could you get to a point of 'near instant' feedback?

How can you, more accurately, track & chart your improvement to improve feedback accuracy?

How can you add key metrics & measurements to speed up - & improve - the feedback loops you're creating?

What did you learn from this chapter about feedback loops & how could you apply it, quickly, to accelerate your learning & skill development?

I assure you, this will accelerate your learning far more than any hack or learning tip ever could.

Take 3 minutes, think about - or journal - on these questions. Then, continue reading.

4 | MENTAL BANDWIDTH:
HOW WE PROCESS INFORMATION

"We would accomplish many more things if we did not think of them as impossible"

- *VINCE LOMBARDI*

When you do anything for the first time, even the simplest part of that skill requires a lot of your conscious attention.

However, over time, those same things, take up less of your conscious thought (*mental bandwidth*) & you're able to do them automatically (like riding a bike, driving or texting).

MENTAL BANDWIDTH

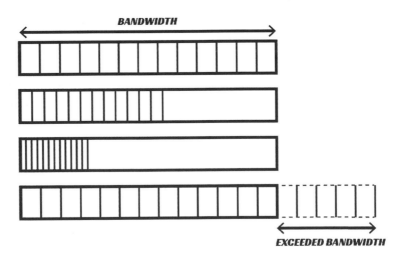

Mental Bandwidth is a concept I learned from a mentor of mine, many years ago. It's a very powerful framework.

I want you to, take a moment, & think about a skill that you've developed in your life. It could be; riding a bike, driving, dancing, an instrument, a sport, or any other skill.

And, now, think back to when you first started learning that skill. Your first lesson, or, first time doing it.

When you first started learning that skill, chances are, even the smallest thing took up most of your attention. Just a few tiny details about that skill - that now you do without even thinking - required your entire focus.

However, as you began to develop that skill, those same things required less & less of your conscious attention, & you could pay attention to more things at the same time.

If your driving instructor told you to text a friend while you were driving, during your *first* driving lesson, you would probably think, *'There's no way to do all these things - drive, talk & text - at the same time; that's impossible.'*

Yet, after some training - a higher level of skill - some people drive while texting a friend, applying makeup, drinking coffee & eating breakfast at the same time.

Same thing when you ride a bike for the first time. At first, it requires your *full* attention. But, with training, people can ride their bikes, without much of their conscious attention required & can do (or thinking about) many other things at the same time.

The first time you were texting, you probably had to find every letter on the keypad and click it consciously. Letter by letter. Now - if you've trained this - you probably don't even look down at the letters at all; you just text.

It takes up much less *mental bandwidth* (mental focus & attention) for you to perform that skill.

Realizing this pattern is great, but, what's even better is understanding it & learning to use it to your learning & skill development advantage.

Why? Why does this happen? How does it work?

And, more importantly, how can you use this to learn faster & train skill more effectively?

That's what this framework, *Mental Bandwidth* is all about. It will help you understand this very clearly.

When we start developing a new skill, every *'sub-skill'* (a smaller skill that makes up a bigger skill; just like 'braking' is a sub-skill of 'driving a car') - every one of those 'sub-skills' takes up a lot of our mental bandwidth.

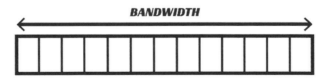

However, the more you develop each one of those 'sub-skills' (through *'Skill Isolation & Integration,'* which we'll talk about in the next chapter), the less of your mental thought process (your *mental bandwidth*) each takes up.

You're doing the exact same things. Same tasks as before *(as visually represented; same number of boxes)*. But, now each box (sub-skill) requires less of your conscious thought & attention (your mental bandwidth) to perform.

This is because, with *repetition*, those sub-skills becomes more & more unconscious (which we'll talk about later).

Just like texting (or typing on a keyboard), if you type your email (or password) over & over again, that process takes less & less of your attention, to the point where you don't even need to look at the letters to type it. You just do it. Without really thinking much about it; it's automatic.

And, as you continue to further train those sub-skills, it continues to take up less & less of your mental bandwidth.

What you're doing is still the same as before, it just requires much less conscious thought.

Just like your first driving lesson (or first time riding a bike), *what* you're doing, then, compared to now, is the same (accelerating, braking, turning, etc), but today, you do those *same* things near automatically (while before, they took up a huge amount of your mental focus).

It's because with skill development - & *repetition* - you turn conscious tasks into subconscious tasks. You make them more & more automatic, more and more habitual & as a result, they take us less mental bandwidth. Which then, frees up your conscious mind to focus on other sub-skills.

Because, although it may seem like a masterful magician, or swimmer, or athlete, is doing just 1 thing, that 1 thing is made up of many different *sub-skills* that they're doing.

Think about it. 'Swimming' (or virtually any other skill) isn't really 1 skill, but rather the accumulation of many,

many *sub-skills*. Effective swimming requires you to move your hands effectively (a sub-skill), while breathing the right way (another sub-skill), while kicking your legs effectively (another sub-skill), as well as other things.

And the reason masters are able to be so masterful is that each of the individual things that would require our full mental bandwidth, for them, takes up only a tiny fraction.

It's because they have trained that skills over & over until it's a deeply unconscious act that they can do in their sleep.

It's a little like brushing your teeth. At first, during early childhood, this skill - brushing your teeth - may have taken some focused effort. Now though, you probably just pick up the toothbrush, put it in your mouth & brush your teeth.

And, as it often is with deeply unconscious tasks, if you were asked to describe *how* you actually brushed your teeth, you might actually struggle to describe the actions that you completed literally seconds ago. We all would.

Why? It's become that skill - that task - has become so automatic, you probably didn't even have to consciously focus to make the toothbrush movements in your mouth.

The difference is that while most people have this automatic, autopilot, execution around skills like brushing their teeth, driving their car, or texting, the world's highest achievers have actually been able to train so hard (& smart) that they've cultivated this similar effect for more advanced skills, including their core field of expertise & skill.

A masterful tennis player is doing - & processing - dozens of little things (sub-skills, or even, sub-sub-skills), often, without much conscious attention required.

A masterful communicator is doing thousands of little things with their words, tonality, facial expressions & body (as well as other sub-skills), without much conscious effort.

Same applies for the world-class Formula 1 driver, the tech tycoon & the masterful DJ.

And, just like most people experience with brushing their teeth, often, the world's most skilled people can't even recall all of the individual things they are doing, because certain things are just so deeply unconscious for them.

In fact, seeing how much of someone's attention (mental bandwidth) a particular sub-skill takes up is a great indicator & tell for how skilled they are at it.

The next understanding is that, if you took *all* of those things that master is paying attention - in order to perform a skill effectively - & you told a beginner to do all of those same things, it would only cause overwhelm.

It's because all of the things that a master can do, for a beginner, would exceed their mental bandwidth. It would be too much. They would get overwhelmed.

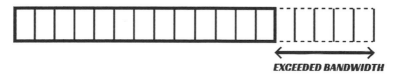

EXCEEDED BANDWIDTH

It's not because their mind has less bandwidth, or less attention, to dedicate to a particular skill. But, rather, because each of the sub-skills, due to lack of training, simply requires much, much more attention.

It's like juggling. You may be able to juggle 2 balls, or even 3, but there will come a point, if you're asked to continually add more balls into the mix, when your mind will just shut off because it's being stretched to focus on too many things.

You exceeded your bandwidth. And, not only does that 4th ball hit the ground, but so do the first 3 as your mind attempts to regroup from this overwhelm.

Another example is a classroom in which, if you keep flooding a student (or group of students) with lots & lots of information, without letting them *train* that information eventually the students will just get overwhelmed.

Think back over your life. If you've felt the feeling of 'overwhelm' while learning anything, it's because of this...

| 'Overwhelm,' is your brain's signal that you've exceeded your 'mental bandwidth'

We feel overwhelmed because the information we have received - or the skill we're attempting to perform - has exceeded our mental bandwidth. It was too much information for us to process (focus on) at one time.

And please note, that this is not a bad thing. Far from it. It's a good thing. When you're overwhelmed, it's simply a sign (like a road sign) telling you to turn back, consciously train the existing sub-skills - through *repetition* - until they use up less of your mental bandwidth, before going ahead.

Just like you've done with brushing your teeth, riding a bike, running or texting. You did it so often that you become *unconsciously competent* (good at something without even thinking about being good at it). Then, the overwhelm will disappear & you can move ahead.

In later chapters of this book, you'll learn specific, practical strategies you can use to accelerate the process of turning the conscious into the subconscious, but for now, it's just important that you understand how *mental bandwidth* works (& how it affects your learning & skill development).

2 MODES: CONSCIOUS & SUBCONSCIOUS

"You have power over your mind – not outside events. Realize this, and you will find strength"

- *MARCUS AURELIUS*

Your brain operates in 2 core, different ways: *consciously* & *subconsciously* (unconsciously).

When your brain operates consciously, it requires your focused thought. You're very aware of it. This is the mode of operation we are most familiar with.

Imagine taking a test & being asked to answer the following mathematics problem:

14 x 31

What's the answer?

The moment you started finding the answer, your conscious mind kicked into high gear. You were thinking.

And as you read these words, you become very aware that you were thinking. It was a conscious process. You know that, because you're aware of the thoughts going through your head right now.

Whenever you learn something (or do something) you've never done before, it always starts as a *conscious* act.

It's because you can't go on 'autopilot' on a route you've never travelled before.

In that same way, your mind can't operate in a subconscious (or, unconscious) way - autopilot - when it's never done that thing before.

Which brings us to the subconscious (or, unconscious) mode of operation that your mind has.

This mode is far more powerful; it's the part of your brain that processes thousands of different thoughts, controls your breathing, blood flow & digestion & keeps you alive, every single hour of the day. It runs non-stop & operates without you having to consciously think about it (just like you don't have to think about your heart beating).

And, our goal, when developing our skill is to train our distinctions deeper & deeper into the subconscious, so we can do them automatically, using less mental bandwidth.

The way you do that is simple; *repetition*.

When you repeat something over & over again, it becomes something you can do more & more unconsciously.

However, it's important for us to understand that repetition is not enough to effectively develop a skill. And, repetition doesn't make you good at something; it simply reinforces an insight & drives it deep; making it automatic.

| Repetition simply makes it more permanent

Repetition doesn't make an action good or bad. It also doesn't make something better. It simply makes something more *permanent*. That's the job of *repetition*.

Let's say you're on the golf course & you swing the club with *very bad* technique. And, then you go repeat that bad technique over & over again. With repetition, your technique doesn't magically get good, rather, it simply becomes more *permanently* bad.

In the same way that smoking cigarettes repeatedly doesn't make them good for you, when you train a sub-skill (or sub-sub-skill) incorrectly, you don't get better. You simply become more automatically - & unconsciously - bad.

There seems to be a perception amongst people that simply doing something over & over again leads to improvement.

It doesn't. *Innovation* - seeking improvement - leads to improvement (as we'll talk about later). Repetition simply reinforces your actions & drives them deeper into the subconscious (making them more *permanent*).

If you repeat the right thing, it simply becomes more automatically & permanently right & if you repeat the wrong thing, it becomes more automatically & permanently wrong. Which makes *'repetition'* a double-edged sword that amplifies your effectiveness - or your ineffectiveness - at a particular skill.

Which, by definition - just like the coaching legend Vince Lombardi put it best - means that:

"Practice does not make perfect. Only perfect practice makes perfect"

And, with that repetition, you drive skills - & sub-skills - deeper into your subconscious mode of operation, which, in turn, frees up more mental bandwidth for you to re-allocate to other sub-skills & tasks.

As we start anything for the first time, it requires a lot of our attention because everything is a *conscious* task, but over time as sub-skills move deeper into *subconscious* mode of operation - through *repetition* - it frees up more mental bandwidth & gives you greater potential to learn more & step to the next level of skill.

And, we mustn't forget, there is always a new, higher level we can get to, with new opportunities, curiosities, possibilities, adventures & rewards.

But to get there, we must we willing. And, we must chase it.

5 | CHUNKING & ISOLATION: THE POWER OF PERCEPTION

"It always seems impossible until it's done"

- *NELSON MANDELA*

EXERCISE: HOW WE CHUNK INFORMATION
It's important you first *experience* what we're talking about before you start reading this chapter.

Below you'll see a sequence of letters. Take 5 seconds, look over them & memorize them.

Now, cover this book (or look away) & see how many of the letters you can remember *(in the right order)*.

Start then your ready. Read on, once you're done.

V   T   D   L   E   M   P   E   N   O   E

Don't keep reading until you complete this first part.

You've been warned; only read on when you're ready.

So, how many letters did you remember?

Did you remember all 9 letters, in the right order?

If so, congratulations. If not, don't worry. This isn't a memory test. It's just an example of what you're about to discover - & learn about - within this chapter.

It's all about how the mind perceives, processes, stores & uses information, as well as how, perception changes.

Now, onto part 2 of this exercise.

Now, take the 9 letters below, on *this* page, & see how many of *these* you can memorize.

Take 5 seconds to memorize them. Look away. And, see how many you were able to remember. Then, read on.

D   E   V   E   L   O   P   M   E   N   T

How many of the 9 letters did you get?

Odds are, you go all 9? Right?

But, why? It may be because the second part spelt out a word, but that only the surface level explanation for it.

Underneath that surface, it's because of the power of *'chunking'* (which you're about to discover).

In case you didn't realize, the 9 letters in both parts of the exercise above were *exactly the same.* The only thing different was the *order* in which the 9 letters were shown.

In the first part, the 9 letters were randomly assorted & if you were to read them, they would spell, *'Vtdlempenoe'*.

Maybe in some other language, that word means something, but in English, it doesn't.

In the second part, the 9 letters were the *same*, but this time they were arranged to spell the word, *'Development'*.

Chances are, you had a much easier time memorizing all 9 letters in the second part of the exercise than in the first.

But why? It's because, in the second part, your mind was no longer attempting to remember 9 letters *(9 pieces of information)*, but rather, was now just focused on remembering 1 word *(1 piece of information)*.

You've seen, read or said that word (& others) so many times that you're mind sees it as '1 piece of information.'

But, it didn't at first. If somebody who had never seen the word *'Development'* before did that exercise, they wouldn't tell the difference between the first part & the second.

Their mind simply wouldn't see 'D E V E L O P M E N T' as 1 chunk of information, but rather as 9 individual pieces.

But, because you've seen that word over & over, your mind has moved the information deeper into the *subconscious*. In other words, it has *'chunked'* it down to make life easier.

And that is exactly how *'chunking'* works & it's how your mind operates in any - & every - learning & skill development scenario you're in.

When you learn (accumulate distinctions through feedback loops), your mind begins to chunk down information to make it easier to use next time *(which is also the reason why the action takes up less 'mental bandwidth')*

Chunking: *taking multiple individual parts and mentally merging them to form one part (1 mental file)*

Chunking is a little like when you take computer files & you merge them together into 1 file. And now, when you send those files *(or do anything else with them)*, your mind isn't having to process dozens of different files, but rather just the 1 file (1 chunk of information).

It's a little like when you drive, bike, walk (or use public transport) to go a particular destination for the first time.

That first time, it's a very *conscious* process & your mind perceives every corner, every road, every turn, etc, as a separate piece of information.

But, if you've been taking that *same* route, to that *same* destination, over & over again, eventually, your mind, mentally chunks it down to just 1 piece of information ('go to that destination'). Your mind no longer treats each step (every corner, road, turn) as a separate chunk, but rather all as 1 big chunk (pieces of information merged together).

And, when it comes to learning in the first place, when you first learned to drive (or any other skill), everything was processed as a separate, individual *'chunk'*.

For example, just the process of 'turning left' would be made up of many pieces (brake, indicator, turn the wheel), but after a lot of repetition, mentally it becomes one chunk ('turn left') & that's how your mind perceives - & uses - it.

As the action got repeated, it drove that information deeper into the *subconscious* mind (instead of the *conscious*), it became 1 mental chunk of information & began to take up *less* of your mental bandwidth.

Which all, in turn, freed up more of your mental bandwidth for further information & instruction.

Your mind does this for a simple reason: *to conserve energy* & *minimize effort*. Your mind wants to do the minimal amount of work possible to achieve the desired outcome. That's why it forms 'habits,' 'chunks,' & 'mental rules,' that it uses to process actions, while saving energy.

By understanding this, it allows us, once again, to more effectively support our brain to 'chunk' down information & free up more mental bandwidth.

SKILL ISOLATION & INTEGRATION

"The things that have been most valuable to me I did not learn in school"

- *WILL SMITH*

A lot of people fail to realize that skills are actually the combination of many *sub-skills* & *sub-sub-skills*.

Which makes any skill you could possibly learn a lot more like a *'learning web,'* rather than a linear element.

Tennis is a skill. Within that, 'serving', 'forehand', 'backhand,' & 'footwork,' are 4 - of many - *sub-skills*. And within the *sub-skill* of 'serving,' 'power,' & 'accuracy' are 2 - of many - *sub-sub-skills*.

By knowing this, we also begin to understand that whenever we go to train a skill (like 'tennis'), only a small fraction of our time, is spent training the whole 'skill', & the *majority* of our time is spent training the specific *sub-skills* - & *sub-sub-skills* - within that skill of tennis.

Think about it. When you spent 2 hours training a skill (let's use tennis as an example), how much of that time is actually spent training the skill of tennis as a whole?

Much less than people think.

Only when 'integrating' skills (by playing a practice tennis match) are we actually training the skill as a whole. The rest of the time, we're training sub-skills, in isolation, like 'serving,' 'forehand returns' or 'backhand returns.'

SKILL ISOLATION & INTEGRATION

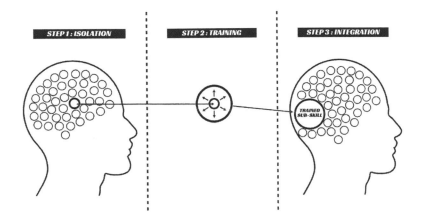

If you've ever seen, studied or read about how top athletes, musicians, magicians or even, entertainers, train, you'll see that they're doing exactly this.

Rarely do we ever train the entire main skill we think we're training (e.g. basketball, marketing, public speaking) - that only gets trained as a whole during 'Step 3: Integration,' - but rather, we spent most of our time training individual sub-skills (or sub-sub-skills), in isolation, to get better.

In the visual, *Skill Isolation & Integration*, you'll see that this process is made up of 3 steps.

STEP #1: ISOLATION

If you're learning tennis & one of the weaknesses to your game is your ability to 'serve' (a sub-skill of tennis), you would go & isolate this sub-skill, take a period of time (like 2 hours) & focus just on this 1 particular sub-skill.

You would probably get a bucket of tennis balls & just fire off serve after serve, over & over again; just training that 1 sub-skill in complete isolation.

STEP #2: TRAINING

As you train that 1 sub-skill in isolation - as you can see in the visual - that sub-skill will improve.

If you just spent 2 hours 'serving' non-stop, chances are, you'll pick up some new *distinctions* that make you better, hence growing & expanding your ability to perform that particular sub-skill.

STEP #3: INTEGRATION

That next step is then to integrate your new & improved ability at that particular sub-skill into the rest of your game.

In the 'serving' example, you would do this by finding a partner, serving the ball & now moving to return it once it's back on your side of the court.

Your job is to integrate the sub-skill with others like 'forehand return,' 'footwork,' or 'backhand return.'

This isn't complex; people have been training their skills in this way for generations. It's not a new concept; it's just widely misunderstood (or not understood at all).

If you're going to the gym to work out, odds are, you're not working out *every* muscle, *every* day.

Chances are, 1 day is 'chest day,' another is 'arm day,' another is 'leg day.' That's just an everyday example of *Skill Isolation & Integration*, in practice.

You're not training everything at every time, but rather you're getting stronger (as a whole) by making the individual parts stronger.

However, here's the most important part *(the reason this is in this book in the first place)*.

This is how *Skill Isolation & Integration* affects your *Mental Bandwidth*.

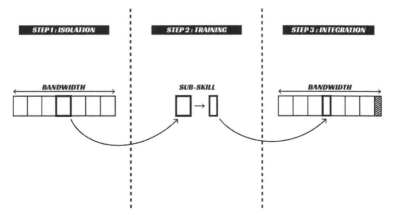

Same concept. Same 3 steps. However, this has potential to bring a lot of new clarity & deepened understanding.

As you take a sub-skill & you train it in isolation, you drive your ability to perform that sub-skill deeper into your *subconscious*. Which, in turn, makes it use up less of your conscious attention (mental bandwidth) when you perform that skill next time. Which, - as you can see in the visual - frees up more 'mental bandwidth' for other sub-skills.

If you're learning how to swim & you take the sub-skill of 'kicking the legs,' & you work on just the legs for an hour, holding onto the wall of the pool, just focused on the correct leg movement, after that hour, that leg motion will be more automatic & will take up less mental bandwidth. Which allows you to 'swim' (the main skill) more effectively when you integrate everything together.

That's our objective; that's how we get increase our skill level at something. We take a sub-skill in isolation, train it & then integrate it back into the overall skill.

And, as we do this, many factors we've discussed in this book already are *working together* to make us learn & improve at something; to give us the result we're after.

And, that's why, in the next chapter - last chapter, in the first section of this book - we'll going to talk about how everything actually comes together to make learning work.

And, by understanding this all, it gives you greater power to design your learning & skill development.

It takes the power away from, *mere chance* & gives it to you, making you the architect of your learning.

6 | PUTTING IT ALL TOGETHER:
UNDERSTANDING GREATNESS

"Education is the most powerful weapon which you can use to change the world."

- *NELSON MANDELA*

With awareness comes greater possibility. It's very hard to change something, get good are something, optimize something or thrive at something without first going out there & understanding it.

If you're attempting to cross the road, but you're walking with a blindfold - unable to see & understand the environment around you - not only is far more dangerous, but plain & simple, it's an incredibly ineffective approach.

It's like a car mechanic who doesn't understand how a care works. That's not going to be a very good mechanic.

And just like it's very hard to win a board game if you don't understand the rules, it's hard to win the game of life & become extraordinary at anything without understanding the rules of learning, improvement, skill & achievement.

Albert Einstein once said...

"You have to learn the rules of the game. And then you have to play better than anyone else."

And although understanding (awareness) doesn't - by any stretch of the imagination - automatically give you results (it takes work) - awareness *is* the first step to new, higher levels of potential, skill & achievement.

LEARNING & UNLEARNING

> *"It ain't what you don't know that gets you into trouble. It's what you know for sure that just ain't so"*
>
> - *MARK TWAIN*

The process of getting better, more skilled & more successful isn't only about learning. In fact, as paradoxical as it sounds, learning isn't just about learning.

While learning - acquiring new information & knowledge - is, undoubtedly, the main part, it's not the only part.

The other part of learning is *unlearning*. And, unlearning (removing information & action) is also an incredibly important part of learning as well.

It's because so often it's not what we don't know that limits our success, it's what we do know, that turns out to be inaccurate, that limits our growth.

If you really scan back through the first chapter of this book, *Re-Defining Genius: The Power Of Learning*, you'll realize that the vast majority of that chapter wasn't about learning new information, per say.

Primarily, that first chapter was all about *unlearning*. It was all about taking existing, inaccurate, beliefs, removing them & replacing them; unlearning the things that may have held you back in the past from that next level.

Because as we go through life - particularly through the education system - we get programmed with a lot of beliefs about skill, success & achievement that don't serve us *(like the beliefs we breakthrough in that first chapter: IQ, talent, genetics, experience & the education system itself)*.

And for a lot of people, simply *unlearning* certain things can make a massive difference in their results. And, by first focusing on unlearning certain restricting beliefs, it allows us to create openness for more accurate, research-backed understandings & strategies.

Hence, from this point forward, if you want to get the most out of every scenario, I challenge you to ask yourself, not only *'What new can I learn?'*, but also, *'What do I currently believe that I could unlearn for better results?'*.

And although that information won't get deleted from your brain, it will now simply become the *nuance* you can use to avoid making ineffective decisions & make better ones.

EXERCISE: UNLEARNING LIMITATIONS

We all have certain things that we believe - or actions we take - that, at some level, we know limit us. Unless you're perfect *(which, nobody really is)*, there are things that we can improve. Always.

In this exercise, I challenge you to take 5 focused minutes & think about what 'beliefs' you have about skill, mastery or success, that could be limiting you.

They may not be, but you could get some life-changing insights just by checking yourself like this.

Now, this requires you to be really honest with yourself. But, in the words of Sigmund Freud, *"Being entirely honest with oneself is a good exercise."*

This is designed to help you raise your awareness of some of the other things you may want to consider unlearning. Everything is learnable & everything can be unlearned. It's a choice. But, it starts with awareness.

Take 5 minutes & think, - or journal - & then continue.

HOW THE PIECES FIT TOGETHER

"Any fool can know. The point is to understand"

- *ALBERT EINSTEIN*

We've covered a lot of moving pieces in this first section of this book, but understanding them in isolation (piece by piece) isn't enough. To really get the most out of learning, *integration* is critical. We must understand how the pieces work together. And, not just know, but truly, understand.

How does The Skill Triangle, Distinctions, Feedback Loops, The Subconscious Mind, Nuance, Mental Bandwidth & Chunking all work together?

As you start learning anything new - anything you haven't learned before - at first, you suck. You have no skill at that thing because, well, you've never done it before.

You haven't gone through the process of creating any *feedback loops* yet, which gives you no *distinctions* (insights, nuances & understandings) to pull from in order to make good decisions (the essence of skill) at the chosen field of expertise.

However, as you are learning *(accumulating distinctions through feedback loops)* even the smallest pieces of information - like holding the tennis racket with the right grip - take up your entire *mental bandwidth* (your full conscious attention).

This is because your mind views each piece of information as its own separate *chunk*. This is all because everything you're learning for the first time is using the *conscious* part of your brain (& not yet using the *unconscious* part). That's where we all start when learning anything new.

But, as we continue to invest time, we begin to form more *feedback loops* (a mental link between *action* & *result*), which then become *distinctions* that we store in our minds.

Every *distinction* (insight) we accumulate gives us more data, understanding & nuance, which our mind can pull from to base its decisions on. And, once again, more data leads to better decisions, which leads to more *'skill.'*

Always remember, a skilled person is only considered as *'skilled'* because they consistently make better decisions - within that area of craft - than others around them.

And, as we, not just accumulate more distinctions, but also reinforce those distinctions through *repetition*, we drive it all deeper & deeper into our *subconscious*, making it easier & easier for us to perform a certain *sub-skill*. This frees up more mental bandwidth to allocate to other *sub-skills*.

Every *skill* is like a web made up of different *sub-skills* & *sub-sub-skills*. And, through the power of *skill isolation & integration*, we can isolate these parts, train them & integrate them to free up more mental bandwidth.

It's a very powerful training methodology because it's the most effective way of driving something deeper into the subconscious. You isolate 1 particular sub-skill, train it, repeat it & make it more automatic, freeing up more mental bandwidth & making you more skilled.

This is how learning really works. And, this is the real secret behind the extraordinary skill of the world's highest achievers. They've allocated hundreds & thousands of hours to the training of their skills, during which time, they've - either knowingly or unknowingly - been more intentional about their skill development.

That doesn't mean that they've necessarily understood everything you now understand. Just like electricity, *feedback loops, distinctions, mental bandwidth - & everything else you've learned in this book* - operates whether we know about it, or not. We don't need to understand electricity to use it. In the same way, you don't need to understand this stuff to use it.

However, if you wanted to become an electrician, now, you would need to understand how electricity works.

In that same way, you can learn whether you understand this or not, but if you want to learn *faster* & train your skills *most effectively*, you must understand how learning works. And, now you do. Now, you have clarity.

And, as you can now see, all of these pieces work together.

Feedback loops create distinctions. A greater accumulation of distinctions leads to better decision making. Better decision making leads to greater levels of skill. And greater skill correlates with greater income, & impact, potential.

Through repetition, your mind processes information differently; it chunks it down to converse energy. By chunking down information, it frees up more mental bandwidth. And more mental bandwidth allows you to execute on more distinctions at the same time. Which then, in turn, links to a great level of skill.

Everything works together. And these pieces of working together to support you to reach new, higher levels of skill (& success). This is what creates the extraordinary.

YOU HAVE THE FRAMEWORK

"All our dreams can come true, if we have the courage to pursue them"

- *WALT DISNEY*

By reading this first section alone, you now have a deeper understanding of learning, skill development & what makes people extraordinary, than 99% of people on the planet. That's not hyperbolized. Far from it.

That's just the sad truth. This is the type of content that, in my belief, every child should learn in school.

But, they don't. And, it's one of the biggest reasons I chose to drop out of the education system.

The education system isn't designed to create world-class achievers, rather, it's designed to create workers. Which, at some level, we all know.

As to why, it's because high achievers (like us) - who understand this - have much more personal power, which makes them far hard to control. Which, they don't want.

On the other hand, it's what gives us freedom. By raising our awareness of skill development, success & achievement, we tap into new, higher levels of personal control, personal power & consciousness.

And, it all starts with a seeking of new awareness. Which, is why I congratulate you for getting here. I wholeheartedly acknowledge you for reading these words.

However, this is just the beginning. This first section is just the foundations, crafted to lay strong groundwork for the more advanced insights in the next 3 sections.

In the very next section, we're going to dive even deeper into the actual strategies, tactics, habits, practices & methodologies of the world's best.

You're going to get an even deeper understanding of, not just the philosophical, but the practical steps you can take, almost immediately, to learn faster, train like the best & become extraordinary at anything you choose.

You took the first step, now continue to the next one. And welcome to the learner's side.

2.

FOUNDATIONS:
THE PATH TO GREATNESS

"You were designed for accomplishment, engineered for success, and endowed with the seeds of greatness"

ZIG ZIGLAR

We all have the potential to become truly extraordinary, yet few understand that the foundations for greatness aren't laid when times are easy. Rather, those foundations are laid in the moments of tough, quit-inducing pressure. Greatness isn't shaped when it's conformable, rather, it's shaped in the hard moments when a part of you feels like quitting - feels like stopping - feels like it's not worth it anymore - but your drive & passion keeps you going. It's during those moments that those seeds of greatness, within you, begin to form the harvest.

7 | STRATEGIC ALLOCATION: ALIGN LEARNING WITH AMBITION

"If you chase two rabbits, you'll catch neither"

- RUSSIAN PROVERB

Becoming extraordinary, as you'll learn, is a game of allocation & the world's highest achievers become that way because they're able to more strategically allocate their time, energy, focus & attention.

And, in today's day & age, there has never been a better time for you to *focus* your energy, do *more* of what you love & become extraordinary at what you do.

What you're about to discover may challenge how you view learning. And it certainly *will* challenge how you allocate your time, not just in the realm of learning, but in life.

The simple fact is...

| Time is the most valuable resource we have

Some may argue that money or possessions are more important resources, but without time they fail to matter.

And while time is most valuable, it's not what, in itself, makes the difference between mastery or mediocrity. I mean, we all have the same 24 hours a day, 7 days a week & 365 days a year; that doesn't change.

But while time isn't what creates success or failure, how one *utilizes & allocates* their time makes all the difference.

THE COST OF LEARNING

"This is the key to time management - to see the value of every moment"

- *MENACHEM MENDEL SCHNEERSON*

There seems to be a misconception that learning is *free*.

I assure you, it's not. Learning - like anything else - has a big cost to it; that cost is your *time*.

And it's this misconception that leads to thinking, such as, *'the more skills I learn, the better.'* Which, based on the stories & patterns of the world's highest achievers just doesn't hold up as a principle we should follow for success.

In fact, learning *more* things can actually lead to *lower* levels of skill or success in our lives.

Learning - like anything else - is an investment of *time*.

Which, in itself, isn't a problem. The challenge is figuring out which topics & skills are the *best* investments of our time & which are just a waste.

We may save $100 by learning how to do your own plumbing, how to design our own business cards or how to make our own pillows, but people fail to account how much of time we are investing to get that saving.

Or, even more so, they fail to realize how much extra progress they can make by paying someone else to do their plumbing or business card design, while they go &

'reallocate' that time to developing their main area (or areas) of expertise.

If you spend 10 hours learning the skill of car repairing to save $100, you're also taking away 10 hours that you could have invested in further mastering your craft.

And this - *how we allocate our time* - is something the world's highest achievers tend to focus on a lot more.

At the end of the day every moment you are spending learning anything other than the 1, or few, things that you really want to master, you're taking away valuable learning & skill development time that, down the line, may just make the difference between success or failure.

And there some investments we definitely should make & others that are simply a waste of our time.

Which is why, we must view our learning & skill development (all of it) as an investor looking to most wisely invest - in this scenario, 'time' - for the best results.

This may seem like a small shift, but in reality, it's huge. There's a clearly-visible difference between how the world's highest achievers allocate their time compared to others.

A GAME OF 'ALLOCATION'

> *"Most people have never thought through how they're going to allocate their time. You need to make a decision in advance"*
>
> - *CLAYTON M. CHRISTENSEN*

There seems to be another misconception that some people are just extraordinary at *everything*, while others suck at *anything & everything* they do. A misconception that you either *'have it all,'* or you have *'nothing at all'.*

On the surface, this may seem accurate, but it's, often, not.

Unlike James Bond in the movies, the high achievers in the real world, *aren't* masterful at 25 different skills.

In fact, the reason they're great at some things (like their core topic or skill) is that they suck at a lot of others.

Throughout their lives they've - knowingly or unknowingly - *re-allocated* a huge amount of time most people spend on other things back into their core area of expertise.

The idea that some people are great at everything is insane. If anyone attempted to be great at *everything*, they would become great at *nothing* because they would be far too scattered with their time to get great at anything.

It's because skill, first & foremost, is *a game of allocation.*

You can compare one kid to another & say that one has lots of skill & the other possesses no skills, but few things can be further from the truth if we really look at it accurately.

They both possess skills. Just very different skills. It's because they both allocated their time very differently.

One kid may have high levels of skill at mathematics, literature, debating & website design, but the other kid may have high levels of skill at the latest video game, social popularity, martial arts & drug consumption.

Technically speaking, they both have knowledge & they both have skills *(by definition, being good at a video game, or even taking drugs effectively, are skills).*

They both have skills, but because of how society views success - based on the ambitions of the majority - the first kid is considered *'skilled,'* while the other, *'lacking skills'.*

What has caused this difference in their skill sets is a big difference in how they've 'allocated' time.

The first kid re-allocated a lot of the time other kids would spend playing video games or hanging with friends & has instead allocated that time to further develop his skills in mathematics or literature.

Which makes him better at *those* specific skills, but worse, at video games or martial arts.

Meanwhile, the second kid is highly skilled at video games & martial arts because he has re-allocated a lot of his time away from getting good grades & has syphoned that time into playing video games or learning martial arts.

If skill is defined as *'the ability to do something well,'* by definition, they both have *skill.*

However, please understand, *not all skills are equal.*

Personally, I've always been like the first kid, focused on developing skills such as mathematics because I personally believe it's a more effective path to achieve results & live a good life. And, I personally don't believe video games or drug consumption are skills anybody should develop,

However, when doing - & sharing - research, sometimes, we have to put our beliefs aside to share that which is most accurate & the most effective representation of the truth. And while I would probably be the first to jump to the conclusion that the first kid is *'skilled,'* while the second is 'lacking skills,' putting my personal beliefs aside, they are both, technically, skilled (just at very different things).

Equally, we must understand that what might be a complete waste of time for one person, might be a skill that another person has always wanted to develop. It's because, as we discussed, different people have different ambitions. It's Einstein's theory of 'relativity,' in the context of skill development & life choices.

And, whether something is a great allocation of our time or a complete waste of it, is dependant on its alignment with our ambitions. So, if you've ever been confused as to what you should or shouldn't learn, adopt this philosophy:

| Align your learning with your ambitions

Generally speaking, those who reach the highest levels of mastery & success, are those whose learning (what & how they learn) is aligned with their future ambitions.

Meaning, if your ambition is to become one of the world's best musicians, you have to allocate a lot of time to that.

The Beatles used to regularly spent between 5 & 8 hours a night performing in front of audiences, often between 5 - 7 days a week. Odds are, if you want to achieve those musical ambitions, you have to allocate time in a similar way.

Furthermore, if you really observe & study high achievers, you'll find that they all - without any exceptions - have areas of inability & lack of skill; they all have shortcomings. And once again, that's what makes them extraordinary.

The simple fact that they've taken the entire time, energy & attention away from certain things & re-distributed it back to their main area of expertise. A great quote says...

"The main thing is to keep the main thing, the main thing"

And that is one of the biggest things that makes the difference between those considered to have ordinary levels of skill & those who have become truly extraordinary.

And if mastery is what you're after, then it's important to understand that that height of ambition requires a huge allocation of your time, energy & focus (as we'll talk about in the next chapter), which in turn, requires sacrifice.

Think of it as a game of 'whack-a-mole.' When you whack 1 in, another 1 pops up. And, this continues over & over.

And this is often what it's like when you look at the world's highest achievers. Their focus (even, obsession) with their craft leaves a lot of moles (weaknesses) all over the place.

But, they don't attempt to fix all those weakness (another big misconception), but rather continue to focus on their *'main thing'* - their strengths - & thrive as a result.

Remember: *you can do anything as soon as you stop attempting to do everything.*

DEPTH OVER WIDTH

> *"I fear not the man who has practiced 10,000 kicks once, but I fear the man who has practiced one kick 10,000 times"*
>
> - *BRUCE LEE*

One of the main challenges with the education system is that they teach you what seems like 142 different topics.

Which is totally bizarre. At first, this range is important for self-discovery, but shouldn't be continued anywhere near as long as it is in schools.

Everybody knows focus is a critical part of success, which really begs the question...

'How exactly can anyone be expected to focus on a topic & gain a level of mastery at it, if they're bombarded with the requirement of learning dozens of different topics & skills?

This lack of focus that leads to *mediocrity* (being average)

The education system, as well as much of society - focuses on *width*: an average, mediocre level of understanding across a large number of topics & skills.

The problem with this is you're spread your time very thin. You're dividing your time across dozens & dozens of topics.

Meanwhile, the world's highest achievers focus far more on *depth*: a deeper, mastery-level understanding of 1 - or maximum, a few - topic & skills. They still can some understanding of various topics, but for the most part, their expertise is mostly in 1 core area of craft.

Which means you're not allocating an hour a day to your music, but rather 5, 6 or 7 hours a day. Which, for obvious reasons, skyrockets your level of skill at that *'main thing'*.

Whether it's sports people like Michael Jordan, business & marketing experts like Richard Branson, or even the greatest war strategists throughout history like Napoleon, they all have the same thing in common; they have become masterful at a select amount of skills (often, 1 skill) instead of becoming mediocre at many. *Depth* over *width*.

KNOWLEDGE VS TARGETED KNOWLEDGE

"Take up one idea. Make that one idea your life - think of it, dream of it, live on that idea. Let the brain, muscles, nerves, every part of your body, be full of that idea, and just leave every other idea alone. This is the way to success"

- *SWAMI VIVEKANANDA*

Most focus simply on acquiring as much knowledge & skill as possible, irrelevant of topic (width), while the world's highest achievers focus their time on acquiring what I refer to as *targeted knowledge* (depth).

They're focused on acquiring the knowledge & skill that are directly *targeted* to their craft & ambitions.

KNOWLEDGE VS TARGETED KNOWLEDGE

They don't learn things simply for the point of learning them, but rather, make *intentional* decisions about which topics & skills they really want to focus on developing.

But, why should we focus on mastering 1 (or a few) topics or skills, rather than simply getting average or good at many like the education system wants us to?

There are many reasons. Of which, the first is that people pay for experts & specialists.

Most employers or companies want people who have high skill in a specific area. Customers, most often, pay people who have a high skill level in a specific area.

If you are selling an online course about how to paint your shed, 99% (if not 100%) of the customers will not care whether you passed or failed your mathematics exams. They care about the core skill they're paying you for.

If you're working at a marketing agency & you begin to develop the skill of playing the violin in your part-time, you're not going to get a pay-raise as a result. It's because you're paid for your marketing skills, not musical abilities.

Hence, unless you're working multiple jobs & professions at the same time, you're many skills are underutilized.

The second reason is that scattering your time & attention across many topics & skills, statistically, decreases your odds of reaching mastery at anything.

Think about it: if you have to divide up your time across 8 different skills, you're not going to spend as much time working on your *'main thing'*. And we know that the top 10% in any field (the masters) usually earn between 80% & 90% of the income within that industry. The upside for those who reach mastery is multiplied.

Another reason is legacy. Those who become the best in the world tend to impact far more people, inspire more people

& leave a far greater legacy than whose you are simply mediocre at a lot of different skills. Masters tend to get remembered & go into the history books.

The *fewer* topics or skills you're developing, the more time you can *'reallocate'* back to your main area of craft (usually the thing you're most passionate about as well) & the greater your odds of succeeding with that skill.

With that said, this doesn't mean you have to focus on only 1 thing. You can focus on mastering 2 or 3 if you want. Just be *intentional* about how you allocate your time & know that the more 'targeted' the knowledge & skill you seek are, the greater your odds of becoming truly great at something.

THE SPECIALIZATION MODEL

> *"Pursue one great decisive aim with force and determination"*
>
> - *CARL VON CLAUSEWITZ*

Greater connectedness has given us a unique opportunity that our ancestors may not have had *(or, if they did, it was much harder for them to seize it).*

This has made it easier for us to *specialize.*

There are 2 sides to the scale of how people allocate their time when learning or developing skills.

1. **Self-sustainability**
2. **Specialization**

On one side of the scale, you have *'self-sustainability'*. Some people go & learn everything they need to be fully self-sustainable. They've learned how to fix their own car.

They've learned how to do their own plumbing. They've learned how to make their own furniture, sew their own clothes & grow their own crops.

And although at first, the idea of self-sustainability - reliant on nobody - seems attractive, it has a lot of consequences.

It often leads to you learning & doing a lot of things you really don't want to - or don't like to - do & also leads to mediocre at a lot of things, with mastery at nothing.

On the other side of the scale, you have *'specialization'*. This is where you become great at 1 core thing, which allows you to earn more & outsource other things. Because you're so focused on your *'main thing,'* you become masterful, you earn radically more & you're able to pay a plumber or mechanic. You're able to buy furniture, food & clothes instead of making them yourself.

The net-result financially may even be similar (although generally, those on the side *'specialization'* will generate far more wealth), but the journey to get there is very different.

This approach allows you to spend all day doing your 'main thing' (which, often, is your passion) & use your mastery to sustain everything else in your life.

One side of the scale represents total *self-sustainability*, the other side, complete *specialization*.

Most people living in first world countries today are somewhere in the middle. Others are massively on the side of *self-sustainability*. And others are on the side of *specialization;* focused on their 'main thing'.

However, the question is...

Where do you think the world's most successful - & highest achieving - people are on this scale?

Or, even more so...

Where do you want to be on this scale?

While both sides of the scale (including the middle) can make you happy, you'll find that whose have achieved mastery, accomplished the greatest feats & left the greatest legacy, are often on the side of *'specialization.'*

Just like any great CEO will tell you the way to grow your business fast is to focus on the highest priority tasks, while beginning to pass off 'low dollar per hour' tasks, in that same way, those who become extraordinary tend to follow this similar philosophy in their life *('specialization')*.

And they will often begin to pass off many things in their lives with the interest of buying back *time* to re-allocate back to their core area of expertise. They're willing to...

| Pay money to save time

And not just 'save it', but rather 'reallocate' it back to higher level priorities (such as mastery of their craft).

Best part, today this is not just doable, but increasingly easy to execute upon.

A few centuries ago it would have been much, much harder. Partially because getting others to do the things you didn't want to do was far harder & required far more effort to finalize. And secondly, because for most topics & skills, it was harder to monetize your 'main thing'.

However, as innovation grew & more things became commoditized & widely distributed (meaning, you're able to buy products & services easier), it become easier to do. And, at the same time, the ways in which you can monetize anything - quickly & efficiently - become better & more effective (as we'll talk about in the next chapter).

By understanding this scale, you're able to be more intentional about how you allocate your time.

Clearly, this chapter is skewed towards 'specialization,' because this is a book about the actions of the world's highest achievers. However, it's your job to tailor this to your ambitions (tailor your learning to your ambitions).

And know that, often, you'll find following the specialization model, at first, is tough. This is because when you're starting out, you're not a master generating the type of financial upside a mastery would.

However, over time, it becomes far more lucrative to focus on your 'main thing' & use that to drive everything else.

INTENTIONAL IMBALANCE

"To succeed in your mission, you must have single-minded devotion to your goal"

- *A. P. J. ABDUL KALAM*

Success at anything requires a level of 'imbalance' & sacrifice. It's a game of allocation & if you're allocating the time required to really become extraordinary at what you do, you'll find that there are things you'll need to sacrifice.

It's near impossible to become the best in the world at something if you're allocating most of your time every day to binge-watching the latest shows. That's the type of time allocation that doesn't create success.

I hope you're beginning to really understand this & starting to think about how you're allocating your time, as well as potential improvements you can make to truly become extraordinary at what you do. Remember...

| You can achieve anything as soon as you stop attempting to do everything

If you research the stories of the world's highest achievers, you'll find that they are tremendously focused on what they've chosen to allocate the majority of their time to. They don't spread themselves too thin; they focus.

They're willing to sacrifice learning one thing in order to re-allocate their time & become extraordinary at another.

And frankly, many of the world greatest throughout history *didn't* have perfect work-life balance because of their fierce obsession with their craft. It's a choice. The key is to really reverse-engineer what *you* want.

How good do you want to get? What are you willing to sacrifice? What's important to you? What do you want? What will really fulfill you at the highest levels?

BECOMING MORE INTENTIONAL

> *"Life isn't about finding yourself. Life is about creating yourself"*
>
> - *GEORGE BERNARD SHAW*

Deciding what is, or isn't, a good investment of your time is very contextual to you.

Its very contextual to your ambitions, your preferences & what you actually want your life to look like.

Perhaps knitting your own sweaters, repairing your own car or putting together your own furniture may be a great investment of your time; it's very contextual to *you*.

And the goal with this chapter is not to tell you to make a big, rapid change in your life - once again, it's contextual - but rather, to give you new awareness & support you to step up to be more *intentional* with your actions.

I implore you to think about learning & skill development like a wise investor, or a chess master. You want to live in the present & enjoy the moment, but you also always want to be 5 steps ahead. You want to treat your actions like great chess moves moving to your ultimate ambitions.

| Align your learning with your ambitions

It's about helping you understanding - & take steps - to tailor your actions & your learning to your ambitions.

The world's most successful - & happiest - people are those whose actions are in great alignment with their ambitions.

Extraordinary levels of skill & success are not a mystery. Nor are they a result of good luck or good fortune. But rather, the result of *intentional* action. Success doesn't happen by accident; it happens with *intention*.

8 | 3 FOUNDATIONS OF MASTERY: IRREFUTABLE KEYS FOR GROWTH

"Success is no accident. It is hard work, perseverance, learning, studying, sacrifice and most of all, love of what you are doing or learning to do"

- PELE

Mastery doesn't just happen. Someone doesn't just magically become great at what they do. As we've well established by now, there's method to the madness. There a process to skill, mastery & achievement.

More specifically, there are 3 foundational keys that those at the highest levels of skill all share. And, each one of these fundamental ingredients in the 'mastery' recipe, opens up new potential for you to become extraordinary.

3 FOUNDATIONS OF MASTERY

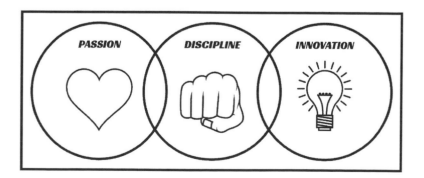

In this chapter, we are going to dive into each of these 3 foundational keys, the stories of how some of the world's best have applied them, as well as, most importantly, how *you* can apply them in your life.

These 3 keys are universal & transferable across all fields & industries. Whatever your 'main thing' is, these 3 foundations serve as a guide of what it takes to get there.

1 | **PASSION:** THE FUEL OF PURSUIT

> *"Those who have a 'why' to live, can bear with almost any 'how'."*
>
> - *VIKTOR E. FRANKL*

Whether it's *Tiger Woods* drawing golf trajectories as a very young child, *Mozart* composing music before his 6th birthday, *Picasso* creating over 50,000 paintings in his lifetime or Bobby Fischer, age 6, playing chess against himself because he had nobody else to play with - the first of the 3 key is exactly this; **passion.**

Passion is the fuel that drives action, hard work & that relentless pursuit many of the world's best are known for.

It's the fuel that starts the process of *mastery.*

Someone can get good at something without passion - children in the education system do this all the time - but real mastery is not achieved without a sense of *passion* - or at least strong *purpose* or *motive* - for what you're doing.

This passion is, in the case of *most* high achievers, an intrinsic (internal) love for the craft itself, but in rare occasions, a passion for a certain result, feeling or extrinsic (external) motive.

Either way, just like a car requires some sort of fuel to move forward, we - human beings - require some sort of passion, purpose or motive (human fuel) to take action.

However, during this chapter, we're going to focus on the type of passion that shows up *most often* in the lives of the world's highest achievers, which is, *a love of the craft itself*; a deep fascination of a particular topic or skill.

While extrinsic (external) rewards, incentives or motives (such as money, fame or recognition - among others) may give you drive to pursue mastery at something, often, these motives will run dry over time leaving you miserable in a job, career or situation that feels like a chore to do.

While, a deep, intrinsic love of the topic or skill itself will very rarely run out & will more effectively drive you to put in the work, get better & thrive.

And if you go & study the world's best, you'll continue to find this pattern arise. They love what they do. For some, that passion is so large, others consider it an 'obsession'.

Which is a feeling a lot of people in this world lack.

In the words of Henry David Thoreau,

"The mass of men lead lives of quiet desperation"

Too often people go through life without any real sense of passion, or higher purpose, for what they do.

And rather than starting their learning, skill development & mastery endeavours with *passion*, many people start with motives of financial or status incentives.

And, once again, those motives may bring short-term motivation & growth, but over time, fade away.

In fact, this is one of the biggest reasons so many hate their jobs. They started their jobs, not based on true passion, but instead, based on money, existing skills, demands from parents, or a number of other reasons besides passion.

And at first, that job was probably pretty ok. In fact, at first, maybe they even enjoyed it.

And the income, perks or potential of a promotion may have brought them that excitement, initially.

Many people start their jobs - & careers - just like *this*. At the beginning, it's great. It's fresh. It's new.

But, over time, the excitement from money or promotions fade away, yet the daily grind of a topic or skill that you have little passion for continues on.

A thought that is only saddened when we account that most people spend the *majority* of their lives working.

Which all leads people to, eventually, reach burnout. They begin to increasingly hate their jobs & careers. And they spend a large part of their work week awaiting the weekend so they can take a break & drink their sorrows away.

They then hear stories of people *willingly & voluntarily* working 70, 80 or 90 a week - without taking weekends off - & they think those people are crazy, without realizing, often, those people are in the best position because they love what they do & have strong *passion* for it.

The people who start their careers with *passion* don't 'work' a day in their lives. It's because, for them, it's not 'work'. They love what they do. They love Mondays.

And they tend to compartmentalize their lives a lot *less* than people who view 'work' as something they hate, but pays the bills so they can enjoy their other life outside of work. They view their 'work' as their purpose, their calling or their mission. It's meaningful. It fulfilling. The key is:

| Start with passion

If you go into learning a new topic or skill starting with the focus on money, fame, or a corner office, over time, you'll begin to hate what you do, no matter how lucrative it is.

Meanwhile, those who *start with passion* & afterwards pile the financial rewards, recognition & fame on top tend to continue to love what they do & are more likely to reach the highest levels of skill as a result.

If you read the backstories of the world's highest achievers, you'll find passion is a recurring theme.

Now, *'passion'* is not necessarily to be confused as a particular topic or skill. Sometimes it is, but often it's not.

Albert Einstein's passion wasn't mere *physics*, but rather a passion & curiosity of the invisible forces of the universe.

Mozart's passion wasn't just playing the piano, but rather composition & creating music. It was his intense love of music & the theatre that fueled his mastery.

It's this passion that, in many ways, enabled him to put in an estimated, 3500 hours of music training, before age 6.

If 'music' was something he was *'forced'* to learn, odds are, he would have settled & put in the bare minimum amount of work possible. However, because it was passion that fueled him, naturally, he was more willing to train harder.

Understanding this *nuance* is incredibly powerful because it allows us to expand our realms of possibility.

Although Martin Luther King Jr, was a minister & activist, his passion was bigger than that. His passion was about equality & human rights, not just 'begin a minister'.

Being a minister or civil rights activist were simply *'vehicles'* for him to fulfil his passions, in the same way, physics was Einstein's *'vehicle'* to follow his fascination.

We mustn't mistake the *'vehicle'* for the *'passion'* itself.

Sometimes the topic or skill is the passion in itself, but sometimes, it's not. We must consider this cautiously.

Either way, we must seek passion in what we do.

And when you *do* find your passion, you'll know because it activates a new sense of energy & excitement in your life, which will pull you towards mastery at something.

HOW TO FIND YOUR PASSION

Unfortunately, there is no one solution - or pattern - that show up repeatedly when people find their passion.

Throughout history, some found their passion deep into their childhood when they received an item, met a particular person or encountered a certain circumstance.

For others, like in the instance of *Mozart*, it was influenced by his family environment in which his father was a pianist & his older sister, *Maria*, was already learning the piano.

For others, they re-connected with a topic or skill they used to enjoy in the past.

For some, their passion finds them. And for others, they have to actively go out there & seek it.

As to how you do that, the best insight is simply to *test, taste & experience.*

The more things you test & experience, the greater your odds of finding something which deeply arouses your fascination & passion.

It's why you've got to be willing to taste a lot of different experiences, topics & skills on your journey of discovery.

Start with a simple list of things you think you might be fascinated by & go out there to experience them.

Test. Experiment. Do things you wouldn't normally do. Travel. Meet new people. Test learning new topics or skills.

And just like you discovered your dream car, dream house or favourite food by seeing & testing *a lot* of them - *testing & experiencing* - in the same way, you'll find your passion.

Mathematically, with every new thing you test *(which we'll talk about later)*, your odds of finding your passion go up.

And as you go on this journey to find your passion (or passions; plural), you want to intentionally spread yourself very thin. You want to ignore the guidance in the last section - for now - *until you find your passion*. Only then begin to re-allocate your time & *specialize*.

In other words, when you're finding your passion, you want to say 'yes' to everything you can & only once you find it, begin to say 'no' to increase focus & *specialize*.

Begin to approach much of life in a new way, knowing...

| Every $1 or hour you spend figuring out what you actually want - your passion - will save you hundreds of $'s & hours in the future

When you approach life with this awareness, you become more courageous & willing to test new things, which as a result, skyrockets your odds of finding your passion.

And understand that...

| Everything is monetizable

There are people whose passion is making their own jewellery, who today, are, not only on a path to greater & greater skill but are also crush it financially.

There are others whose passion is a fascination with nature & plant, who create wealth by monetizing this passion.

Everything is monetizable if you're creative. Beyond that, everything is monetizable in dozens of different ways.

In the day & age we live in - especially thanks to modern technological capabilities - we can monetize anything.

And, if you're still in doubt of this, go & search the internet & will find people making a living - or building a fortune -

from the craziest things. You'll find the strangest examples, which may just build up your belief that it's really possible.

However, as we know, we don't start there. We start with passion & only layer the money, fame, recognition & other extrinsic factors on top later on *(just like so many high achievers)*. It is important to think about this though.

EXERCISE: BECOME A 'YES' PERSON
If you've already found your passion, feel free to skip this particular exercise. However, if you're still chasing your calling, this exercise is something you should do.

Create a list of *everything* that you *could* potentially be passionate about, including everything that's a *'maybe'*.

If you really go & see the diversity of people, you'll find that there are literally thousands - yes, thousands - of different 'passions' that people are pursuing.

Create a list of everything you find fascinating - or that you've never experienced before - & begin to test each & every one of the things on that list.

If you're really honest with yourself, there should be at least a hundred things on your list to test out.

Sign up for every lesson, every class, every experience, you possibly can, constantly testing & experiencing, knowing that everything is moving you closer to finding that which you are deeply passionate about.

And only once you find it, begin to focus on the contents of the last chapter, re-allocate time more strategically & *specialize*. But, first, you have to find your *'main thing'*.

2 | **DISCIPLINE:** THE DRIVING FORCE OF WORK

"Discipline is the pathway to freedom"

\- *JOCKO WILLINK*

In the summer of 2012, professional trainer, Rob, had an opportunity to see *discipline* like he had never seen before.

He had just been hired to train the USA basketball team.

During his first interaction with Kobe, they talked about what was possible by the end of the summer. At the end, Rob gave Kobe his number & told him to call him anytime, if he wanted to do some extra conditioning work.

2 days later at 4:15 am, Kobe gave him a call.

"Rob, I hope I'm not disturbing anything right?"

"No, what's up Kobe?" Rob replied.

"Just wondering if you could just help me out with some conditioning work," Kobe asked.

"Sure, I'll see you in the facility in a bit."

This phone conversation happened at 4.15 am.

Approximately 20 minutes later, Rob walked into the training facility expecting to meet Kobe there to start the conditioning work. However, Kobe was already there.

He saw Kobe there - alone - completely dripping in sweat already deep into his conditioning. It wasn't even 5 am yet.

After about 2 hours of conditioning work together - 7 am - Rob went back to his hotel to get some quick rest before the actual day's practice began. During that time, Kobe went to the court to practice his shooting.

11 am. Rob arrived back at the facility to meet the rest of the USA basketball team. They were talking and chatting waiting for training to begin; expect one player; *Kobe*. On the far side of the facility, he was there shooting hoops.

"Good work this morning" Rob said to Kobe.

"Yeah, thanks Rob. I really appreciate it" Kobe replied.

"So when did you finish?"

"Finish what?" Kobe replied.

"Getting your shots up. What time did you leave the facility?" Rob asked Kobe.

"Oh, just now. I wanted 800... so yeah, just now."

Rob was shocked. Kobe was drenched with sweat before 5 am, worked with Rob on strength & conditioning for 2 hours, then made 800 shots over 4 hours until 11 am.

Most impressive of all, this was all *pre-training*. Meaning, training was only about to begin.

He did all that - 6, almost 7 hours of work - before official training with the team had even begun; that's *work ethic*. That's *commitment*. That's world-class *discipline*.

Hence it's no wonder that Kobe - *Kobe Bryant* - at age 34, had already won 5 NBA championships, 2 NBA Finals, Most Valuable Player award & 2 Olympic Gold Medals.

Beyond that, it's important to note that this wasn't a one-time occurrence during which Kobe wanted to impress the new coach. We know this because there are literally dozens of examples like this of *Kobe Bryant*, during his career, outworking those around him, similar to this one.

So often we often talk about hard work, we talk about work ethic, we talk about discipline, yet, we don't live it.

Yes, Kobe may have had the physical advantage of height - 1.98 metres - but so do millions of others - yet they never achieve what Kobe achieved in the sport of basketball.

It's because his physical advantages aren't what gives him the edge, his *skill* - developed through back-breaking discipline & work - is what gives him that advantage.

It *wasn't* talent that made extraordinary. It *wasn't* his natural born gifts. It was his *work*. His discipline and astounding work ethic; that's what made him one of the best basketball players of all time.

And that's what world-class skill & achievement requires; *you've got to be disciplined & put in the work.*

TESLA, SPACEX & THE MAN BEHIND IT ALL

He built 4 billion dollar companies, in 4 different markets (industries). A feat even the best would be proud of.

But, how did he do it? How did he achieve this? How did he become so extraordinary at what he does?

As always, there were many factors that contributed to it - not just 1 - but a huge one that stands out in this particular case is, of course, *discipline & hard work.*

Elon Musk often talks about his *'100-hour work week'* & is known to regularly work exactly that; *100 hours per week.*

While most attempt to become extraordinary at what they do, & achieve their goals working 9 - 5 - & taking weekends off - Elon Musk's approach is different. He works 100 hours per week (an average of 14.28 hours per day)

Which means he's work twice - & sometimes 3 times - as hard as many people around him. A big difference.

Too often we look at the world's greatest without realizing all the 5 am wake-ups, the sacrifices & the incredible workloads - the *discipline* - that formed the foundation on which their achievements are born. It's because they know:

| No amount of wishful thinking can replace the work it takes to get there

Positive thinking may make you feel good, but without the *discipline* & work, dreams will simply remain dreams.

For some reason we have actually been persuaded to believe that the 'secret' to success is to simply think about what we want. Yet, latest research - as well as the study of the world's most successful people - continues to show us that few things can be further from the truth.

Positive thinking (or, the law of attraction) definitely has its place in success. It's often what drives a lot of 'passion' & 'discipline' in the first place; that optimistic outlook on the future, however alone, it doesn't contribute to success.

Just like a great dish is the combination of multiple ingredients, success is too & we can't simply take 1 ingredient in isolation & call it the 'secret' to success as many people have done in the personal development space.

A great ingredient may add to a great recipe, but only as long as other ingredients are in place. Of course, *discipline* is a core ingredient to skill & success at anything.

It's why discipline & hard work are such common threads amongst successful people. And odds are, as you read this book, you can't name a single person who has achieved anything great - over the long term - without discipline or hard work. It's because those people don't exist.

Which is what makes *discipline* the second foundational key for mastery & success mastery & success.

THE '10,000-HOUR RULE' REVISITED

Although I often question the accuracy of the *'10,000-hour rule,'* the essence of it is very practical & can be followed.

The number '10,000' may vary wildly (in the next section, we'll dive into acceleration strategies), but it's always a great target to aim for, that will inspire greater *discipline*.

The rule, once again, states that it takes 10,000 hours of 'deliberate practice' to reach *mastery* at your area of craft. This originated from Anders Ericsson's research & is based on studies of high achievers, like The Beatles & Bill Gates

The Beatles, during early stages of their career, went to Hamburg, in Germany & regularly performed for between 5 & 8 hours per day, between 5 & 7 days per week. And did this multiple times a year.

Most musicians might do a 3-hour-long concert every few weeks (or months), while The Beatles performed for up to 8 hours per night. It really brings their success into greater perspective & helps us realize the value that *discipline* & the willingness to outwork others has in process of success.

Bill Gates used to sneak out during the night to code while everybody else was sleeping, only to climb back in through his window before his parents came in to wake him up.

They thought he just liked to sleep a lot, failing to realize that he spent many hours - while they thought he was sleeping - on computers, developing his mastery.

Then, from the age of 20 to the age of 30 (10 years) he never took a single day off work.

Almost everybody knows about Microsoft, Bill Gates & the impact he - & his company - have had. However, few know about the all the nights of work & the '10 dark years' that led to the success of Microsoft & the accumulation of his fortune, valued at over 90 billion dollars (net worth).

It's that day-in, day-out grind that allowed him to become extraordinary at what he does.

Whether you want to dominate an industry (or many industries like Elon Musk), or you simply want to get a pay-raise in your career, the path to get there is similar.

That path is the sequential & strategic acquisition of skills, acquired through *discipline. Hard work is irreplaceable.*

And it's this is the type of discipline, focus & effort that is required to become world-class at what you do. We know this based on countless examples of the world's best like Kobe Bryant, Elon Musk, The Beatles, Bill Gates & others.

Nothing significant is ever achieved overnight; it requires discipline & work. And, the highest levels of achievement require a disproportionate 'allocation' of your time.

This doesn't apply just to learning & skill development, but rather, to everything in our lives. The very things we value most in life, never come without discipline & hard work.

Great health & fitness doesn't come overnight. Six-pack abs don't just appear. The ability to run marathons doesn't come overnight. It all takes hundreds & thousands of hours of disciplined training, sweat & work.

Great relationships, friendships & partnerships are never formed overnight. It takes quality time, connection, shared experience & understanding to build a great friendship, intimate relationship, family bond or business partnership.

Same applies to business & career success; it takes work.

Can each process be optimized, improved, heightened & accelerated? Absolutely. But, it still takes *discipline.*

And this is all something that, at the deepest levels, we all know. We know success doesn't just happen overnight, yet sometimes we are misled to believe that it does by online money schemes, infomercials or the media (& media bias).

Motivation & self-discipline is your ability to activate your own drive, focus & effort when you choose & it's an ability to do what others are not willing to do. Which, is trainable.

Discipline is about a hunger for something greater, combined with a commitment to follow through & make it happen, no matter how tough the journey may be.

When you're disciplined, committed & relentless about achieving what you want, *nearly anything is possible.*

However, it all starts with the small things. Discipline is rarely about huge feats of will, but more often, it's about the day-in, day-out execution of the basics & foundations.

In the words of Jim Rohn,

"What is easy to do is easy not to do."

And discipline is about doing the things that others are not willing to do. It's not about starting a diet, a business or a relationship - that's the easy part - it's about following through even during the days when you may not feel like it.

And it's in those moments - when you're down & don't feel like getting back up - that your *discipline* is really tested.

Everybody experiences challenges. Everybody fails. However, it's our response to those circumstances that matters most. The world's highest achievers have the *discipline* to keep going, even in those tough moments.

Also, people think that by avoiding working hard by working smart. And, they can, to some extent.

But, if you want to truly become extraordinary, the fastest, most effective, way to get there is do both.

There are many ways to gain a competitive edge. One way is to *work harder* than everybody else. Another is to *work smarter* than others. Another is to be more *skilled*. Yet another is to be *more consistent & outlast* others.

And while any 1 of those strategies can give you an edge, a combination of them gives you an *exponential advantage.*

Elon Musk is a great example of this. He works harder than pretty much everybody else (100 hours a week). He works smarter & more strategically than most people. He works more skillfully. Estimates say he used to read up to 10 hours a day during his childhood; he clearly prioritizes learning. And, he's consistent; willing to outlast others.

Which all gives him multiple points of advantage, which combined, give him an *exponential* advantage that leads to the incredible things he's been able to achieve.

Remember: *a combination of lot of small advantages, combined, makes a big advantage.*

So, if you really want the greatest advantage, greatest odds of success & the fastest, more effective way to achieve your ambitions, don't just look to do 1 but use all of the methods of gaining a competitive advantage above.

However, there is nuance to this as well. And this nuance comes from this simple, yet powerful, question:

| Are your actions & ambitions aligned?

Not everybody is going to work as hard as Elon Musk, Kobe Bryant or Bill Gates. And, not everybody should.

The key is to align your *actions* (how hard you work or train) with your *ambitions* (how lofty your ambitions are).

If you want to become a trillionaire, yet you're working 3 hours a day, you're not striking that alignment between *actions* & *ambitions*. It's because that height of success requires massive work ethic, focus, sacrifice & discipline.

Meanwhile, if your ambitions are simply to make a comfortable living, travel the world & sightsee, & you're working few hours a day, that's great. Your actions & ambitions are aligned & you'll be happy.

And remember; there is no right or wrong with this. Different people want different things. It's about aligning what we want *(ambitions)* with the required *actions*.

EXERCISE: ALIGN ACTIONS WITH AMBITIONS
The first step is to answer this question:

What are all the things that I actually what to achieve - things to learn, skills to master, goals to attain, experience to have, ambitions to fulfil - that I'm equally willing to work for & dedicate my time to?

Take 7 minutes (minimum) & journal on that 1 question alone, in detail. List out the ambitions you have.

Most people would stop there; we're not like the rest.

Part 2; answer this question in detail:

What is really required of me for me to accomplish these ambitions that I've set out to achieve?

This is crucial. Take as long as you need to answer this question to the absolute best level you can.

Go through each goal & think about what it requires.

One of the best ways to do this is to find other people who have achieved what you want & see how much time, energy & effort they put to achieve that goal.

How much time, energy, focus & effort will it take? What are you going to have to sacrifice to make it happened?

Dig deeper & journal on this. It will give you greater awareness of what's required & will help you get aligned.

3 | INNOVATION: THE SEEKING OF GROWTH

"Success in life is founded upon attention to the small things rather than to the large things; to the everyday things nearest to us rather than to the things that are remote and uncommon"

- BOOKER T. WASHINGTON

If you count up all the hours, you - or someone you know - has probably spent thousands of hours preparing food, yet that doesn't make you (or them) a masterful chef.

You (or someone you know) has probably spent thousands of hours behind the wheel, driving, during your lifetime, yet, this doesn't make you (or them) a Formula 1 driver.

Equally, over the course of your life, you've probably spent a few thousand hour's talking & having discussions with people, yet it doesn't make you a masterful public speaker.

Although repetition - which stems out of first 2 keys, *passion* & *discipline* - is essential to mastery, it alone, will not make you great at something.

What's also required is this third - often overlooked - ingredient in the recipe; **innovation**.

Innovation, meaning, making constant & strategic tweaks, changes & improvements to what you're doing.

When most people drive, prepare food or talk, they don't do it with mastery in mind. They just do it. No *'innovation'*.

Which is the reason why people aren't that much better drivers today than they were many years ago.

It's also the reason why, as we talked about in chapter 1, *'experience'* doesn't correlate strongly with skill or success.

It's because somebody may have years of experience at something, but they stopped applying this third key - *innovation* - & hence aren't really getting any better.

Which is ok; the goal isn't to get better at things that we don't particularly care about getting better at. You may not really care about becoming a better driver, chef or speaker.

The key is to identify the topics & skills that we *do*, in fact, want to get better at & approach them with *innovation*.

I refer to this as an *'optimization mindset'*. Getting into a state of mind where you're seeking to optimize, refine, improve & accelerate what you're doing..

And the first step to tap into this is very simply; *decide*. You just decide that you want to get better, knowing that...

| There is always a better, faster, more effective way to do anything

More experienced doctors often score lower on tests than *less experienced* doctors because after a certain point they settle & never continued to *decide* that every day, week, month & year they want to get better at what they do.

Decide. Wake up each morning & commit - make a mental declaration to yourself - that, whatever topics or skills you want to develop, you're going to get better at them *today*.

Beyond that, it's about being willing to constantly research, test, question, experiment, fail & improve what you do.

EXERCISE: HOW CAN I MAKE THIS BETTER?
A very simple, yet powerful, question you can keep at the forefront of your attention in order to approach life with an *'optimization mindset'* is this one:

How can I make this better?

The exercise is simple; ensure that you think about this 1 question at least 5 times a day.

You can set a reminder on your phone that rings every few hours reminding you of it, you can hang it on your fridge, you can set it as your phone or laptop background. The 'how' is really up to you.

By doing this you're conditioning your mind to not just see the best in every scenario, but also see the greater possibility in everything you do. It will help you activate an *'optimization mindset'*, which in turn, will help you experiment, improve & get better every single day.

DELIBERATE EXPERIMENTATION

The *10,000-hour rule* talks about *'deliberate practice,'* but it's also important we value *'deliberate experimentation'*. The idea of intentional, strategic & consistent testing.

It's a framework that, at first, may seem to contradict the *'10,000-hour-rule,'* but actually perfectly compliments it.

Further research shows that the impact & value of the *'10,000-hour rule'* differs depending on the topic or skill that your time is put towards.

They found that when you put 10,000 hours towards the mastery of an instrument, sport or other skill in which the rules rarely change, *'deliberate practice'* is top priority.

However, in topics or skills which change rapidly - such as business, marketing or tech - less emphasis is on the 10,000 *hours* (deliberate practice) & more is on strategic testing & innovation (deliberate experimentation).

Meaning, while in sport or music, the emphasis is placed increasing on the 2nd foundation - *discipline* (deliberate practice) - within high growth & rapidly changing topics & skills, more emphasis is on this 3rd key - *innovation*.

All 3 keys still matter in all topics, skills, professions & industries, however, their order of importance changes depending on *what* you're learning or developing.

The *'10,000-hour rule,'* has a stronger correlation to mastery in skills, such as music, sport or chess, while the *'10,000 experiment rule'* has a greater correlation to success in high growth & rapidly-changing topics & skills.

Once again - & this can't be emphasised enough - both *discipline* (the '10,000-hour rule') & *innovation* ('the 10,000-experiment rule') are very important in both cases.

The *'10,000 experiment rule'* states that it's not always the number of hours that you dedicate to your craft, but rather the number of *experiments* you do within the topic or skill.

"Our success at Amazon is a function of how many experiments we do per year, per month, per week, per day," Those are the words of the man worth over 100 billion dollars (net worth), *Jeff Bezos.*

Another example comes from an interview with Facebook founder, *Mark Zuckerberg*, in which he said:

"One of the things I'm most proud of that is really key to our success is this testing framework ... At any given point in time, there isn't just one version of Facebook running. There are probably 10,000."

Facebook is estimated to perform over 100,000 tests & experiments per year. Hence, is there any wonder why it's so successful, with over 2 billion users & great engagement compared to other sites & apps. It's because everything is tested, tracked, optimized & improved, all the time.

And just like Facebook, as well the other biggest businesses in the world thrive because of an incredible emphasis & obsession with *experimentation (innovation)*, we too can emphasise it as it's what helps create *'feedback loops'*.

INNOVATION = FEEDBACK LOOPS

The process of *innovating* - & more specifically, experimenting - is what creates *feedback loops*, which create distinctions & move us to new, higher levels of skill *(as we initially discussed in the first section of this book)*.

So, in case you were thinking, *'How exactly do I create feedback loops & distinctions?'* The answer is: through constant experimentation & 'innovation'.

Every experiment leads to a new *feedback loop* (a new distinction), which gives you more data to base your decisions on, which makes you more skilled.

Experimentation is the ability to come up with ideas (hypothesise) within a topic or skill, test them, look at the results & create new conclusion & understandings (distinctions) within a topic or skill.

And assuming you're acting on the data, every experiment moves you to a new, higher level of skill & success.

For example, if you want to become a master at the topic of marketing, you should put in 10,000 hours, but more importantly, during those hours of development, perform at least 10,000 experiment within your craft.

Once again, the number '10,000' is very generic, but it's simply a good benchmark to aim for to achieve mastery.

If you want to become a masterful marketer, you should be consistently experimenting; testing new marketing channels, new ad types, new visuals, new call-to-actions, new follow up methods - the list goes on & on.

If you want to become a musician writing your own music, you should be writing & experimenting with new rhythm's, new lyrics, new speeds & new songs all the time.

You should become very prolific at what you do (especially if your passion is driven by creation like it is for songwriters, authors, creators, fashion designers & others).

Often those who create a lot - experiment a lot - are those who gain a huge advantage. Often, it's the artists who paint the most paintings, songwriters who write the most songs, comedians who write the most jokes, authors who write the most books, who - not always, but often - have the greatest advantage & go on to win. It's because they experiment a lot more than the average person in their field.

And with each experiment, their taking *new actions* - which lead to *new results* - creating new feedback loops (distinctions) which makes them more skilled.

And if we look at this from a mathematical, analytical perspective, we'll realize that the more experiments we do, not only the more knowledgeable & skilled we get, but also the greater our chances of success at anything.

Assuming you're building each experiment on top of insights from the others, if you do enough experiments, your odds of hitting on a breakthrough go up radically.

Think about it. If you're new to a topic & you know absolutely nothing, the first experiment, hypothetically, is like a guess. It has a 50% chance of being successful & 50% chance of being unsuccessful; just like flipping a coin. This is because you have no prior understanding in this field to skew the odds in the favour of success.

But when you get take the results of the first experiment & you go on to do a second experiment, now, your odds of a successful experiment are *more than 50%*.

Why? It's because you're now factoring the results of your previous experiments into the hypothesis for the next one, increasing the odds of the second one being successful.

And, this trend continues. The more data you from previous experiments you've done, the more data you can use to base your next experiments on, consistently boosting the odds of success for the next experiment.

Meaning, not only is each individual experiment giving you more distinctions (making you more skilled), but it's also increasing your chances of a breakthrough, exponentially.

And even if the experiment is *not* successful, it's still a win because you're accumulating distinctions (data) which make you more skilled at your craft.

Ultimately, if the experiment is successful, it's a win & if it fails, it's also a win. Big upside; no downside. It's like playing Poker, but no matter what card is drawn, you win.

The world's most successful companies know this, the world's most successful people act on this & now it's time for you to as well if you haven't already.

Or - if you have - to stretch yourself, experiment more, test more & accelerate your learning further.

IT'S ABOUT THE SMALL THINGS

Too often we think 1 opportunity is going to make us rich, 1 intensive week of training is going to make us world-class or 1 big gesture is going to make someone like us forever.

Yet, as you may have realized from this book - or from the works of many great philosophers & thought leaders - success, is much less about the big events & far more about *consistency* & *accumulated effect* of small things, together.

And this really applies to learning & skill development; it's rarely about that 1 big innovation - or insight - that's going to change everything, but rather the accumulation of small experiments & innovations, working together, that makes someone extraordinary at what they do.

ALL 3 KEYS ARE REQUIRED

It's easy to take these 3 keys & pawn them off as 'obvious,' or 'simplistic;' partially because that's exactly what they are. They are simplistic & they may appear obvious.

However, there's a lot of nuance to each one & it's why these 3 keys required this entire chapter to cover in detail.

Beyond that, although they may be simple, the reason I often refer to them as the '*3 irrefutable keys of mastery*,' is because nobody can name anybody who achieved mastery at anything, missing any 1 of these 3 keys.

Every master throughout history - without exception - has all 3 of these foundational keys in place.

They have a *passion* - or at least, a purpose or motive - for what they're doing. They all have *discipline* that enabled them to put hundreds & thousands of hours into their craft. And they all have a level of *innovation* that allows them to filter for new improvements to actually get better. It's why:

Passion + Discipline + Innovation = *Mastery*

Together these 3 powerful keys form a powerful framework anybody can use to become extraordinary at anything & serve as a constant reminder of what it really takes.

9 | ELITE-LEVEL MINDSET SHIFTS: THINK LIKE THE WORLD'S BEST

"Change your thoughts and you change your world"

- *NORMAN VINCENT PEALE*

Our mind is tremendously powerful; it's one of the greatest - if not *the* greatest - assets that we have.

But, it's also much like a hammer; it could build you your dream house or it could be used as a weapon to bash in somebody's skull. It's a tool. In itself, it is not good or bad; that's dependant on how you use it.

And some people use their mind to develop tremendous levels of skill, achieve their ambitions & live a fulfilled life, while others use their mind to be mediocre, fail to achieve their goals & live with a lot of regrets.

I know that's not popular to say, but it's just the most accurate version of the truth.

However, as we briefly covered in the first section of this book, our thoughts are also, often, not our own.

Many of the thoughts & beliefs that we have, we did not consciously choose but rather were passed down to us by parents, grandparents, friends, teachers & mentors (as well as others we've interacted with on our life's journey).

And if your current beliefs (that often are not your own) got you to where you are today - good or bad - some new, altered beliefs can take you to that next level of success.

That's why this chapter is focused on the 3 core mindset shifts - modelled of the world's best - we can (& should) make if we want to become extraordinary at what we do.

1 | FAILURE IS THE KEY TO SUCCESS

"There is only one thing that makes a dream impossible to achieve: the fear of failure"

-   PAULO COELHO

"What have you failed at this week?"

Those were the words she would hear from her father on a regular basis.

Often, when they would be eating dinner, he would ask her, *'what have you failed at this week?'* & they would discuss her failures from that week.

The same question; over & over again.

"What have you failed at this week?"

She would tell him about her failures, but rather than get disappointed or disheartened, they would celebrate these failures. They viewed them as positives.

As she grew up & got older, she started chasing her dreams.

She wanted to be an attorney. She started studying, however, reconsidered very quickly after scoring low on the LSATs. She failed.

So, she got a job at Disney World in Florida, where she worked for the next 3 months. However, she wasn't happy with this job & wanted something more.

"What have you failed at this week?"

Next, in that pursuit of more, she accepted a job at an office supply company selling fax machines door-to-door.

During this time, she had an idea for a product of her own. She started her own business, but the failures didn't stop.

She had no business experience, business education or clue about how retail works.

When she first presented her product & business idea, she was turned away by every representative she spoke to.

"What have you failed at this week?"

But she kept going, pursuing her dreams.

Skip forward to 2014, and she was listed the 93rd most powerful women in the world by Forbes.

Her name... Sara Blakely. Founder of Spanx.

Her net worth, as of 2017... over $1.1 billion.

In an interview she said;

> *"My dad, growing up encouraged me and my brother to fail. The gift he was giving me is that failure is (when you are) not trying versus the outcome. It's really allowed me to be much freer in trying things and spreading my wings in life"*

In the words of Sara Blakely,

| **"Failure is the secret to success"**

And although, just like we talked about before, there is no 1 'secret'; only factors that correlate to success strongly. However, just like Sara Blakely's father helped her realize, failure is an incredibly important factor in success.

Her father helped her redefine her mindset around failure. And that's, in her own words, one of the biggest things that she attributes her success to.

It allowed her to view (& approach) failure far more positively, which allowed her to test more, experiment more, learn more & push through challenges easier.

And, if you go & study success & the world's highest achievers, you'll find this isn't the exception, but the rule.

The vast majority of the world's highest skilled - & highest achieving - people view & approach failure far more effectively & positively than the majority of society.

FAILED SO OFTEN HE BECAME THE BEST

> *"I missed more than 9000 shots in my career, I've lost almost 300 games, 26 times I've been trusted to take the game-winning shot, and missed. I've failed over and over again in my life, and that is why I succeed"*

Those are the words of basketball legend, *Michael Jordan*, in the famous Nike commercial, 'Failure'.

In 1978, 15-year-old Michael went to sign up for his varsity basketball team, however, he never made the team. And was asked to play on the junior team instead.

Later in his career, Michael recalled that moment, *"I went to my room and I closed the door and I cried. For a while, I couldn't stop. Even though there was no one else home at the time, I kept the door shut. It was important to me that no one hear me or see me."*

But Michael - just like Sara Blakely - never let failure define him. He uses failure as fuel. It made him work harder & train harder until he got what we wanted.

And, as you can see from that commercial transcript, he doesn't view failure as a negative. He didn't view failure as something that stops him from his goals, but rather, he views failure as the very reason for his success.

And, it's a big factor that allowed him to become, arguably, the greatest basketball player of all time.

It's because failure, in itself, is a huge key to success.

And, while everybody failures - *that's inevitable, the only people who don't fail are those who never do anything* - it's those who react to failure most effectively that thrive.

The world's highest achievers know that failure is simply a *stepping stone* to success, as well as, something they can learn from to become better at what they do.

And beyond that, history tends to cover the failures & emphasise the successes.

Michael Jordan may have scored more game-winning points than anyone else, but he also missed more last-minute shots than any other player.

Yet, few ever blame him - or even talk about - the failed last-minute shots. Those failures get wiped away through history & icons get remembered for their successes.

FAIL OFTEN

In his book, *Bounce, Matthew Syed*, talks about a study conducted in the sport of figure skating back in the 1990's.

They found that one of the biggest differences between elite skaters & their less skilled counterparts was simply how frequently they failed in training.

They discovered that, quite simply, elite skaters fell over far more often during their training sessions.

Which, now, makes perfect sense. It's because each failure is an opportunity for learning. And, it's why...

| Failure shouldn't be avoided, it should be encouraged

Failure should be applauded. It should be celebrated. It should be encouraged because 'failure', at its core, is not only a sign someone is *'going for it'* & *'taking action'*, but is also a stepping stone to success in itself.

Imagine how different society & life would be if we were all, throughout life, encouraged to go for it, take action, fail often, learn from failure & view failure as a stepping stone.

We would see not just a radical improvement in skill level, but also a massive increase in human happiness.

By avoiding failure, we're avoiding the opportunity to learn & get better & it's why we must challenge ourselves to view failure as a positive in our lives. As something that supports us to get to where we want to go on our journey.

FAIL FAST

Beyond just failing often, we should strive to *fail fast*. Especially if we're learning something for the first time.

It's because when we learn something new - something we haven't yet failed at before - a part of our mind is actually holding us back from our full learning potential.

It's because when we've never experienced failure in a particular topic or skill, our mind begins to over-emphasise & over-exaggerate the worst-case-scenario in our heads.

My greatest experience of this comes from a skiing trip in France, during which I was teaching my grandma to ski.

At first, she was terrified. In fact, you could see the fear of falling written all over her face. She wanted to learn, but fear was taking up so much of her focus & attention that all she was doing was getting increasingly frustrated.

Because she hadn't fallen before, her mind was over-emphasizing how bad & painful falling over would be & it was stopping her from learning.

And maybe you've experienced this before; where you want to learn, but most of your attention & focus isn't spent on 'learning', but rather on 'avoiding failure'. I sure can relate.

As to how you get through that, you simply *fail fast*. Which means if you have to fail on purpose; go ahead.

And that's exactly what I did on the skiing trip. I went & pushed her over on purpose (safely, of course) just to help her remove that fear of failure. An action that may sound evil without context, but an action that allowed her to experience what I call the, *'that-wasn't-so-bad-effect'*.

This is based on the understanding that fear is much worse in our heads than it is in real life. Perhaps, you've experienced this effect before, where you were scared or terrified about something only to later say to yourself, *'Oh, that wasn't as bad as I thought it would be'*.

So, if you're ever paralyzed - or limited - by fear, free yourself by stepping into that fear (on purpose if you have to) instead of avoiding it. *Failing fast* is a strategy we can use to remove ourselves from a state of being paralyzed by failure & begin to step back into more focused learning.

DON'T LET FAILURE DEFINE YOU

He had produced about 2100 works, including around 900 paintings & 1100 drawings & sketches in his lifetime.

During that lifetime he had sold just 1 painting. That's it.

He committed suicide at age 37, following years of mental illness & poverty.

Vincent Van Gogh was considered a failure during his life.

He became famous only after his death, & today is regarded as a misunderstood, artistic genius.

Unfortunately, he wasn't able to see the legacy he left. But, odds are, if he did, he wouldn't consider himself as a failure, but rather a huge success (just like he is viewed amongst society today).

What do you think he would have said if he saw the legacy that he has had since his death? How do you think he would have viewed his life if he saw what we see today?

Van Gogh was an extraordinary artist but made the fatal mistake of letting failure define him. He let his *current reality* define who he was, which amongst other reasons, caused his to suffer emotionally, despite his amazing skill.

And what we can learn from this very abridged & rather tragic story of *Vincent Van Gogh* is not to make the same mistake & let our failures define us.

He had created over 2100 works of art before the age of 37, with many of those painting later selling for millions - & tens of millions - of dollars. Imagine how much more he could have created & contributed if he never let failure define him, but rather viewed it positively.

This is one of those rare instances in which we are not modelling the behaviours of a successful person, but rather, learning from their mistakes.

Michael Jordan, Sara Blakely & other high achievers never let failure define them & went on, not only to become extraordinary but also to live lives filled with happiness.

We mustn't let our past shape how we view ourselves because we don't know what the future holds. If only Van Gogh did this, it would be fascinating to see how we would interact & inspire the world today.

We must view failure positively & have faith in the future we're creating instead of letting short-term failure stop us.

| Fall in love with failure

That's only fully achieved when we, not just 'tolerate' failure, but rather, learn to fall in love with it.

EXERCISE: FALLING IN LOVE WITH FAILURE
Every day, for the next 7 days, before you go to bed, write out a list of things you have failed at that day. Just list a few things, no matter how small they may be.

And after you finish your list for the day, stand up & celebrate. Go crazy. Go nuts. Just celebrate like a maniac.

Then sit down for 2 minutes & think about how each failure served you. *What did you learn? What problem could it have helped you avoid? How did it help you?*

This exercise is designed to recondition your thoughts about failure & enable you to associate each failure as a positive event. Just like Sara Blakely, you can condition yourself to love failure & achieve whatever you want.

Challenge yourself to do this exercise for the next 7 days.

Approach learning - & life in general - knowing that...

| When you fall in love with failure, nothing can stop you from achievement

It's time for all to, collectively, step up into higher levels of thinking, to fall in love with failure, to celebrate failure, to view failure as a positive & to use each failure as a stepping stone to greater learning, skill & success. It's time for us to, now just know this, but to *live it* in our lives.

When we do this, not only will we live happier lives, but we'll also step into greater levels of our true potential.

2 | FEEDBACK IS FUEL FOR GROWTH

"We all need people who will give us feedback. That's how we improve"

- *BILL GATES*

China, in the 2012 London Olympics, won 6 out the 8 possible gold medals in the sport of diving.

4 years later - the 2016 Rio Olympics - they came back & won gold in 7 out of the 8 diving events.

On top of that, Chinese diver *Wu Minxia*, became the first athlete to win the same diving event 4 times.

What the Chinese diving team achieve in the sport of diving is nothing short of extraordinary.

Very few individuals, or teams, dominate any sport to this extent, making it a great place to model for insights.

How can we tap into this level of extreme achievement in our lives? What is it that they do differently that allows them to achieve these extraordinary results?

And most importantly...

What can we learn from the Chinese diving team to optimize our own learning & skill development?

In order for us to find these answer, we must dive deeper into the rituals & routines of the Chinese diving team.

A typical training dive looks like this:

1. They go up to the diving board & perform the dive *(often a very basic dive; they focus on mastering the foundations)*.

2. They get out the pool & instantly get *feedback* - constructive criticism - from a coach about what they can do better next time.

3. They then walk over a TV screen & proceed to watch a replay of the dive they just performed to get a second layer of feedback from themselves.

Let's dig into why this is so impactful. The core of it is something called *feedback*.

Not the type of feedback we talked about in the chapter about *feedback loops*. This is similar, yet different.

Feedback loops are what your brain uses to accumulate *'distinctions' (it's the internal workings of the brain)*, while the type of *'feedback'* we're about to talk about is, plain & simple, getting a list of 'things to improve next time. Often labelled as *'constructive criticism'*.

It's often about the things that we may not want to hear but should hear to really get to the next level at what we do.

And while most people avoid feedback or receive it very rarely, the Chinese diving team have structured their diving training to give 1) consistent & 2) multi-layered feedback for each & every dive a diver performs.

First, they receive feedback from the coach *(we'll discuss the value of coaching in a later chapter)*.

Second, they watch a replay of their dive on a TV screen which allows the diver to give themselves further feedback - constructive criticism - about what they can do better.

Most people rarely get feedback, while the Chinese diving team are rigorous, consistent & adamant about it. More so than pretty much any other training team in the world.

And because of years of training, this feedback structure has conditioned members of the Chinese diving team to love feedback as it leads to higher levels of skill.

Just like Sara Blakely's father helped her condition to love failure, the Chinese training structure has helped these Chinese divers condition a love & respect for feedback.

| Fall in love with feedback

Instead of avoiding feedback, or taking it personally, fall in love with it & use it as insight into future improvement.

Feedback can come in many forms: a suggestion (e.g. from a co-worker), a complaint (e.g. from a customer), advice (e.g. from a boss or mentor), amongst other sources.

Your role is to, no matter where you receive that feedback from, find ways you can use it to improve what you do.

And know that simply accepting feedback when it's given to you is not the same thing as *falling in love* with it.

Falling in love with feedback is about you going out there and *actively seeking* & *asking for* feedback. It's a mindset.

It's all about your willingness to constantly ask your friends, family, mentors, coaches & teachers for feedback. Constantly ask them *'What can I do better?'*

It comes from an *'optimization mindset'* - as we talked about in the last chapter - but manifests itself as a question to others rather than a personal thought process.

David Copperfield, one of the world's greatest illusionists, had an insatiable desire for feedback. He would perform magic tricks for everyone around him & ask for feedback from them all about what we could do better with the trick.

At one time he couldn't find anybody else so he asked a janitor to give him feedback.

David Copperfield, very early on, fell in love with feedback & it helped him master his craft.

And feedback can help *you* learn anything many times faster, but you have to be willing to seek it.

And as you read this, odds are this makes a lot of sense & you can see how getting more constructive criticism can help you learn faster, but what stops many people is fear.

Often we know the right things to do, but we fear them. Our ego or self-pride can get in the way sometimes & we don't ask for feedback (although we know they should).

It's the reason we don't ask the staff at the gym for feedback on our workout technique, why we don't ask fellow players on the team for feedback of how we can get better, or why an aspiring artist doesn't ask for feedback from the teacher of the art class.

It's because hearing what we've done badly - even if it's said in a nice way - can, at first, be hard to take. However, I assure you, like any habit, it gets easier over time.

It's why we must push through the initial resistance to get to the other side where feedback becomes a way of life.

We must be courageous, willing to hear what we should have done better, knowing that feedback is fuel for growth.

The first step is to begin asking. Set an intention to ask people for feedback as often as you can. At the beginning of the day, tell yourself *'I'm going to ask for some type of feedback 5 times today'* & don't go to sleep until you have.

The next step is to, just like the Chinese diving team, begin to structure feedback into your skill development (as we'll talk about in the next chapter). You can leverage the power of coaching, or just create great systems & procedures, to ensure you get feedback every time, no matter what.

Lastly, surround yourself with people who are willing to tell you the brutal truth - even if you may not like it.

Often, people ask the wrong people for feedback.

They ask people who are likely to say something like...

'No, I don't have any feedback, you're doing great. You're perfect. Keep being awesome.'

This is great encouragement - which is important for other reasons - but it doesn't help you get the feedback (the fuel for growth) that you need to progress & get better.

It may make you feel good in the short term, but in the long term, it only slows down your learning & limits your true potential. You have to find people who are willing to tell you the brutal truth that you need to hear.

And sometimes, the best feedback you'll ever get is from people who *don't* like you. I've found this quote very fascinating, especially when it comes to feedback:

"Keep your friends close, and your enemies closer"

Your competitors, your rivals or your haters are often great sources of feedback, but only if you're able to take the emotion out of what they say & treat it as simply, *feedback.*

From sources like these, the feedback is often covered by tons of dirt & hate, & it's your job to really dig deep to find the nuggets of insight in what they're saying.

"Your most unhappy customers are your greatest source of learning" - Bill Gates

Someone who doesn't like you may say *"you're never going to achieve anything because you're so lazy,"* & you have to interpret that as, *'you should be more disciplined'.*

And when it comes to uncovering the things you should improve, it's best to think of this like a stolen credit card.

If your credit card was stolen, when would you rather hear about it: straight away, so you can do something or in 2 weeks after the thief has spent all your money?

Personally, I would prefer to find the things that I am doing wrong - through feedback - as soon as possible.

Another example. Let's say that you are a professional diver on the Chinese diving team.

When would you rather find out that you are making a mistake in your dive: before or after the big competition?

My bets are you would rather 'before', so you can improve as soon as possible before the competition.

| Feedback accelerates growth

The faster you can get feedback, the faster you can make improvements & become more skilled at what you do.

That's how the Chinese diving team - just like so many of the world's highest achievers (& highest achieving teams) - think about learning, skill development, peak performance, failure & feedback. They think very differently.

And it's the combination of a love of *failure* (as discussed previously) & love of *feedback* that gives you a huge edge.

But, let's take it to an even higher level with another insight from the hugely dominant Chinese diving team.

Imagine you are standing on the edge of the diving board.

And the other team members are watching you eagerly as you attempt a dive that's never been successfully landed.

You look down. You see the water below you. You can feel the fear, but you do the dive anyway.

You start twisting & turning in the air, performing this dive that has never been successfully landed before.

And, smash. You misland it.

You start to think *'what did I do wrong?'* or *'maybe this dive is just too hard to complete'*

However, as you get out of the water, everyone is cheering & applauding you. You get out to a complete round of applause from the other diving team members.

Which inevitably makes you smile as you stand there with everybody clapping & celebrating your *'significant failure'*.

This is how the Chinese diving team react whenever any diver attempts a new dive or does something outside the realm of current possibility. They...

| Celebrate significant failures

What they're doing is encouraging their divers to 'go for it,' & push themselves to go for the seemingly impossible.

What this, rather unconventional, practice is doing is actually *inspiring courage*. Which makes it very powerful.

It makes the divers far more likely to push themselves & go for it again next time. They support them to view failure & feedback as huge positives. They train 'mindset'.

Once again, imagine how different society would be if these views (ways of thinking) were the norm, not the exception.

How different would lives be? That's what I want to create.

3 | RESPONSIBILITY GIVES YOU POWER

"The price of greatness is responsibility"

-   *WINSTON CHURCHILL*

The world's highest achiever take greater responsibility.

This is a pattern & success principle that has been passed on by the greatest philosophers, thinkers & thought leaders for generations, yet, it's still wildly under-utilized.

Studies across various fields continue to reaffirm the power & impact of our beliefs, thoughts, decisions & action, but the world's highest achievers, not only know that but actively act on this understanding by taking a greater level of personal responsibility for everything in their lives.

When something goes wrong, they don't blame those around them, but rather they point the finger back at themselves, willing to take *personal responsibility*.

This way of thinking enables them to stop making excuses, take more action & tap into greater *personal power*.

And when it comes to learning, so often people blame their circumstances, blame their lack of equipment, blame their coaches & teachers, blame their friends, blame their family, blame their lack of IQ, talent or superior genetics, instead of taking full responsibility for their skill & focusing on what they can control to shape their future.

'Victim thinking', 'blaming,' & 'finger pointing,' strip people of their power to change, improve & take control.

The reason for this is because, psychologically, as soon as we blame our failure, challenge or problem on a co-worker, our mind thinks to itself, *'hey, I'm off the hook. It's their fault, meaning we can't do anything about it & we can't change it, so why bother attempting to do anything'.*

In essence, when we put the blame on somebody else we are giving them the power over that situation, which strips away our personal power & control over that outcome.

For example, when we blame our IQ for our lack of skill, now we have given our power & control of our destiny over to our IQ. Psychologically, our mind knows that we can't change things that we have no control over & so it never attempts to make a change because that's 'IQ's' fault.

Meanwhile, those who take control of their learning, skill development & results have control over their destiny. It's because, if something is 'your fault,' you have the control over that situation required to change it as you wish.

In other words, you want things that go wrong to be 'your fault,' because that means that you have the control over that situation to respond effectively & make it better.

If it's somebody else's fault, sure, it may make you feel better in the moment, but over the long term, it gives you absolutely no control over that situation.

As Stephen R. Covey once wrote:

"Look at the word responsibility - "response-ability" - the ability to respond. Highly proactive people recognize that responsibility. They do not blame circumstances, conditions or conditioning for their behavior. Their behavior is a product of their own conscious choice, based on values, rather than a product of their conditions, based on feeling"

By taking full responsibility for our learning & skill development - in every scenario - we give ourselves the possibility to respond strategically for the best results.

It's a mindset that, once you adopt, changes everything.

And this very much fuels the 2 other elite-level mindsets we've discussed in this chapter - *failure* & *feedback*.

When you take full responsibility for your thoughts, decisions, actions & results, falling in love with failure & loving to receive feedback become many times easier to do.

Individually, each 1 of the 3 mindset shifts we've discussed has great power, but together, that impact is compounded.

In the same way that each of the chapters in this book can help you learn faster, develop your skill more effectively & become extraordinary, together, the concepts in this book have a greater, more exponential, effect.

Remember: skill or success isn't the result of 1 big, magical act or understanding, but rather the accumulation of many simple, but powerful, understandings, practices & habits.

And we must move forward in our lives approaching failure positively, viewing feedback as fuel that propels our growth & each action as our own, taking full responsibility for it.

We must step into the true power we have to shape our learning, skill development & life results.

10 | THE LEARNING PROCESS:
A STRATEGIC LEARNING PLAN

"Learning is the beginning of wealth. Learning is the beginning of health. Learning is the beginning of spirituality. Searching and learning is where the miracle process all begins"

- *JIM ROHN*

Effective *learning* is more than simply taking notes & attempting to memorize important facts, figures & info.

In that same way, effective *skill development* is more than just repeating something over & over hoping to get good.

We are all born with the capability to learn (it's a gift), but we are *not* born with the ability to learn *effectively*; that's a skill we must go out there & develop.

When you look at the world's highest achieving people - those truly masterful at what they do - they don't just *think different*, but those new ways of *thinking* also drive *new actions, habits, practices, methods, routines & rituals.*

And it's only by deconstructing these learning & training 'best practices' that we can quickly move into world-class, fast-paced, progress & improvement at any topic or skill.

In this chapter, you'll discover a *9 step learning process* which puts together the philosophical, high-level-thinking concepts we're covered so far into a practical, actionable, step-by-step plan for learning anything faster.

This *9 step learning process* is built on the backbone of the routines, disciplines, practices & regimes of many of the greatest individuals & teams.

All distilled into 9 simple, actionable steps you can begin to implement almost immediately.

Most people utilize just step 1 of this process & never tap into the power of other 8 steps. Which means they are only utilizing a small fraction of their entire learning potential.

Let's say you want to develop the skill of sales. You might go & buy a book or training program about sales & consume the information inside. And, a lot of people would consider that, in itself, 'learning'. But, that's really only the first step (of 9) in the learning process.

And while this step alone may help you get some new understandings about sales, it's an approach that leaves a lot of learning & skill development potential on the table.

However, as you learn more about this complete, start-to-finish learning process in this chapter, you can begin to add more of the other 8 steps & learn the skill of sales - or any other topic or skill - far more effectively.

It's because each of these 9 steps has a specific purpose in the process of learning & the more of the 9 steps you're using, the more of your full learning potential you are tapping into & the better the results you will get.

THE LEARNING PROCESS

A strategic, 9-step process for learning anything faster

1. COGNITIVE LEARNING
Cognitively & consciously learning new information, new strategies & new distinctions about your craft.

2. REPETITION & INTEGRATION
Repeating & integrating information for greater recall.

3. ACTION-BASED LEARNING
Implementing learning. Turning 'learning' into 'skill'.

4. TRACKING & TESTING
"What gets measured, gets improved," tracking key performance indicators & constantly testing.

5. CELEBRATION & REINFORCEMENT
Celebrating successes & creating forward momentum.

6. COACHING & FEEDBACK
Leveraging the power of feedback & coaching.

7. BREAKDOWN & REVIEW
Reviewing performance for further insight & growth.

8. FUTURE IMPROVEMENT ANALYSIS
Identifying specific future improvements to make.

9. REPETITION
Strategic repetition for greater mastery.

LEARNING VS SKILL DEVELOPMENT

Learning is the acquisition of *knowledge*, while training (or, skill development) is the acquisition of *skill*.

They are similar, yet different. They follow similar rules, yet differ in nuances. However, both fit under the category of developing *'mental assets'*.

A *mental asset* is anything valuable you can use - knowledge, information, skill - to achieve future results.

Effective *learning* is about consuming information in a way that you can easily recall & act upon it at any moment.

Effective skill *development (training)* is about acquiring a skill & being able to demonstrate that skill at any moment.

Learning basketball would mean that you learn the information - the rules, statistics, gameplay, best practices, theory - of the game so you can recall it at any time.

Training (or developing the skill of) basketball, on the other hand, is not about information, it's about training the skills of passing, defending, dunking, 3-point shooting - amongst others - in a way in which you're able to do them (demonstrate those skills) at any moment.

When you *learn* something new (theoretical) about how to dunk more effectively; consuming that information is labelled as *learning*.

When the coach explains & gives instruction on how you can dunk more effectively; that's still *learning*.

When you get on the court, pick up a ball, & begin to execute on that information, repeating it over & over again, until you get it - that's *skill development* (training).

When we consume information with the intention of remembering it & using it in the future, that's *learning*.

However, when we take that information & begin to train it, it quickly moves into the label of *skill development*.

This is important to understand before we dive in this 9-step learning process because while they are similar, they're also different & follow slightly different rules. However, both learning & skill development are critical.

It's tough to effectively *'train'* or *'develop' a skill,'* without first *'learning'* the information (the briefing) required to actually begin. It's why most of *'skill development'* will first begin with *'learning'* (consumption of new information).

And on the other hand, the deepest *'learning'* comes from, not just consuming information, but also *'training'* it.

For example, I could learn how to dunk a basketball by theoretically understanding how it's done, but it's most effective when that textbook learning becomes skill development & you actually develop the skill.

Learning is about simply *knowing* the information, skill development is about being able to *demonstrate it.*

You need to effectively combine both *learning* & *skill development* together to get great at anything.

And that's exactly what this 9 step learning process will help you do.

STEP #1 | **COGNITIVE LEARNING**

"New knowledge is the most valuable commodity on earth. The more truth we have to work with, the richer we become"

- *KURT VONNEGUT*

Cognitive learning is what we're most familiar with. It's about using our mind - & senses - to learn something new.

Let say you want to learn the topic of *'leadership.'* You buy a book about the topic & begin to read it. And, as you do that, your mind begins to memorize information.

That what *cognitive learning* is; the consumption of new information with the intent to remember it & use it.

And while some consider his alone as 'effective learning,' it's really only the first step in the learning process.

While by itself it has little value, it is a critical step because all progress, change, improvement & skill must first start with new awareness. And that's what this step is all about.

By exposing ourselves to new information - new awareness - we create opportunities for us to implement & get different results than we have gotten before.

| New awareness creates growth opportunities

And although simply repeating this step alone, will *not* make you a master at your craft, it does have its place in the learning process, as the gateway to progress & growth.

You may have heard the quote *"knowledge is power,"* but really, knowledge is simply *potential power*. It's only when knowledge is *applied* does it turn into power.

Most people stop here in the learning process. The world's fastest learners & highest performing people don't.

It's because watching a tutorial video, reading a book or scanning through an article isn't enough to create actual bottom-line improvement or results. The next step is to take that information from *awareness* into *understanding*.

As referenced in the first section of this book, this quote by *Albert Einstein* shares this point so eloquently:

"Any fool can know. The point is to understand"

And, unfortunately, while this step - step 1 - is where most people stop in the learning process, this step alone doesn't create a deep level of understanding.

Think of this step as tipping your toe in the water of *'new awareness,'* while the next step - step 2 - is about diving into the deep end of *'understanding'*.

STEP #2 | REPETITION & INTEGRATION

"The noblest pleasure is the joy of understanding"

- *LEONARDO DA VINCI*

This is the next immediate step after you learn something new & is often implemented in combination with step 1.

The purpose of this second step is to drive information from surface-level memory into deep understanding, greater internalization & to a point of greater future recall.

> **Recall:** *bring previously acquired information & experience back into one's mind; to remember*

It's because, just like a mentor of mine told me, *we don't have a memory problem, we have a recall problem.*

Despite what we may think, we don't have a problem remembering things. If you were asked questions about your life in a multiple-option format. For example:

> *Where were you on the 24th of October, 2009?*
>
> *Option 1: Top of the Empire State Building*
> *Option 2: At your holiday home in France*
> *Option 3: On holiday in Australia*
> *Option 4: At your neighbour's house*

If you received a question like that with real options based on your actual life, odds are, you would get the answer right & you would remember where you were on that date.

However, if without the pre-given answers, someone came up to you, out of the blue & asked you where you were on that date, your odds of remembering would drop radically.

This is the reason why multiple-choice questions, across almost all topics & skills, are usually easier to answer than questions without pre-given options.

It's because, 1) we don't have a memory problem, but rather a *recall* problem & 2) the options are like hooks that allow us to effectively recall information back to memory.

Whenever we learn anything, that information is stored in our subconscious (or, unconscious) mind. Every piece of information. Every experience. Every memory. It's all stored. However, often, unless we follow through with *this* step, that information is often left inaccessible to us.

And that's why, when we learn anything new, we must act on this second step in this learning process, during which we focus on 1) *repetition* & 2) *integration*.

Firstly, don't just read, listen to or watch some information *once*. Studies show an exposure to information only once has very little chance of being remembered (recalled) by us in the future. Rather, focus on *repeating* that information. Re-read that new insight. Be willing to re-listen, or re-watch that same information. Deploy *repetition*.

There's a reason why so many people can remember their email address, phone number or home address; it simply because they've repeated it so many times.

Secondly, it's about boosting our ability to *integrate* the information we learn. This is where *metaphors, stories, emotional learning & memory triggers* - amongst other tools - come into play.

Think about it. *Why do we, so often, remember stories, yet struggle to recall facts, figures or statistics?*

It's because metaphors, stories, emotions & triggers are *'recall tools,'* that enable greater recall of information.

A lot of these 'integration' techniques also fall under the category, labelled as *'accelerated learning techniques'*

Think about it; there are probably certain books, articles or posts that you read a few months - or even years - ago that you can still remember, while others that you read a few days ago, that you've 'forgotten'.

It's not a memory problem, it's a recall problem. Which is why we must support our mind to recall information.

Often, the things that you can remember over time, & can recall easily, are the things which, while learning them, we better utilized this second step; *repetition & integration*.

There are two ways to accelerate learning:

1. Teachers to become better at teaching
2. Students to become better at learning

Good teachers know how to convey information in such a way that it gets remembered. Bad teachers don't.

Hence, the fastest & easiest way to leverage this second step is to simply find a great teacher, coach or mentor that can effectively convey the information you want to learn.

However, we can't simply hope we get a good teacher to teach us. Although we have a large element of control around this, we don't control it entirely.

As well as that, if we want to fully tap into this power, we must also work on ourselves & internally create strategies for greater memory & recall of information we learn.

To fully optimize this step, you should leverage both. Find a great teacher, coach or mentor to structure learning with repetition & integration built-in. And, at the same time, continue to become a better learner by deploying this step.

There an entire section on this later in the book, but for now it's just important that we realize that there are certain strategies that help you learn faster, remember information longer & be able to recall it anytime you need.

STEP #3 | ACTION-BASED LEARNING

"Tell me and I forget. Teach me and I remember. Involve me and I learn"

- *BENJAMIN FRANKLIN*

This step is when you switch from *learning* (consuming information) to *skill development* (training).

The first two steps are about 'information recall,' while all the rest of the steps in the process are more accurately categorized under *'skill development'*, with the purpose of maximizing the acquisition & development of skill.

Once again, almost every skill that you'll ever want to learn is a combination of both 'learning' & 'skill development'

For chess, 'learning' is about mentally remembering the rules of the game, how the game works & the best strategies for winning it. Meanwhile, 'skill development' would include leveraging past experience to move the right pieces at the right time to win the game. And 'training' chess wouldn't be about remembering information, but rather about taking existing information, sitting down at the chess board & moving pieces to get better at chess.

And this part is critical for many reasons.

Imagine attempting to teach a toddler to walk by getting him to listening to a lecture or watch a tutorial video.

The outrageousness of that visual makes me laugh, yet it isn't written for comedic purposes. It's written to show that the way we learn is often backwards.

In society, we tend to over-prioritize theory or information & under-prioritize actually getting up & training a skill.

Imagine buying a new bike & learning how to ride it by buying textbooks about bike riding. Sure, that may be a great first step - like the first 2 steps in this learning process - but unless you actually get on the bike & *do* (skill development) your progress will be very limited.

We may laugh at these examples, but this is what people do all the time in schools, at events & at lectures. They attempt to learn photography, art or business purely through the consumption of more & more information.

The challenge for you, if you really want to learn faster, is to follow this learning process & quickly move from the first 2 steps - *learning* - into this step - the start of *skill development* - by taking fast action on whatever you learn.

If you're learning sales, don't just read that sales book. Read a chapter, then stand up & re-do your sales pitch; now including the new sales tactics you just learned.

If you're learning photography, as soon as you get an insight from the photography guide you're reading, take out your camera & test it. Take action fast.

Go from reading the guide - *learning* - to implementing the information - *skill development* - as fast as possible.

Move into *action-based learning*, instead of the old, ineffective lecture-style learning that schools still use.

That's what this step - step 3 - is all about. And it may be common sense, but it's definitely not common practice.

Too many people are attempting to learn public speaking by listening to lectures instead of getting up & speaking.

It's time for us to implement that which is common sense & make it common practice in our lives.

STEP #4 | **TRACKING & TESTING**

"What gets measured, gets improved"

- *PETER DRUCKER*

After learning something new - steps 1 & 2 - as well as implementing that knowledge through *action-based learning* - step 3 - the next step is *tracking & testing*.

Think back to the *'feedback speed'* concept we talked about in the first section. By effectively tracking, you're able to create near-instant feedback loops which turn into 'distinctions' & make you more skilled at what you do.

Without accurate tracking measures in place, you don't know if you're getting better, but most importantly, your feedback speed slows down dramatically, which leads to slowed distinction accumulation & slower overall progress.

Comparatively, by creating accurate tracking measures, you're able to get greater insight into what's working & what's not. They key is to...

| **Chart learning & skill development**

Just like the biggest businesses in the world know the metrics they're focused on, the targets they're aiming for & the objectives they're looking to hit, when you begin to track & chart your learning & skill development, it allows you make better decisions & move forward faster.

When you add this step to the existing 3 steps, it will radically add to your learning speed.

It's because science has shown us that *tracking* helps us get better at what we do. Sometimes, even near-automatically.

One study showed how individuals lost weight by making no purposeful changes to their diet or exercise routines, by tracking their actions. The only change they were asked to make in the study was to write down what they ate & what exercise they did every day. That's it.

At the beginning, people doubted the study, claiming that there is no possible way that getting people to write some stuff down (tracking) could actually lead to weight loss.

So they did the study & shockingly, individuals started losing weight. They repeated the study multiple times & the results came back the same each time.

By getting individuals to simply *track* what they ate & what exercise they did lead them to lose weight. This is a great example of the power of *tracking*.   ·

| Tracking leads to improvement

When you track, it leads to greater *self-awareness*, which in turn, leads to, sometimes, near-automatic improvement in performance (just like in the 'weight loss' study above).

Another psychological study showed how, getting people to look at themselves in the mirror more often, improved their overall performance at particular tasks.

Why? It made them more self-aware. When we track our actions & results, it brings us more self-awareness & leads us to strive for the goals, objectives & targets we set out for.

Equally, when we start seeing progress, it increases our willingness to keep going & continue the progress. It's momentum *(which we'll talk about in step #5)*.

TRACKING MINDSET: TRACKING TO MILLIONS

When the great American, oil industry titan, John D. Rockefeller was a child, he would track every single cent he ever made & every cent he ever spent.

He did this simple exercise for many years growing up.

And this helped him, not just train his skills of money management (no matter how small the amounts he managed as a child were) but also develop a *tracking mindset*, which later helped him accumulate his fortune.

He grew up to become a billionaire. He thrived in the oil business beating out - or acquiring - competitors in his way, to grow the largest oil company in America.

His company, *Standard Oil*, became so successful it became considered a monopoly & was forced to split up into 34 separate companies.

Although we can't - by any stretch of the imagination - attribute his success to tracking alone, based on what we know about him, his mindset about *tracking*, money & money management did have a big impact on his success.

And that largely started when he was a small kid tracking every cent he made & every cent he spent.

Tracking and testing are hugely beneficial & impactful parts of this 9 step learning process.

It allows you to see what works & what just doesn't, so you can optimize & accelerate your growth.

And beyond tracking, this step is also about beginning to *test* & implement the *'10,000-experiment-rule'* we talked about earlier. It's about using your *'optimization mindset'* to create new hypothesise you can test to accumulate new distinctions that lead to greater skill.

STEP #5 | CELEBRATION & REINFORCEMENT

"Celebrate your successes. Find some humor in your failures"

- *SAM WALTON*

Celebration is one of the most powerful forms of morale-building, reinforcement & momentum-building.

And *'reinforcement'* is something that the world's highest achievers often do unconsciously with their own self-talk (the mental voice - chatter - in their heads).

This step is all about conditioning future achievement & creating powerful forward momentum.

So after you've accumulated new information - steps 1 & 2 - & you've trained, tracked & tested - steps 3 & 4 - the next step is to celebrate your efforts.

Just like the Chinese diving team celebrate 'going for it' - irrelevant of whether they succeed or not - the challenge for this step is to celebrating your efforts to condition in your mind that every step you take, every hour of training, every new insight is moving you closer to mastery. And you execute this step - celebration & reinforcement - irrelevant of whether you get a result you want, or you don't. It happens either way because you're celebrating effort (not outcome).

Over the years I've consumed so many articles, videos, books & teachings, where people approach learning, skill development & achievement in a very robotic way, without understand the strengths & weaknesses of humanity.

Other's, both in the topics of learning & skill development, but also in topics such as motivation or productivity, will tell you to remove all the quote-on-quote *'fluff,'* like celebration, morale-building, acknowledgement, feel-good, & pretty much all *emotion* from your work. And rather, focus only - exclusively - on data, math & what appears rational & logical. A little like robots on a production line - *no emotion, just more repetition.*

And that might seems like a good argument... *wouldn't it be more effective & faster to just scrap all the celebration & positive emotion, to focus only on efficiency?*

The answer: *yes & no.* Short term, yes. Long term, no.

As much as we would like to think that we are rational, logical beings that act purely on logical pro's & con's, often, we are not. We are equally emotional beings.

And studies in human psychology continue to reaffirm that what we think *matters.* How we feel *matters.* Enthusiasm, passion & optimism *matter.* Not just for our personal happiness, but also in how we perform.

When we feel empowered, engaged & excited, we learn better, perform better & achieve more. Which is something that, it appears, the education system has failed to learn.

Which is why so many children grow up hating learning. It's sad. Learning - the unleashing of the creative spirit & act of gaining new insights - shouldn't be a chore, but a gift.

Yet, for a lot of people growing up, it's not viewed that way. And, it not the children's fault. And, it's not even the teacher's fault. The teachers simply do the best they can.

Rather, it's a problem with the system itself & how far it has fallen behind the curve of innovation, modern research & understandings of what actually drives success in life.

If your goal is to maximize the effectiveness of your learning or skill development over the short-term, the way to do that is to, *yes*, remove all the celebration, remove the emotion, remove the encouragement & focus only on robotic, quantifiable, production-line-style work.

However, if you want to maximize the effectiveness of your learning & skill development *over the long-term*, the focus on energy & emotion is a critical part of that.

If the local sports team cut everything emotional from their trainings (celebration, care, emotion) they would, most probably, get better, faster (in the short term) because they can reallocate that time to more repetition.

Over the long term though, they are likely to be overtaken by a team that places an equal priority on the *intangible* (emotion, celebration, state of mind) as on the *tangible*.

That's why *celebration* is in this 9-step learning process.

Firstly, this step is independent of success or failure, meaning you complete this step - *celebration* - no matter how good, or bad, the outcome from the first 4 steps was.

Basic personal development talks about how when we celebrate, we attract more celebration into our lives, but that's not the reason celebration is in this process.

Training isn't easy, it's hard. And it's meant to be hard. It's designed to push, challenge & stretch you.

Celebration is the equivalent of you going to a fuel station & filling up your car with fuel. It's what helps you re-fuel & reignite your passion during the learning process.

And at the same time helping you reinforce positive behaviours (to make them into habits faster) & help you build positive forward momentum.

THE POWER OF MOMENTUM

Momentum is what makes the rich get richer & the poor get poorer. It's what makes the healthy get healthier & the unhealthy get more & more unhealthy. It's what makes the loved increasingly loved & the hated, more & more hated.

And momentum is always in action, working either for us or against us, whether we want it to or not.

It's a law of nature. And, if you've ever seen momentum work in someone's favour - or against them - you'll know how powerful it is for learning, skill & overall achievement.

Momentum is made up of 3 core parts.

1. **Belief**
2. **Action**
3. **Result**

To understand momentum we must understand how these 3 parts works, separately, as well as together.

It all starts with *belief*. Belief is all about your level of certainty & confidence that your efforts will transfer into the results you're after. If your belief in something is high, you're naturally going to pay more attention to it, focus more on it & put in more effort into the task at hand.

Think about it. *If you believed, with 100% certainty, that what you were going to do would turn into the exact result you want, how much attention, focus & effort would you be willing to put into that action? A lot, right?*

It why higher *belief* leads to more *action* (the second part).

Action is about the effort you're putting it. It's about your level of commitment, discipline, willingness to go above & beyond, as well the willingness to do whatever it takes.

And when you put in a lot of focused, deliberate, committed action (effort), what's likely to happen?

It's likely to be matched by great *results* (the third part).

And if that high level of action turns into high levels of results - you believe it would happen, you put in the effort & you got the results you expected - now what happens to your belief next time?

It goes through the roof. And it re-ignites the cycle.

Higher *belief* leads to higher levels of *action*. Higher levels of *action* lead to higher levels of *results*. And higher levels of *results* go to refuel your *belief* to restart the cycle.

This is one of the biggest reasons - if not the biggest - why successful people continue to achieve more & more.

It's because they're in an upward spiral of momentum.

However, this is also one of the biggest - if not the biggest - reasons why those who fail continue to fail over & over.

It's because they're in a downward spiral of momentum.

Their low *belief* leads to a low level of *action* (half-assed effort; lacking commitment) which creates poor *results*.

And then their mind goes *'I told you it wouldn't work out,'* which further lowers their *belief*. Which makes then take even less committed action. Which leads to even lower results. And creates this downward spiral.

However, simply becoming aware of this momentum cycle already gives you a massive advantage.

The other advantage is created by *celebration* (which we'll talk about in just a moment).

A good example of *momentum* demonstrated very clearly is in sports & seeing a team come back from nowhere to win.

The team may be losing badly. But, then, out of nowhere, they get a point - or score - & suddenly momentum shifts.

The team stops thinking about losing & starts to attack harder, faster & better than they did previously.

What happened? Did they become better players?

No. They just started to believe (higher *belief*) which fueled a higher calibre of action (more committed, willing effort).

Fans at the stadium watching, before, were also in low levels of belief. Which, for many, made their cheering very half-assed (low action driven by low belief).

But now, they're shouting, screaming & jumping with optimism. Their new higher *belief* is fueling more *action*.

And for the players that greater belief, leads to greater, faster, sharper, better action. Which leads to better *results*.

And the whole momentum cycle repeats. Over and over.

This new action gets them another point - or goal (new *result*). Which fuels *belief* & creates more *action* & results.

And its this upwards spiral of momentum that leads to amazing comebacks or unexpected feats. But, it's also the downwards spiral of momentum that leads individuals - & teams - from being miles ahead to end up losing. Momentum is always working for us, or against us.

And this matters so much because at a certain point in your mastery, your psychology, state of mind & belief become as important as skill itself.

It doesn't at first. Your first training, it doesn't matter if you're having a good day or bad day, you suck either way.

But, at the elite level - especially at the point of *incremental improvement,* where the best in the world is only a small fraction better than second best - now, how you feel, your belief & state of mind makes a big difference.

And now that you understand how momentum really impacts skill & performance, one of the best ways you can skew momentum in your favour is by doing one simple thing: *celebrating your efforts* (this step right here).

When you *celebrate your efforts*, mentally, you reinforce that what you're doing is good & you should keep doing it.

Which makes you want to do more. Which then leads you to take more committed *action* & creates better *results*. Celebration helps you create powerful forward momentum.

And this is especially important when you don't see immediate *results* from your actions. That's when the true power of celebration comes into play.

Let's say you have high *belief*. Hence, you take a high level of *action*. However, your high level of *action* doesn't create - or doesn't seem to - a high level of immediate *results*.

And this happens all the time. It's because while 1) *belief* & 2) *action* are very controllable factors, *results* are less controllable & often require more time to actually show up.

Sometimes people go the gym for 2 days, look at the mirror & get surprised that they can't get see *results*. It's like that. High *effort* in the gym doesn't lead to *results* straight away.

Which, for a lot of people kills their momentum because they lose *belief*.

So, what should you do?

You do what the Chinese diving team do & you celebrate your *efforts* - irrelevant of the results. You celebrate *'going for it'*. That way, you're able to maintain your high level of *belief* & *action*, even when *results* take some time to show up *(just like going to the gym; it takes time to see results)*.

Celebration allows you to build morale, build enthusiasm & flip the momentum cycle in your favour.

And that's why this step is this in this process. Your job is to apply it & *celebrate your efforts* consistently.

STEP #6 | COACHING & FEEDBACK

"Feedback is the breakfast of champions"

- *KEN BLANCHARD*

After you've learned new information, taken action on it (step 3), tracked it (step 4) & celebrated your efforts (step 5), the next step is to get accurate, insightful feedback into what you can do better next time.

And, it's during this steps that the power of coaching is really demonstrated. This is when you turn to a coach or mentor (a topic an entire sub-chapter in the next section is dedicated to) & get feedback from them.

However, the key is to build feedback into your learning; to make it a way of life. Make it something you don't just do once, but rather, just like David Copperfield or the Chinese diving team, you do it *consistently.*

If you're an artist, as soon as you complete your next piece, celebrate (step 5) & quickly get feedback on it (this step). It has to become automatic; something you do *every time.*

This is where your new mindset of *'loving feedback'* fits into the process (step 6). And this is where you implement everything we covered in the last chapter about feedback.

STEP #7 | BREAKDOWN & REVIEW

"Mistakes should be examined, learned from, and discarded; not dwelled upon and stored"

- *TIM FARGO*

Just like athletes watch game tapes to get an even deeper personal set of insights that they may not have spotted in the heat of the moment - during the game - & just like many top businesses run rigorous performance reviews to improve results, this is your opportunity to do the same for the topic or skill you are developing.

Have you ever seen yourself on camera, only to find you looked different than you thought you did in your head?

It's because what we think we're doing when we're learning often, when reviewed on video, is very different than it appeared in our heads. For example, we thought we were doing the technique perfectly, but upon review, we cringe because it didn't look anything it should have.

And it's why we must, firstly, document what we do. If you're a singer, voice record every time you sing. If you're a sales rep training your sales skills, film every sales presentation you ever do. However, know that documenting is only the first step & is only valuable if you actually take the time to review the 'game tapes'.

There a reason why athletes watch game tapes & why the Chinese diving team have their divers watch back instant replays of their dives. It's no accident; it's intentional.

It's designed to give that extra layer of, not just feedback, but opportunity to break down your performance into smaller details which you can deeply analyze & improve.

And remember: *each one of these 9 steps applies to each & every skill you're developing.*

Even if you're a writer training your creative writing skills, you may not film yourself writing (the writing itself is your documented 'game tapes'), but you still should take time to sit down, break down, analyze & review every piece of work you produce as it will give you insights to get better.

STEP #8 | **FUTURE IMPROVEMENT ANALYSIS**

> *"I think it's very important to have a feedback loop, where you're constantly thinking about what you've done and how you could be doing it better"*
>
> - *ELON MUSK*

After you've gone through steps 4, 5, 6 & 7, this step is all taking everything you can improve & breaking it down in the exact, specific steps you can take right away.

This step is all about taking the conceptual & grounding it in deep practicality.

It's where the following questions really come into play:

What are the 3 specific things I'm going to focus on next time to serve the tennis ball more effectively?

What are the 2 things I'm going to focus on, right now, to improve my sales ability?

What are the 5 steps I'm going to take to accelerate my learning right now & how can I implement each one?

It's about grounding everything in deeper clarity, specificity & practicality. It's about removing confusion.

Because while confusion is a great sign that you're about to learn something, it's not great when you're giving others - or in this case, yourself - instructions for what you should focus on & do differently next time.

Let's say you want to learn the skill of leadership.

So, step 1 of learning process if you wanted to improve your leadership skills would be reading, listening to or watching (consuming) new information about effective leadership.

You might read a leadership book. You might listen to your mentor. You might attend a leadership lecture. That all fits into step 1 (cognitive learning). The intention is awareness.

Step 2 would be you highlighting key points, making notes, re-reading key points, asking questions of the lecturer or mentor, re-listening to the information, reading leadership examples & stories for better information recall, amongst other things. It's all about *repetition & integration*.

Step 3 would be you going out & actually leading people, because, you're not going to master leadership by simply consuming information about it; it requires *training*. This step - *action-based learning* - represents you actually leading people (skill development, not learning). Be resourceful. The world needs leaders; find people to lead so you can effectively train your leadership abilities.

For step 4 - *tracking & testing* - you would find the key metrics you can track, such as team morale (tracked through ongoing surveys), generated results, project completion speed or others. The key is to find the metrics that will give you most accurate data & track them.

Step 5 - *celebration & reinforcement* - you would celebrate your *efforts* irrelevant of whether your new insights were successful or not, knowing it's all moving you forward.

For step 6 - you would ask for feedback from the team you're leading, from your mentor & from everybody else you can get feedback from. And, you begin to sort through this feedback knowing not all feedback is equal & shouldn't be treated equally. You're looking for those golden nuggets of feedback that can move you forward to greater skill.

Step 7 - is when you review the recordings from your recent leadership meetings (which, of course, you filmed) looking for that extra layer of feedback & insight from yourself.

And this step - step 8 - you take the feedback & insight you accumulated & turn it all into actionable steps - grounded in practicality - you can apply quickly for better results.

And it's these 9 steps - *combined with the last step, repetition* - which form an effective blueprint & process for developing your leadership skills *(as well as any other topic or skill you want to develop in your life).*

And while each step may take a different length of time - for example, step 3 may take 2 hours while the step about celebration might take 20 seconds - each step contributes to the bigger picture & leads to optimized learning.

STEP #9 | **REPETITION**

> *"So many of our dreams at first seem impossible, then they seem improbable, and then, when we summon the will, they soon become inevitable"*
>
> - *CHRISTOPHER REEVE*

Although *repetition* alone isn't enough for anyone to become extraordinary at anything, it still is an irreplaceable ingredient in the recipe of greatness.

| Repetition is essential to skill development

This step is simple. It's about finishing off with the previous 8 steps & repeating the whole process over & over again, constantly learning, implementing, developing skills, tracking, optimizing & improving at your craft.

Imagine this 9 steps less like a bullet point list & more like an infinite loop where this step - step 9 - simply loops you back to step 1 & the whole process starts again.

Because, as we've discovered in previous chapters, it takes a lot of *passion, discipline* & *innovation* to become great.

As you can see, there's a lot more to effective learning than simply reading a book, listening to a lecture or watching a tutorial video about your topic.

Each step has a specific purpose & together, these steps create a powerful game-plan anyone can you begin to follow, almost immediately, to learn anything faster.

3.

ACCELERATION:
TRAIN LIKE THE BEST

"Citius, Altius, Fortius"

THE OLYMPIC MOTTO
(Latin for 'faster, higher, stronger')

While others may settle for conformity, mediocrity or comfort, we must continue to seek, question & experiment in our ways of doing because the future belongs to those who have the courage to chase a better way. It belongs to those who have the strength to question the socially accepted norms & pursue the seemingly impossible. There truly is a better, faster, more fulfilling way to do anything. But, we must seek it to find it.

11 | ACCELERATING THE PROCESS:
SUPERCHARGING LEARNING

"Good, better, best. Never let it rest. 'Til your good is better and your better is best"

- *ST. JEROME*

Unless you've been hiding under a rock, you've probably realized the world is moving faster than it has ever before.

Innovation is speeding up. Competition is continually heightening. Change is accelerating. Today...

| We live in accelerated times

And in this accelerated world, it's time for us to step into that same level of *acceleration* & *optimization*.

Outdated learning & skill development strategies that used to work well, just don't cut it anymore. Especially not if you want to stand out & become extraordinary at what you do.

What we need is a new tool belt for this new world. We need new tools, strategies & tactics for accelerated learning & more effective skill development.

While the previous 2 sections were focused on crucial understanding & foundational keys to skill & success, this third section is focused on *acceleration* & *optimization*.

It's focused, not on answering the questions *'how does learning work?'* or *'what keys do all master's share?'* - that was in the first 2 sections - rather on answering:

How can I take a learning or training situation - any topic or skill - & accelerate, optimize, heighten & improve it?

That's the journey we're going on during this third section. And this all starts with this foundational belief...

| There is always a better, faster, more effective way to do anything

This is a mindset - a belief - that the vast majority (if not all) of the world's highest achievers share.

Their insatiable desire for growth, improvement & acceleration is nothing short of extraordinary. It's what allows them to do the seamlessly impossible.

While a pessimist will tell you something is *'impossible,'* or an optimist will tell you *'nothing is impossible,'* a high achiever will find a way to turn the *'seemingly impossible'* into something that's they've achieved & accomplished.

THE 4 MINUTE MILE

> *"The most difficult thing is the decision to act, the rest is merely tenacity. The fears are paper tigers. You can do anything you decide to do. You can act to change and control your life; and the procedure, the process is its own reward"*
>
> - *AMELIA EARHART*

People used to believe that running a mile in 4 minutes was impossible. They thought it just couldn't be done.

Then Roger Bannister, in 1954, broke the 'four-minute barrier.' A feat considered 'impossible' had been achieved.

Chances are you've probably heard this example of the *'4 minute mile'* before. But few realize he didn't just break a running record, but he also shattered a paradigm that had limited many other runners at the time.

The ripple effect he had created was, in my opinion, the most fascinating part of the story.

Over the next few years, dozens of runners also crossed this barrier, running miles in under 4 minutes. And today, this is a standard among professional middle-distance runners.

This is the rule, not the exception. The 4 minute mile - or any other *'impossible feat'* achieved was not a miracle, rather the norm of how improvement works.

Many (if not, most) of the things that, at one point, are considered *impossible*, through innovation, growth & improvement, end up getting achieved.

Examples from history that come to mind include Martin Luther King Jr & the civil right movement, The Wright Brothers & flight & Graham Alexander Bell with the phone.

All these things - as well as many other great feats - at one point, where defined as impossible. Yet, were achieved.

In fact, what Graham Alexander Bell first produced - the first phone - seems light years behind what we have today. Compare what a phone can do today to a decade ago & you'll see the massive innovation that occurred.

The same applies to the computer, the car, the airplane & pretty much everything else we have today.

Beyond that, the same applies to performance. A masterful entertainer, photographer, illusionist or tennis player of the past wouldn't seem so masterful today if compared to the skill level of individuals today.

Another example from sports; the 200m record in 1908 Olympics was 22.6 seconds. As of 2017, it's 19.19s.

However, that's not the best part. The best part is today the average high school sprinter runs 200m in less than 22.6 seconds; faster than the Olympic champion did in 1908.

It's because everything goes through this similar cycle.

It starts as a dream, often considered 'impossible'.

Then it gets achieved by some individual (or team) for the first time. Which shifts the paradigm of what's possible.

This then causes many people to quickly catch up to this raised level, as what was previously 'impossible' is not defined as 'possible' or 'achievable'.

Beyond that, it often gets innovated on further & becomes increasingly achievable. And, that initial breakthrough often ends up as simply a legacy which led to a new, better, more advanced, versions of the original achievement.

We see this pattern over & over again. And we'll continue to see it in the future.

What we consider extraordinary - or masterful - today, in a few years, likely, won't be considered so amazing anymore.

A new, higher level will be achieved by then. And the things that we consider 'impossible' or 'too difficult' today will have been accomplished as we continue to innovate, improve & build upon existing knowledge & information.

Remember: *we are an accumulative species.*

And it won't be because of some big feat of will, or overnight shift, rather, thanks to an accumulation of little things - little actions & efforts - coming together.

The impossible turns into the accomplished because of exactly this; the combined effect of little things working together. It's the combination of hundreds & thousands of little improvements that turn into extraordinary results.

And that's what this section is about. Each of the tools, strategies & tactics alone may give you a 2%, 5%, 15% or even 50% improvement in your *learning speed*, but together (combined) they allow you to achieve extraordinary - sometimes, seemingly-impossible - things.

Each chapter - & subchapter - will give you new tools you can add to your tool belt - new distinctions & nuances - so you can pull out the right tools at the right time to build up your skills & achieve what you want to achieve.

Each of the tools shared in these chapters will also give you the potential to accelerate your path to mastery.

We talked about how the number '10,000' in the '10,000-hour-rule' or '10,000-experiment rule' is a generic number & varies wildly. One of the biggest - if not the biggest - things that influences it is *learning speed*.

One person can reach a higher level of knowledge, understanding & skill after 2000 hours than another can after 3500 hours. It's because *learning speed* is so crucial.

Which is why, at the end of the day, each strategy & tactic in this section has the potential to shave hundreds & thousands of hour off your path to mastery at what you do.

Each upcoming chapter in this section will approach & tackle optimization & improvement from a different angle.

In the following chapter - chapter 12 - we're going to cover 3 powerful *learning* acceleration strategies. These are tools you can use to *learn* (consume, recall & use information) better. These aren't necessarily about skill development but are focused on learning (the first 2 steps in the 9 step learning process we covered in the last section).

The next chapter after that - chapter 13 - we'll dive deep into *skill development* acceleration & optimization strategies, tactics & tools. These are focused, not on learning, rather on skill development.

In the last chapter in this section - number 14 - we cover 5 of the biggest learning speed killers; 5 things that radically slow down - & kill - people's learning speed. This way you can see these obstacles before they come up, remove these hurdles & progress faster at any topic or skill you choose.

Everything can be improved, tweaked, optimized & accelerated with the right strategies, tactics & actions.

And that's what this section is about; giving you an entire tool belt of *acceleration* & *optimization* tools for better learning & skill development. Let's get started...

12 | ACCELERATED LEARNING: TOOLS FOR FASTER LEARNING

"Curiosity is the wick in the candle of learning"

- *WILLIAM ARTHUR WARD*

Reading a book, listening to a lecture or watching a video, alone, is an average way to learn (consume information).

A huge amount of information we consume, we forgot (we can't recall it when we need it) or we don't apply (caused by a lack of deep understanding & integration).

Which all opens up a huge amount of potential for us to learn faster, more effectively & with deeper understanding.

And that's what *this chapter* is about; sharing *tools* you can use to learn any topic - or piece of information - better.

1 | MEMORY TRIGGERS

"Memory... is the diary that we all carry about with us"

- *OSCAR WILDE*

Have you ever started reading, listening to, or watching, something, thinking you've never seen it before, only to realize you have, in fact, seen this exact thing before?

For example, you start reading a book, article or post thinking you've never read it before, but, as you read the first few lines, you realize you have, in fact, read it before.

That's the power of our memory. We're able to remember (recall) things even when we've seemed to forget them.

It's because when we forget something, we haven't actually forgotten it. We simply aren't able to *recall* it & bring it back to conscious thought at that time.

However, what changes that is what I refer to as a *'memory trigger'*. While you reading that book, article or post you've read before - but can't remember you have - you might come across a phrase, heading, description, name or image that makes you go *'oh wait, I have read this before'*.

That's a *'memory trigger'* & it's what allows you to recall that which you had previously seemed to have forgotten.

And note, this isn't some one-time occurrence. Your mind operates in this way all the time.

A certain line in a song - trigger - keeps that song stuck in your head all day. Or, you hear someone say something & it brings back the memory of an old friend. Or, you see something & it makes you remember something you had on your to-do list that you had forgotten about.

This happens all the time; it's how memory works.

A *'memory trigger'* (when created *intentionally*) it's much like a wake-up alarm. At the right time, it will help you recall the information you need to remember. It serves as a reminder that allows you to recall & use information better.

And it's why, in this subchapter, we're going to dive deep into, not just how memory works, but also how you can intentionally create *'memory triggers'* that help you remember more, recall what matters when it matters; all with the intention of *accelerating* & *optimizing* learning.

A *memory trigger* can be anything. It could be as simple as a drawing or graph, a certain chair in your living room, a certain tonality or gesture, a particular location. Anything.

For example, for many people, their childhood toys are powerful *'memory triggers'* for their childhood memories.

Just imagine if someone suddenly showed up at your doorstep & gave you all your childhood toys back.

Chances are, those toys would not only inspire you to reminisce about your childhood but will actually help you remember more details about your childhood.

In that same way, imagine if you went back to your childhood home (location). Think about how that would affect your memory of your childhood.

Everything we see, hear, taste, smell & feel - & yes, learn - gets stored in our mind. It's there, waiting for us to recall it.

The challenge, again, is that most people never consciously create *'memory triggers'* that allow them to effectively recall those past memories or learnings into their thoughts.

And while a great teacher will naturally use powerful memory triggers, metaphors, stories & examples to accelerate a students learning, to step up to an even higher level of learning, we must personally understand the power of *'memory triggers'* & begin to consciously create them.

Many things can become *'memory triggers'*...

1. **Images/Visuals/Doodles:** If I showed you a picture of a holiday home you stayed in, you'd remember more details about that holiday, easier. In that same way, the visuals in this book, like *'Mental Bandwidth'*, *'Feedback Speed'* or *'Skill Isolation & Integration'* help you recall more of what you read about in those chapters.

   How can you associate images, visuals or doodles to your learning for better recall?

   This is something I do all the time. I don't just read books. I create visuals - like the ones in this book - from what I learn, which, help me better recall the information I had read in the future.

2. **Locations/Decor:** If you've ever seen a proud adult pass their old high school building, you'll know that certain *locations* can create a huge recall of memories, experiences & information.

   And just like a school building is a powerful *'memory trigger'* for high school memories or how Christmas decorations *(decor)* are powerful triggers for Christmas memories, you can consciously turn *locations or decorations* into powerful learning triggers that help you recall important information.

   Don't just read a book. Go & read it in a location you don't often go to; like a forest or fancy library. And, that location (or piece of decor) will serve as a trigger for better recall of that information.

3. **Metaphors & Stories:** This book is built on a lot of metaphors & stories. This is to create a deeper understanding of information *(which boost recall)*.

   Growing up, we hear stories & metaphors with life lessons contained within them. Those stories & metaphors are powerful *'memory triggers'* that remind us of powerful principles & concepts. Knowing this you can *consciously* wrap stories & metaphors around the information you're learning.

4. **People/Environment:** It's may seem strange how meeting an old friend can bring up so many memories that you wouldn't otherwise remember.

   In that same way, if you're learning with others - or in a different environment - this can be a powerful *'memory trigger'* that helps you remember more.

5. **Objects:** Certain objects can amplify learning because they are powerful *'memory triggers'*.

   A great prop - object - can be a great teaching tool from a teacher's point of view, but can also be a very powerful *'memory trigger'* for learning.

6. **Names/Titles/Phrase:** Our mind recalls short names, titles or phrases better than long blocks of text. It's why book names can often boost the recall of the concepts within that book. Or, why the title of a movie than trigger the memory of the scenes in it.

   In that same way, when you can summarize large blocks of information into short sound-bites *(like 'we live in accelerated times')* that can boost recall.

And this is just the tip of the iceberg.

Almost anything can serve as a powerful *'memory trigger,'* for greater recall of information you learn.

It's because our mind links one thing to another. Memory (recall) works much like a web...

RIPPLED RECALL

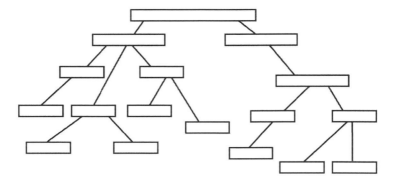

Our mind recalls based on what I call *'Rippled Recall'*.

We don't recall things by accident. Thoughts are triggered by other thoughts or *'memory triggers'* & - unless interrupted - go on to create *webs* of thoughts. This is sometimes referred to as a *'train of thought'*.

1 thought, thing or person triggers the recall of something *(a memory or thought)* which triggers another & another.

Those new thoughts now trigger other thoughts & it forms an ongoing cycle; creating a ripple effect.

Here's an example of how this works. Let's say someone in conversation tells you the title of a movie. The thought of that movie has now entered your conscious thinking.

MOVIE TITLE

Then that title - often, instantly - triggers other thoughts.

Your mind recalls (remembers) other memories, thoughts, experiences or learnings...

Now, these thoughts - unless interrupted or stopped - will continue to turn into further thoughts.

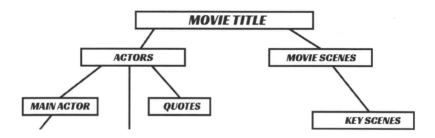

Which, in turn, continue to create more thoughts...

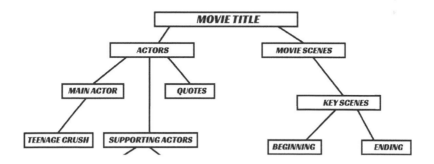

And often, because of *'memory triggers'* - as well as how our mind links our life to external things outside it - the thoughts about the movie might trigger other thoughts.

RIPPLED RECALL (MOVIE EXAMPLE)

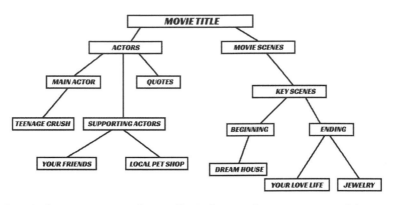

This is how our mind recalls information. It uses 1 thing as a reference, link or connection to another thing.

Hence, memory, in many ways, operates based on *'Rippled Recall'*. What it recalls is dependent on what has been recalled previously, unless interrupted, stopped or a new *'memory trigger'* starts a new set of thoughts.

Knowing this - how our mind stores, remembers & recalls information - opens up greater opportunities for us to better understand, recall & use what we learn.

If you want to learn faster, learn deeper & recall learnings better, you've got to be creative & find ways to add *memory triggers* into your learning. Constantly ask yourself:

How can I create 'memory triggers' that continue to bring back past information & learnings to memory at the right times so I can make optimized decisions?

How can I learn in various locations so those locations become triggers that help me recall key informations?

How can I use objects - or props - that my mind can associate certain lessons to for better information recall?

How can I - as I learn - create images, graphics, visuals or doodles for deeper understanding of the information?

How can I summarize & categorize pieces of information I learn into headings, titles or bite-size phrases I can repeat that will help the rest of the information ripple down?

By asking these questions consistently - & by consciously creating *'mental triggers'* around your learning - you'll recall information better & turn it into results you want.

We mustn't forget that the goal *isn't* just to hold information in our minds long enough to answer questions on a test, only to forget that information soon afterwards.

That's not the goal. Rather, the aim is to learn information - & build deep understanding & recall into it - in such a way that key information comes back to us when you need it, so we can make the best decisions & get the best results.

2 | EMOTIONAL LEARNING

"All learning has an emotional base"

\-   *PLATO*

Think about your most embarrassing moment.

Now, think about the most romantic moment in your life.

Now, start to think of a moment in your life in which you were proud of something you did.

In each of these experiences, chances are, you were able to recall (remember) a lot of details. Many memories (good or bad) probably came to mind for each.

And, odds are, if you continued to think about your most embarrassing, romantic, passionate, loving, terrifying or proud moments, your mind would continue to dive deeper & recall these experiences in mind-numbing detail.

Remembering (recalling) these *emotional* experiences isn't a problem. In fact, often, it comes with a lot of ease.

However, what if I asked you:

Do you remember the email you sent your 5th email to?

Or, can you recall the 5th word in the 1st book you read?

Attempting to remember (recall) these experiences is probably much harder for you to do.

But, why? What's the difference?

The difference between the 2 is simple: **emotion**.

Our mind remembers *highly-emotional* experiences better than highly-logical (or, *non-emotional*) experiences.

If you think through a timeline of your life, often, the first thoughts that will come to mind are *highly-emotional* events & experiences in your life. It's because...

| Emotion skyrockets recall

This is yet another understanding that we can use to radically increase our learning speed & ability to better recall that which we have previously learned.

Simply put, if you ever struggle to remember something, you simply have to find a way to jam-pack that moment with *emotion* & odds are, you'll begin to remember (recall) it much more easily going forward.

Knowing this makes me put the education system under further investigation & scrutiny.

If *emotion* helps us remember experiences - & learnings - better, why does the education make learning so boring, mundane & non-emotionally stimulating.

I say this not only based on my personal opinion, but also on the opinions of children in the education system who tend to believe it's a rather boring experience. Especially, compared to how emotionally-stimulating it *could* be.

Boring lectures. Hours of rigorous note-taking. Little-to-no emotional engagement. What a waste of learning potential.

The key is make learning *emotionally-stimulating*.

If you want to learn something in a way in which you're able to easier remember it in the future, think to yourself...

'How can I add emotion to this?'

For example, if you're reading a book & you come across a particular phrase you want to remember, think of ways you can add *emotion* to the experience.

For example, shout the phrase out loud. If you're in public, this may embarrass you a little. Which is good. This strong emotion (embarrassment) will help you remember that phrase better in the future. It will anchor it deeper into your memory for better recall in the future.

If you're at home alone, shouting this important phrase may just make you laugh. Which is another emotion that will help you retain & recall information better.

Better yet, find ways to turn *learning* into *experience*.

Don't just consume information, instead, find ways to really *experience* it. Go on a field trip. Go on an educational adventure. If you're learning about insects, go out to the wild & turn that *learning* into an actual *experience*.

Experiences tend to create of stronger level of emotional engagement than lectures or endless note-taking.

We - as human beings on this incredible planet - learn better when we're *actively engaged* in what we're learning.

When we raise our level of emotional engagement & involvement, it's going to help us raise our *learning speed*.

When people learn while bored, they tend to forget more of what they learn, however when they're fully involved, they'll learn faster, understand more & recall more, easier.

Which is yet another reason why *passion* is 1 of the 3 foundational keys to mastery (as we discussed in the last section). When people are passionate about what they do, it creates a natural level of emotional stimulation & deeper involvement that accelerates & improved their learning.

And this is also another reason why *celebration* is such a critical element of the 9 step learning process (as we talked about in the last section as well). When we *celebrate*, we raise our level of emotional engagement & we deeper reinforce our learning & skill development for better recall.

Your challenge is to find ways that you can turn your learning situations into more emotionally-rich experiences.

By adding emotion - *emotional learning* - you drive up your ability to recall important information in the future.

3 | LEARN TO TEACH

> *"No law or ordinance is mightier than understanding"*
>
> - *PLATO*

If you can't explain something to someone, you don't really understand it (or you don't understand it *deeply*).

Which is why explaining something to someone forces you to - near automatically - learn information deeper.

It encourages you to learn, not just at the surface-level of *'knowing,'* but at the deeper level of *'understanding'*.

And it's why, when you learn with the intention of passing that information on (teaching), you'll tend to learn faster, remember more & be able to recall it easier in the future.

However, please understand this doesn't mean you have to become a professor, author or speaker, teaching others.

This is a strategy you can deploy even if you don't like people & never want to teach them anything.

It's simply about you asking yourself:

'What would I need to learn about this topic or skill to be able to effectively explain it to someone - if I had to?'

This approach politely nudges your brain to focus far more on creating *deep understanding* (which your mind recalls better) & not just surface-level *awareness*.

And if you want to push it to an even higher level, whatever topic or skill you are learning, find someone to learn with you & explain everything you learn to each other.

This will drive that information into deeper understanding for both of you. Also, by explaining it, that process in itself, further deepens learning & boosts recall.

Test this. Next time you read a book, read just the first chapter, then find someone who you can explain that chapter too. Once you do that, continue to the next one.

And the same applies when you listen to information or watch it. After a lecture or video, take time to deepen the learning by talking about it with someone (explaining it)

In the short term, this may actually slows down learning as it requires more time to do.

However, in the long term, it saves you from having to re-learn the same things over & over, making it a huge learning accelerator you can begin to leverage today.

13 | ACCELERATED TRAINING:
TOOLS FOR SKILL DEVELOPMENT

"The biggest room in the world is the room for improvement"

- *HELMUT SCHMIDT*

Skill development - like anything else - can *always* be accelerated, improved, heightened & optimized.

In this section, we're going to dive deep into 5 powerful skill development tools (strategies) you can start using, almost immediately, to optimize your skill development.

1 | PRE-LEARNING STATE

"Energy and persistence conquer all things"

- *BENJAMIN FRANKLIN*

The *state* (feeling) in which we enter a learning or skill development situation has a far bigger impact on how quickly we learn (progress) than most people realize.

If you start reading a book, reviewing a textbook, listening to a lecture or training a skill while you are in an angry, annoyed & frustrated *state of mind*, clearly, you're not going to learn as fast, remember as much, or in general, get the most out of that learning time, as you could.

Meanwhile, if you are in a great *state* (excited, enthusiastic & ready to improve), you'll learn & develop skills faster.

High achievers put a lot of focus on ensuring they approach their learning, skill development & crucial life situations in the right energy (*state*) to ensure the best results.

It's because they understand the impact of *state* (energy).

If you're passionate about what you do, you'll naturally have a higher level of energy - a better *pre-learning state* - approaching any learning or skill development situation. However, we will still have days where our *state* (how we feel) may not be quite where it should be.

Fortunately, *state* (like a lot of other important things) is deep within our control; it's very controllable.

And, at any moment - if you've trained this ability - you can change your *state* (energy; how you feel).

Meanwhile, most people feel a huge *lack of control* over their *state*. They feel controlled by their emotions, their energy & their feelings, instead of *being* in control.

The underlying belief to change that is that, you are *not* your body, you're *not* your feelings & you're *not* your urges.

Rather, *you* - your spirit, your true essence, the real '*you*', or whatever you want to call it - are a higher version of consciousness - beyond your body - that can override temptations, urges & negative emotions.

You are a higher consciousness & energy that's in control of your future (your destiny).

This understanding allows you to control your *state* & move into a life of, not just more skill, but more happiness.

Your state (how you feel) is made up of 2 core things...

1. **Focus** (Mind)
2. **Physiology** (Body)

It's this combination of what you're focused on (mind; your current thoughts) & how your body is showing up (physiology) that forms how you feel (your *state*).

For example, if you're thinking about how stupid the person who just cut you off on your drive to the office was (focus) & your body is demonstrating that rage by tensing up (physiology), you're going to be in the *state* of anger; a state that doesn't tend to produce the best results in learning, skill development or most other situations.

However, you can change your *state* by changing what you're focused on (what you're thinking about) & the positioning - & intensity - of your body (physiology).

In moments when you're in an ineffective *pre-learning state*, approaching a learning situation, ask yourself a question like, *'What can I be excited about right now?'* or *'What are 5 things I'm grateful for in my life?'*

These types of questions will help you change focus (mind). Then, proceed to change your body. Stand up straight. Smile. Do something silly with your body. And, this will quickly change your *state*. It will put you in a better *pre-learning state,* which will lead to faster learning.

Beyond that, you can create *rituals* that consistently & predictably get you into a more effective pre-learning state.

HOW TO CREATE STATE-CHANGE 'RITUALS'

One of the best ways to repeatedly & consistently tap into a great *pre-learning* (or pre-action) *state* is through a *ritual*.

We know that people who feel empowered, optimistic, confident, excited, passionate, committed to following through & willing to learn are those who perform best.

In the same way, we know that those who show greater emotions of gratitude, appreciation & passion in their lives are those who tend to be most happy, most often.

The best part; particular emotions & feelings (including the ones listed above) can be triggered with a great *'ritual'*.

A ritual, simply put, is something you do that creates a certain result (often, that result, is a *change of 'state'*).

Think of Ellen DeGeneres & her mint toss. That's a small ritual that she does that brings her into a better, more charismatic, more joyous, state.

She tosses a mint into the air & attempts to catch it before getting onto the set to film an episode of her show.

It's simple. It's a little silly. A little funny. And that's exactly what it's meant to be. It's a great little ritual she has that helps her, consistently, get into a better *state*.

Another example is Barack Obama, who always played basketball on the morning of an Election Day's. A *ritual* that allowed him to get into a better state of mind.

And no, this isn't about superstitions. It's about an action that you consistently condition to get you into a particular *state of mind.* His basketball helped him release some of the pressure & helped him get into a better state of mind.

There are countless examples beyond these of athletes, musicians, performers, investors or entrepreneurs who have rituals that condition them into a great pre-learning (or pre-action) state, however, the key remains the same: *create a ritual that consistently gets you into a great state.*

Whatever way you do it, start to place a higher level of priority on the *state (energy)* in which you enter each & every learning & skill development situation, as it makes a huge impact on your learning speed & effectiveness.

2 | COACHING & MENTORING

> *"All coaching is, is taking a player where he can't take himself"*
>
> - *BILL MCCARTNEY*

There's a reason so many of the world's best - the greatest athletes, the greatest investors, the best musicians, the best entertainers - have coaches & mentors to support them.

I'm here to tell you; it's no coincidence. It's because the power of coaching or mentoring is clear; it works!

It has helped people learn faster, progress more effectively & supercharge their process to mastery for generations.

It's because a coach or mentor can see what you may not see. A coach (or mentor) offers an external point of view - a different outlook - for greater feedback & insight.

A great coach (or mentor) is worth their weight in gold.

Tim Grover is a great example of this. He's the coach who coached both *Michael Jordan* & *Kobe Bryant* - 2 of the greatest basketball players of all time - to reach new, higher levels of performance. And has received dazzling words of admirations from both of these incredible athletes for his support & coaching. Both of them have commented on the value of him as their coach.

And this doesn't mean *Tim Grover* is better at basketball than Michael Jordan or Kobe Bryant - he'll be the first to tell you, he's not - but he knows how to push athletes to reach new, higher levels of performance. That's his skill set.

If you're really serious about getting great at a topic or skill, don't attempt to do it alone. If you want the fastest - & best - results, hire a coach (or find a mentor) who can help you.

COACHING VS MENTORING

As mentioned, I've always found the mentor-apprentice dynamic fascinating. And, I've always found the dynamic between coach & coachee very interesting too.

And both - *coaching* & *mentoring* - have massive merits when it comes to learning, skill development & mastery.

But, what's the difference between them?

A coach is usually someone you hire (a paid service) to help you get a particular result you're looking to achieve. It doesn't have to be like that, but, usually is. It's someone who, isn't necessarily better than you at what you do but knows how to coach you to the next level. And, especially at the highest levels, high achievers will tend to have multiple coaches for various roles & sub-skills they're developing.

A mentor on the other hand - at least, throughout history - is often *not* a paid service, but rather a *partnership*. It's usually based on a mutual agreement between mentor & apprentice (the person being mentored) which consists of guidance for the apprentice (or, mentee) to get better.

Based on the study of the world's highest achievers, both - *coaching* & *mentoring* - are powerful methods you can use to accelerate your learning, skill development & success.

THE POWER OF MENTORING

Oprah Winfrey was mentored by Maya Angelou. Henry David Thoreau was mentored by Ralph Waldo Emerson. Mark Zuckerberg was mentored by Steve Jobs. Leonardo Da Vinci was mentored by Andrea del Verrocchio. Raphael was mentored by Leonardo Da Vinci. The list goes on & on.

An incredibly high percentage of those who have reached a world-class level had mentors to help them get there.

This doesn't mean you can't succeed without a mentor, but research continues to show how positively *mentoring* (or *coaching*) impacts learning speed & progress to mastery.

And clearly for all the people above, based on their results, as well as their comments in interviews or in their works, early *mentoring* was of huge benefit.

However, the key is to 1) pick the right mentor & 2) gain the greatest possible *proximity* to that mentor. That's how you get the most out of *mentoring*.

One of the mistakes people make initially after hearing about the power of mentoring is picking the wrong mentor.

Nowadays, there are so many people out there who say they are coaches, life coaches or mentors, who - if you dig a little deeper under the surface - have little previous success to actually be able to successfully coach upon.

If someone has never achieved something for themselves - with rare exception - will they be able to effectively teach it.

That's like a fat person wanting to mentor you about fitness, or a broke person teaching you about finances.

It's why you want to pick a mentor whose 'been there & done that' & has achieved that which you want to achieve.

Better yet, find someone who has achieved it *repeatedly* & *consistently*. They haven't just done it once, but they've done it many times; an even stronger track record.

Lastly, you want to pick a mentor who's achieved in a similar industry, profession or path as you want to head down. This, once again, makes a huge difference.

If your mentor has achieved their success in an industry, profession, category or even, business model, far outside the path that you're heading down, their guidance may be misleading (lacking accuracy).

You want your mentor (or mentors; you can have multiple) to have experience in similar industries, professions, topics & skills to yours.

And when you've picked a great mentor, understand that there are multiple levels of learning from a mentor.

I've narrowed these down to the 4 core layers of 'proximity' that arise in a mentor-mentee dynamic.

1. A mentor **from afar**
2. A mentor **in range**
3. A mentor **in person**
4. A mentor **in association**

A mentor from afar is someone you're learning from, from afar. You might read your mentor's book. Or, watch their video training. They're *mentoring* you from afar, often through their products or services, rather than in person. And although this is only surface-level mentoring, it is a form of *mentoring*. It may be the least effective form of mentoring - very surface-level - but, is still valuable.

At first, you may not know (or have the capability) to meet your dream mentor in person, or convince them to mentor you, however, you can always learn from their work. This is the stage where most people start.

A mentor in range is the next level. This level, you're coming into closer *proximity* with your mentor. You're not only researching them, studying their work, reading their books or watching their videos *from afar*, but you're also going to any events - or meetups - they're running or you're working at - or with - the companies they run; all with the intention of getting into greater *proximity* so you can pick up greater nuances that you can use to progress.

A mentor in person; a face-to-face, 1-to-1 type of interaction with your mentor. You're not only studying their work, but you'll also receive specific feedback & guidance, from them, tailored to you & your ambitions.

This may be the result of working beside (or underneath) them in an organization or company. Or on a personal level, you're spending time with them like you would with a friend. And, at this level, your mentor is your friend. You know them & they know you.

There are dozens of reasons why this level will give you greater insight than the previous levels, including the personalized guidance, the behind-the-scenes access to them, as well as their friendship.

A mentor in association is the highest level. It's the level you should strive for if you want to be influenced by your mentor at the highest level. At this level, your mentor isn't just your friend, but a dear friend. It's also the level where you're in deep *association* with your mentor. There's no holding back. You receive their best guidance & personalized wisdom as they support you to become great. You're actively spending time with them. Often, directly with them; working side-by-side.

And, with each level, your *proximity* increases. And know...

| Proximity matters

When you're learning *from afar*, there's only so much your mentor can influence your learning & skill development.

However, at the highest level (*a mentor in association*) your mentor is largely influencing - & uplifting - you to new high levels. By spending time in-person with your mentor, you're - often unknowingly - making small tweaks to your actions that make you better at what you do.

With each level up, you're learning more & progressing faster at the topic or skill you're developing.

Your goal is to go up the stages to greater & greater levels of friendship, association & proximity to your mentor.

However, don't expect to jump to stage 4 (*a mentor in association*) immediately. It rarely happens that way.

Most of the time, you'll start at 1 of the first 2 stages. And, you may progress up in the future.

As to how; you must find ways to add value to your mentor.

And know that a great mentor is sowed after. Almost every aspiring film director would love the opportunity to be personally mentored by Steven Spielberg, almost every aspiring magician (or illusionist) would love to be personally mentored by David Copperfield & most aspiring investors would love the opportunity to have Warren Buffett mentor them. You're not alone; I assure you that.

It's why you'll often start on phase 1 or 2. And to progress up, you must find ways that you can add value.

How can you add value to your mentor's life?

That's the question you should be focusing on.

Not, *'how can I get this from them?'*, but *'what can I give?'*

That's what will make them want to mentor you in the first place. Bring value & you'll receive value back.

And yes, even the world's highest achievers still have things that they want, that they would love support with.

It may be a project that they're working on that they're missing things for, or a dream that they lack resources to achieve. Or, perhaps, they're concerned about their legacy & want someone to carry the torch in the future. You have to find what *they* want & provide value to get in the door before you can start building a friendship (& moving up).

And, be humble. Value the learning you get as great compensation. If you're really committed to world-class skill (mastery) at what you do, be willing to work for free under them if you have to - to get into closer proximity - knowing the short-term sacrifice is nothing compared to the long-term upside that will come from their mentoring.

Put self-pride aside & be willing to sacrifice in the short-term for massive long-term upside.

And equally know that, just like any friendship or business relation, you have to start by simply becoming known to your mentor. They have to be aware that you exist first.

It starts there. And beyond that, it takes patience & time to build that association or proximity with your mentor.

Like anything worth doing, it doesn't happen overnight. It takes time to form that strong mentor-mentee dynamic.

However, the right mentor can massively supercharge your progress making it a very worthwhile effort.

3 | IMMERSION

> *"Concentrate all your thoughts upon the work at hand. The sun's rays do not burn until brought to a focus"*
>
> - *ALEXANDER GRAHAM BELL*

We arrived. We didn't know what to expect. However, we were excited for the possibilities & opportunities ahead.

My parents made 1 big life decision, with little preparation, that changed our lives entirely. However, let's rewind a bit.

I was born in Gdansk, Poland. Me & my brother were raised in Poland for the first few years of our lives.

My dad had been running a reasonably successful furniture business in Poland for many years at the time.

However, my parents aren't the type of people who settle for good, when they can strive for something greater (one of the many things I admire about them).

So one day their ambition guided them to make a decision. A decision that radically changed all our lives forever.

We weren't fully prepared but did it anyway, with faith.

My parents decided to close it all down, pack it up & move.

We moved from Poland to London, UK - a place where so many people, especially in Europe, moved in search of greater success & abundance.

However, we didn't know the culture. We didn't know the people. We didn't know what to expect.

We didn't even know the language. We hadn't had a single lesson of the English language in our entire lives.

With that, me & my brother started going to school.

My parents started a construction business.

We all struggled our way through the first few months, slowly learning the language so that we could actually communicate with other people.

We continued, struggling through it, knowing we had no other choice. Fortunately, we started getting somewhere.

If we really wanted to live in this country, we had to learn the language; we needed to communicate.

Then, after a few months, we started picking up more & more of the English language.

In fact, within just a few years (if not less), my English was completely fluent. So was my brother's.

Furthermore, after those few years of living in London, my English was far better than my birth language of Polish.

As you read this you may be thinking, '*Bogdan, why are you sharing this story; how's it relevant?*'

The essence of the story is the power of *immersion*.

If we lived in Poland & just took English language lessons, it would have taken us 2, 3, 4, maybe even 5, times longer to learn fluent English. And, even then, we may not have been *completely* fluent.

At that time, I hadn't even started my research into accelerated learning or skill development (the contents of this book), so I didn't have that on my side.

Nor, did I have a knack for language either. In fact, I spent 2 years in primary school learning French & today, I can say, perhaps, 20 words in French. And I then spent 3 years learning Spanish, before forgetting most of that too.

Same time periods (a few years), yet the results were so different when I was learning English, compared to learning French or Spanish. And, having travelled all around the world teaching, observing & talking to thousands of people, I've found this pattern is similar.

The first difference was *intention*. I actually had a strong passion, desire & intention to learn English. We've talked about this a lot already & we'll talk more about how detrimental *a lack of intention* can be in the next chapter.

However, the biggest difference was *immersion*.

A lot of people go to learn a new language but never dive in *immersively* enough to learn it effectively.

Statistics show it takes numerous years (often, many) to become fluent in a new language through study.

Through *immersion*, me, my family, & probably hundreds of thousands of other people around the world were able to skip years of study to achieve the same desired result.

And this doesn't just apply when learning a new language, but rather, applies to almost anything we could ever learn (or do). In my life alone, thanks to this 1 concept, I've been able to radically accelerate the learning & achievement of many things; from learning to gallop a horse in just 2 hours to writing 200+ page books in a just a few days. It was largely thanks to this 1 very powerful concept; *immersion*.

Immersion: deep mental involvement in something

Immersion, simply put, is *sustained focus*. And by applying greater *immersion*, we'll able to learn anything far faster.

If you're learning a new language, go to the country, speak only in that language for a number of days, set everything around you to that particular language. Completely immerse yourself in that new world & you'll learn faster.

If you're learning the guitar, don't just play for 10 minutes a day, but rather, schedule a weekend where you spend 10 hours *immersed* in the topic & skill of the guitar.

Beyond that, listen to great guitar songs - or guitar solos - as you drive to work or while you do the dishes. Instead of buying cinema tickets, buy concert tickets & watch great guitarists play in front of your very eyes. Be *immersed*.

If you're learning marketing, go to marketing conferences, hang around with friends also passionate about marketing, allocate a few days where the majority of your focus is just on improving that 1 skill & you'll learn it much faster.

These are all various examples of how you can be more *immersed* (focused) in your learning & skill development.

For some, they may already be doing this, but for the vast majority, when they learn something new, they dabble.

They allocate little time to it, scheduled that time irregularly (lacking consistency) & act without *immersion*.

It's like they're dipping their toes in the water, compared to getting in & actually seizing the opportunity fully.

You can learn anything you want many times faster by being focused & sustaining that focus (*immersion*) over a longer period of time as you learn & progress.

And this doesn't just apply to learning & skill development, it applies to life. Focus & immersion are powerful keys for accelerating the accomplishment of any ambition you have.

CASE STUDY: HELD HOSTAGE IN A HOTEL

When I write books - as well as work on other projects - I don't do it like most. I don't follow the conventional, yet often ineffective, wisdom that gets passed around. Instead, I leverage the power of *immersion* to achieve things faster.

Most people when writing to write a book get told to dedicate 10 minutes a day to writing as much as they can. Or, they get told to write 2 good pages per day. Or, told to focus on writing 1 solid chapter per week. That's the conventional guidance that gets passed around.

Meanwhile, when I was writing my second book, I decided to lock myself in a hotel room for 4 days straight & write it.

I had an idea & I wanted to, by the end of the 4 days, have a completed, 200+ page, published book, ready to ship out to customers all around the world.

So, I checked into the hotel. I turned off my phone. I turned off all social media. I didn't check email. And made sure all other work projects were taken care off so I didn't have to focus on them during these 4 days.

Remember: *immersion* - at its core - is *sustained focus* & is broken when interrupted (hence, the precautions).

And all I did during those 4 days - besides eating, drinking, sleeping & other essentials - was writing (*immersively*).

10 - 15 hours *per day* of immersive, non-stop writing & book creation work. Total, full-on immersion on 1 thing.

At the end of the 4 days, technically, I had failed. It was about 90% done. It actually took 4.5 days - total - to write the book & get it completed, ready for publishing.

Which, was still a massive success that I celebrated enthusiastically. And goes to show the power of *immersion*.

It's not like I'm some great writer - I'm a high school dropout - it's that these concepts are just so powerful.

Before that experience, my first book - the initial version of this book - was written in 6 days, also thanks to *immersion*.

And please note, these books are not 40-page ebooks. They were full-blown 200+ page, 50,000 word + books written in such very short periods of time (thanks to *immersion*).

Immersion is so incredibly powerful for a few key reasons.

Firstly, any time you change focus (breaking immersion) your mind requires time to adjust & you lose efficiency.

Think of it like a car having to change direction. When you have to turn to head in a new direction, the car (your mind) needs time to adjust before progressing at full speed again.

When you can remove this need to change direction (focus) constantly (through immersion) - at least for a certain time - you maximize your efficiency & achieve things faster.

Secondly, you maintain a greater state of flow when you're immersed in something. Your mind isn't scattered; it's focused, allowing to zero-in on the best ideas, possibilities & opportunities to help you achieve faster. This is a big reason why you'll tend to have the best ideas in immersion.

Thirdly, *immersion* creates a huge blast-off of momentum which propels you to higher levels of *continued* progress.

This level of compressed focus into a short, condensed period of time allows you to make huge leaps forward.

The best example of this is by looking into the fuel usage of a rocket ship as it takes off.

When a rocket ship takes off, approximately 50% of its fuel is used just to get it off the ground - in the initial take off.

In that same way, starting anything is the most draining, energy-consuming & hardest part of doing anything, while continuing what you're already doing *(sustaining focus)* uses far less energy to produce the same - or better - result.

And while most people spend their entire time, energy & effort starting, stopping & changing direction (switching focus) those who are *immersed* - sustaining their focus over longer periods of time - can achieve far more & accelerate their learning, skill development & achievement.

It's because it requires radically less energy & effort to *keep going* (momentum) than it takes to get started.

In your learning, get started & then focus on staying in that upwards momentum as long as you can. In other words, be *immersed* (sustain your focus) for optimized results.

Lastly, sheer *time allocation* (as we talked about before) dictates you're able to achieve much more, much faster by compressing time like this (immersion).

Simply put, if you're putting in the same number of hours of focused work others are putting in over the course of an entire month in just a few days, you're going to be able to achieve the goal you're after much faster.

And know that this type of *time-compression* (immersion) doesn't take away from the quality of your work, but rather, tends to improve it. This is because we tend to do our best work when we're fully focused (not distracted).

Immersion means you are focused. You're not distracted. You allow your mind to focus exclusively on 1 thing, boosting the speed & quality of your learning & progress.

Here's the nuance; it's near impossible to spend our entire time (our entire life) in *complete immersion* & focus on 1 thing only. Life has many moving parts. And, variety is the spice of life. Which is why, while you may spend a few days immersed in a certain topic, skill or ambition, it's also important to *counterbalance* & focus on other priorities.

And *immersion* must be combined with *consistency*. We learn fastest when we are immersed over a period of time, but we must also be consistent in our learning & skill development if we want to become truly extraordinary.

4 | TRAIN HARD TO EASE EXECUTION

"We don't rise to the level of our expectations, we fall to the level of our training"

- ARCHILOCHUS

There seems to a shared belief that high achievers flourish when it matters most; that they rise to the occasion.

When often, it's the contrary. Champions don't rise to the occasion, but rather sink (fall) to the level of their training.

Meaning they'll push harder, work harder & perform better in training than they ever will when it matters.

They'll tend to dip from that highest level of performance to a level that's still better than anybody else's during a competition, test, assessment or career-defining moment.

In other words, champions *train hard during training* (behind the scenes) to make competitions, performances, tests or assessments much, much easier later on.

While others, on the other hand, train lightly (don't push themselves during training) & hope to rise to the occasion.

For example, a school might teach high-school-level math for years & then expects students to flourish at college-level mathematics. When they should, in fact - if they're looking to optimize results - challenge students far beyond where they need to get to in order to make exams easy later on.

The goal is to make training incredibly difficult & challenging; harder than the competition would ever be. That way, it will be easier & better when it matters most.

For example, the harder you push yourself during your marathon *training*, the easier the actual marathon will be. Or, the harder you push yourself during your guitar training, the easier performing on stage will be. By making training harder you're making success easier.

HOW BRAZIL CREATES FOOTBALL STARS

In the book *The Talent Code*, Daniel Coyle talks about specific *'talent hotbeds'* in the world; specific geographical areas which produce a shockingly high percentage of high achievers, compared to other places in the world.

A key thing that most of these *'talent hotbeds'* have in common is the difficulty of their training & how they train so much harder - with greater difficulty - than others.

One example of this came from a tiny location in Brazil which was producing far more football (soccer) stars than any other place in the world of the same (or sometimes, substantially larger) size or population.

After research, it showed their progress & skill improvement was radically accelerated because instead of training football (soccer) as we know it (on a big grassy pitch) they were training it in a very compressed space.

Meaning that in the same amount of game time as normal football training, each player was getting far more touches of the ball, with far less space to pass or move with the ball, making each player think faster & play better.

They call this sport *'futsal'* (or, street football). And it's largely responsible for many of the world-class football stars that have come out of Brazil.

It's a lot like football (soccer) as most people know it, but a scaled-down version. The pitches on which they play are much, much smaller. The pitch isn't grass-covered, rather a far more rough, solid terrain. And the goals into which players have to score are much smaller.

This all leads the players to train with much greater difficulty. They were forced to think faster, dribble better, control the ball better, aim better & overall, play better, tighter & more rigorous football.

And when these players went from playing futsal to playing actual football (soccer) on a normal-sized football pitch, the amount of space they had in comparison to move and pass the ball was huge, allowing them to flourish.

They had trained themselves to control, pass, move & aim the ball in a much smaller space so much so that playing actual football become so much easier. And, they thrived.

| Train hard to ease execution

These Brazilian footballers were, unknowingly, training harder than they would ever be expected to perform thanks to the nature of futsal.

And this is a lesson that we can all take into our own learning & skill development, irrelevant of the topic or skill that we are developing.

Don't train easy expecting to flourish when the time comes. Don't expect to rise to the occasion. Instead, make training overly-difficult & challenging - more challenging than any teacher or coach would ever be expecting you to complete - so that the end result becomes easier to achieve.

Train under those difficult circumstances & you'll be pleasantly surprised at how good you are when this extra difficulty is removed later on.

Let's say that you are training your skill of sales. Instead of training your presenting & closing to people who don't challenge you with objections or challenges, start training with champion intensity (greater difficulty).

Get your training buddies to flood you with objections. And, with harder & tougher objections than you would ever expect to experience for real. That way, when you do step out into the real world, & you're presenting to real business prospects, objection handling will be much easier.

Another example; if you're training your skill of football (soccer) shooting, instead of simply training to shoot with no defender, no obstacles or no challenges (like most do), you should increase the difficulty of your training.

Make the goal 5 times smaller. In the background, play a booing soundtrack to attempt to get you off your game. And, add 3 defenders charging at you from 3 various angles attempting to block each shot you take.

Beyond even that, add a world-class goalkeeper & give yourself only 5 seconds to take the shot.

Now, repeat this type of training drill & you'll begin to make accelerated progress.

However, you may not realize this accelerated progress you're making until later when you're in a regular football situation with normal difficulty.

The key: structure your training to be more difficult than the competition, performance, test or assessment ever could be & you'll flourish when it counts. In other words...

| Train hard to ease execution

This is something we (the team) used to do when we were training our public speaking skills. We intentionally increased the difficulty by getting other team members to throw stuff at the person presenting on stage.

This way, during the actual speech, any distraction that could come up from the audience wouldn't matter as they've already trained with this extra layer of difficulty.

A crying baby or slammed door doesn't seem like such a distraction anymore when you've trained to present flawlessly even while others are deliberately chunking stuff at you to distract you. *Train hard to ease execution.*

This also comes from the understanding that...

| Pressure exposes weaknesses

It's crucial to understand that *pressure* - an amplification of an existing situation or environment - doesn't change you (or your skills). Rather, it *exposes* the weaknesses & flaws hidden underneath the surface.

Someone can do something well a hundred times without pressure, but as soon as pressure is applied, their competence (skill) can seem to fall apart.

For example, a musician who plays a song well every time, but then messes up the song on stage in front of a large audience (a form of *pressure*) or the golfing pro who has made a similar putt successfully hundreds of times, yet cracks under the pressure during a big tournament.

Just like you can't really see how strong a building is until it gets hit by an earthquake, in that same way, you can't really see how strong someone's foundations at a certain topic or skill are until moments where *pressure* is applied.

Pressure exposes the weaknesses you can't always see.

By knowing this, it allows us to better follow the philosophy of *'train hard to ease execution'* & intentionally apply greater pressure to get better at what we do, faster.

We should be enthusiastically excited about uncovering our weaknesses *during training*, as it allows us to deal with them in private (during practice) rather than when it counts (a performance, test or career-defining moment).

Meanwhile, most people hide their weaknesses. They don't want to uncover them; they want to conceal them.

However, the simple fact is, those weaknesses will come out at some point (likely, in moments of the highest pressure) whether we like it or not.

Knowing that, it's far more beneficial for us to squeeze out weaknesses as soon as possible (preferably, during training) so we can address them & get better.

We don't want them to erupt during a critical moment in our lives, rather, we want them to come out during training so we can address them. We can do this by deliberately - intentionally - applying *pressure* to test our foundations.

By training harder than it's may seem logical to do so, we're applying a greater level of pressure on ourselves, which quicker uncovers our weaknesses, allowing us to address them & get better at what we do, faster.

And, the harder the *pressure* we have to deal with, the stronger our foundations have to be. Another thing that training with heightened difficulty allows us to do is train our foundations & better pressure-proof them.

It's like running a business. When you starting out - when you're working alone or with a few employees - you don't necessarily need operating procedures, standards, codes of conduct, policies, or other guidelines like those in place.

Frankly, you can manage the business without any of that.

Those weaknesses won't get exposed because there's little pressure on a new business. However, if you're managing a Fortune 500 company with thousands of employees, now you need to eliminate those weaknesses & develop much better systems to manage what's going on, else those weaknesses will be exposed & things may get ugly.

And when it comes to personal mastery of a skill, when we know *pressure exposes weakness*, we can use that.

It may seem stupid to throw stuff at someone to help them train their public speaking skills, or to reduce the size of a pitch (like in futsal), but when we train with this higher level of pressure (difficulty), it allows us to discover our weaknesses in training (instead of when it really counts) as well as allowing us to strengthen our foundations so we can perform well even when the pressure is on.

5 | REST & RECOVERY

> *"It's very important that we re-learn the art of resting and relaxing. Not only does it help prevent the onset of many illnesses that develop through chronic tension and worrying; it allows us to clear our minds, focus, and find creative solutions to problems"*
>
> — *THICH NHAT HANH*

Some people view *rest* or *recovery* as weakness. They think rest is only for those who aren't truly committed. They think they don't need it. Or, that it's not important.

And they believe that *rest & recovery* slows down learning, skill development & overall success.

And yes, in the short term, it does, as you have to allocate time to it. But, in the long term, *rest & recovery* in itself is a method of accelerating learning & skill development.

Over the long term, rest & recovery brings a net positive boost to learning speed & skill development effectiveness.

With sustained focus, intensity & effort, over time, your performance declines. It's not something bad; it's simply a sign from your mind or body that you need to take time to rest & recover, before continuing. It's normal. It's like working out at the gym; you're supposed to get tired.

If your topic or craft requires a lot of physical intensity (like most sports) you'll begin to feel a performance decline. You'll feel the tiredness kicking in, *in your body*.

That's easier to spot; what's harder is in topics or skills that require less physical & more mental intensity (like chess, art or creative writing). In those topics or skill, it's not your body that's getting exhausted, but rather your mind (your brain). And, your brain - just like any muscle - gets tired & declines in performance over time too. Hence, either way, *rest & recovery* is important & hugely beneficial.

Taking time to rest is not slowing you down, rather, helping you learn faster because your brain performs far better when you give it regular rest.

However, the main resistance that arises when people think about rest & recovery comes from short-term thinking. They make decisions for the short-term. And, in the short-term, it's often less effective to rest & recover effectively; it's better to just push through it & keep going.

However, *in the long term*, this way of thinking has detrimental effects. It's one of the biggest reasons you see people burn out - even, collapse - as they work or perform.

The world's highest achievers - especially those who outachieve others over many decades - place a huge importance on rest & recovery.

Not because they feel *'forced'*, but because they know the place *rest & recovery* has in the process of learning.

Rest & recovery, over the long term, allows you to push yourself harder, learn faster, achieve more & sustain high levels of performance. A massive net positive over time, however, it requires long-term-thinking to see it.

With that, if you want to rest & recover like the world's highest achievers, there are insights into this as well.

Yes, even in a topic that seems as simple as *'rest & recovery'*, there are still better (more effective) & worse (less effective) ways to do it. Effective *rest & recovery* is...

1. **Intentional**
2. **Intervaled**
3. **Immersive**

All 3 of these keys are crucial for optimal rest & recovery.

Intentional: A lot of people rest by *accident*. They rest when they have nothing else to do, when somebody tells them to, or when they burnout & can't do any more. None of these are particularly effective approaches.

Instead, the world's highest achievers are far more *intentional* about their rest & recovery. Often, it's scheduled. It's consistent. It happens predictably. And it's so important for them, it rarely get skipped. They'll often have people (coaches) whose job is just to help them rest. Coaches that they deliberately, intentionally, decide to hire.

They don't tell themselves *"I'll rest when I have nothing left to do,"* or *"I'll rest when I feel like it"* but rather, they make the time, block it out & rest with *intention*.

They know that rest isn't binary. It's not that you're either *fully rest* or *fully exhausted*. It's not that black & white. Rather, it's a scale. You start fully rested after allocating time to rest, however, with sustained effort, you gradually get more & more tired.

And they don't wait until they are *fully exhausted* to rest.

That's not a good strategy for long-term success. Instead, intentionally & mindfully, allocate time for rest & recovery.

Intervaled: A lot of people will work as long & hard as they can, without rest & will then go & rest for many weeks or months. However, we know that, most often, taking 8 1-week-long breaks during a year is more effective than taking 1 long 2-month break.

In that same way, taking 9 spread out 10-minute breaks is, often, more effective than taking 1 long 90-minute break.

Why? If you rest too long at one time, your recall of what you learned before starts to suffer (& so does your motivation to keep learning). Taking a 2-month vacation makes you lose focus & momentum far more than taking multiple 1-week breaks. Plus, often, if you're passionate about what you do, you don't need (or even want) to take a long break; you'll prefer to take many bite-sized ones.

Even taking short 2 - 5 minute breaks every hour has shown to increase productivity & effectiveness. Create strategic intervals of rest in your life.

Immersive: We all know people who, even when they are resting, are still thinking about their business, career, or items on their to-do list. They never let themselves rest *fully*. They lack focus (*immersiveness*) in their rest.

Immersive rest & recovery is about resting at 100%. Work hard, but remember to rest hard as well.

While resting, don't continue to think about the tasks at hand, rather, allow yourself to rest immersively (fully).

Challenge yourself to take your mind off learning, skill development or work (a tough, but possible, act) & place your attention entirely on rest & recovery during this time.

This is also one of the biggest reasons why meditation is such a great tool for rest. It allows you to empty your mind, be more present & more focused on your rest & recovery.

Look at how you're resting (or forgetting to) now & ask:

Is my rest & recovery intentional? Am I choosing it? Is it consistent? Intervalled? Immersive? Am I resting fully?

These 3 factors will form a powerful foundation for you to rest & recover optimally (like the world's best!)

And these 5 strategies (tools) we've covered in this chapter - if, & when, applied - will help you move into new, higher levels of learning, skill development & success.

14 | 5 LEARNING SPEED KILLERS: REMOVING THE OBSTACLES

"You have to handle adversity well. There are roadblocks you will have to fight through"

-   ZACH LAVINE

So often we're finding ways to, metaphorically, run faster towards the finish line (which is important & what a huge portion of this book is focused on), however, we sometimes forget another way to get to the finish line *faster* is by simply removing the obstacles - hurdles - along the way.

Success at anything isn't all that complex. At the core, it's about 1) doing the right (effective) things, while at the same time, 2) avoiding the wrong (ineffective) things.

Just like great health is the result of going the effective thing (good nutrition, exercise, etc) while avoiding the ineffective things (unhealthy foods, toxic drinks, alcohol, smoking, high stress, etc), the same applies to every ambition & achievement in life.

It's about knowing & implementing the effective things, while - at the same time - avoiding the ineffective things.

And while many of the chapters in this book were focused on applying the effective things, this chapter is focused exclusively - & extensively - on avoiding what's ineffective.

This chapter is all about removing the *learning speed killers*; the things that people do, that tend to radically slow down - kill - their *learning speed*.

By learning these, you'll be able to avoid the pitfalls & therefore learn even faster & more effectively.

1 | LOW TEACHABILITY LEVEL

"I don't think much of a man who is not wiser today than he was yesterday"

- *ABRAHAM LINCOLN*

All learning starts with *willingness* & *choice*.

If somebody doesn't want to learn something, they won't learn it - irrelevant of how good the teacher is, how well-structured the training is or how important it may be.

All of *that* will perish in comparison to that person's lack of *willingness* to learn; their low level of *teachability*.

Teachability: one's capability to be taught; one's apt, tenacity & willing to learn.

Maybe you know someone in your life like this: they are given the best guidance from the smartest people, yet don't learn because they've closed themselves off from learning.

Maybe it's because of their sense of righteousness (a need to be right), their self-pride or perhaps a lack of interest in the topic; there are many reasons why one may be closed off from learning, but they all lead to a lack of progress.

And it's all because of a *low level of teachability*.

If you (or someone else) is not *teachable*, what you do doesn't matter as a lack of *teachability* will block learning.

Think of this like wearing a pair of tinted glasses. If you're wearing *red-tinted* sunglasses, it doesn't matter how spectacularly *green* the object may be, to you, it's still *red*.

That's how a low level of *teachability* affects your learning. The opportunities for learning may be right in front of you, but you won't see them because of a low *teachability* level.

On the other side of the spectrum, those who have a *high level of teachability* (high willingness to learn), can learn anything much faster. It's because they're *teachable*.

And that's what we must strive for. If we really want to learn anything faster, we must raise our *teachability* level.

We must become more teachable. We must become more coachable. We must realize our beliefs are often not our own - rather, passed down from others - & understand others may know things what we may not yet know.

We must be humble. We don't 'know it all'. And probably never will. That's where teachability starts.

As the great philosopher, *Socrates,* once said...

"The only true wisdom is in knowing you know nothing"

The person who is righteous, who over-attaches to a certain way of being, or lacks the humility to learn from others is going to learn much, much *slower* than they could.

While the person who is humble, opening to seeing other points-of-view & prioritizes results over an attachment to a certain belief or method, will learn *faster* & achieve most.

It all starts with teachability, which in my work with customers, clients, readers & fans globally, I've measured with a simple assessment: ***The Teachability Index.***

Unlike most of the concepts in this book, this one wasn't one I personally created. I first learned it many years ago & it has had a huge impact on my life since; hence it's here.

A high ranking on this index - *a high teachability level* - is a mindset that supports you to learn faster in any situation.

A low ranking on this index - *a low teachability level* - is a mindset that doesn't support you. It holds you back. It stops you from learning, growing & progressing.

First things first though, the very fact that you are reading this book already shows me (& the world) more about your willingness to learn than almost anything you could say or do. Reading a book like this is an act of high teachability.

However, there's always a higher level. Teachability *isn't* binary (it's not something you either have or lack). It's *not* like a light switch; on or off. It's more like a scale. And you can always reach a higher level of teachability.

The Teachability Index consists of 2 key questions:

1. **What is your willingness to learn?**
2. **What is your willingness to change?**

Both parts play a critical part in your level of teachability.

QUESTION #1: *What Is Your Willingness To Learn?*

Lessons are everywhere. However, if someone who's closed off from learning receives those learning opportunities, they're *not* very likely to learn or implement those lessons.

Alternatively, if you teach someone who is very eager to learn new information, they are far more likely to consume, learn & implement what you have taught them. It all comes down to your willingness to learn.

And your willingness to learn is made up of a few different elements. It includes your willingness to invest time to learn new things, your willingness to invest money into learning (if you need to), your willingness to continue learning even when it gets tough, among other elements.

However, often as human beings, we have learned something, yet we haven't actually *implemented* that new information into our life to achieve the results we want.

This is where the second question comes into play.

To achieve different outcomes, you not only need to *learn* but also *implement*; make *changes* to what you do.

QUESTION #2: *What Is Your Willingness To Change?*

Too many people are terrified of change, yet *change* is life's only constant & is an ongoing part of anything.

We live in the most constantly-changing, unpredictable time in history, & our willingness to *accept change* is a big factor in our level of long-term success.

There is no point *learning* something if you're not going to implement it; make some type of *change* in what you do.

Question 1 addresses your ability to find new knowledge, meanwhile this question - question 2 - addresses your ability to take that new knowledge & use it (make *changes*).

And both parts work together synergistically. They are dependent on one another. And, to have a high level of *teachability*, you must be strong at both parts.

EXERCISE: THE TEACHABILITY INDEX
Start by ranking yourself - with total, brutal honesty - on the first question.

1) On a scale of 1 - 10, where 1 is completely closed off from learning & 10 is as open to learning as they come, what is your willingness to learn?

Closed Off 1 2 3 4 5 6 7 8 9 10 **Eager**

Write down your number. Now, part 2:

2) On a scale of 1 - 10, with 1 being totally closed off from change & 10 being loving change & high eager, what is your willingness to accept change?

Closed Off 1 2 3 4 5 6 7 8 9 10 **Accepting**

Write down your number for this second part.

Now multiply the 2 numbers together to get your teachability index: (_____ / **100**).

This represents your *willingness to learn*.

To be even more specific you can do this exercise again for different categories, topics & skills in your life as your teachability level may change from one area to another.

Your goal, now, is to increase this number; to raise to higher levels of teachability - & coachability - in your life.

To be increasingly, humble, open to learning, willing to disassociate from methods & rather place the attachment on higher-level objectives in life.

And please note, your teachability index isn't something that you get at birth, something that is hardwired into you or something that you can't change, rather, your teachability level is constantly changing throughout life. You can change it through choice - it's in your control.

A low teachability will kill your learning speed, while a high level of teachability will accelerate it. It's a critical mindset shift we must make if we want to learn anything fast.

The truth is there are opportunities for learning anywhere & everywhere. We live in the information age; everybody has a greater access to information & knowledge that they'll ever even need. But, it requires a high level of teachability to seize this opportunity. And your level of teachability is like a filter that runs 24/7/365, that filters all the information & knowledge you consume accordingly.

Anything can be turned into a lesson in your life, yet most people aren't seeking learning and improvement, hence they don't get the lessons. And they keep making the same mistakes and struggling.

They make a big mistake, but rather than learning from it, they whine, complain, get annoyed & then, a few, days, weeks, months or years later, they make that same mistake.

And then they continue to make that same mistake over & over again, wondering why they aren't getting anywhere.

Insanity, right? Yet we have probably all done this at some point. I know I definitely have.

The reason why in the last section we talked about failure as such as a massive key to success is that it assumes you're actively learning from your failures; you're learning from each mistake, fall & setback to get better next time.

I don't get annoyed or frustrated to make mistakes or to fail. I find making mistakes a critical part of the process.

What isn't required is making the same mistake 10 times. That's just ineffective learning. Something that can be avoided - & improved - by raising your level of teachability.

And those with a *high teachability level* don't just wait to learn something, but rather seek learning.

| Seek learning. Don't just wait for it.

A pattern of high achievers is that they don't wait for things to come to them, but rather, they actively seek for what they want. In the same way, seeking learning is far more powerful than waiting to be taught something.

"Always walk through life as if you have something new to learn and you will" - Vernon Howard

If you approach learning & growth with that mindset, improvement becomes the inevitable result.

Think to yourself, '*What can I learn from this situation?*'

Don't let this learning speed killer - a low level of teachability - sabotage your potential.

From this point forward in your life, make a commitment to, not just wait to learn something, but rather to, actively seek learning, growth & improvement in every situation.

2 | A 'FIXED MINDSET'

"Why waste time proving over and over how great you are, when you could be getting better?"

- *CAROL DWECK*

In Carol Dweck's brilliant book, *Mindset,* she revealed research that one of the biggest restricting elements that slows - kills - *learning speed* is having a *'fixed mindset'.*

In the book, she talks about the 2 categories under which people fit when it comes to their *mindset* approaching a learning or skill development situation.

On one side of the scale, you have those who have a *'fixed mindset'.* On the other side, those with a *'growth mindset.'*

The primary difference between the two, as she explains, is whether they believe skill (ability) is something binary (you either have it, or you don't) or something that can be trained & cultivated (a recurring theme of this book).

*A **'fixed mindset'** assumes our abilities, characteristics & skills are binary qualities which can not be changed in any meaningful way. We either have artistic gifts or we don't. We either have high intelligence, or we don't. We either have it, or we lack it. Period.*

*Those with a **'growth mindset'** on the other hand, view skills & abilities as trainable, changeable & able to be improved through focused effort. They don't view abilities as binary (you have it, or you don't), but rather as trainable (even if you don't have it now, you can train it to have it later). And this allows these people to thrive on challenge & further view failure as a stepping stone - or springboard - for growth & improvement.*

A lot of the work in this book - especially the first section - builds upon the understanding that those with a *'growth mindset'* tend to outperform those with a *'fixed mindset'.*

Carol Dweck found - in her years of research - that those with a *'growth mindset'* tend to react better to failure, challenge themselves more, persist during hard times, learn from constructive criticism (feedback) better & put in greater effort (discipline) to reach their goals.

And this all comes from their belief that skill is something that can be *controlled, trained* & *cultivated*, rather than something that is binary & can't be changed.

Furthermore, you can quickly tell which category you (or anyone else) fall into by viewing the language they use.

Those with a *'fixed mindset'* will tend to say *"I'm smart at this,"* or *"I'm just bad at this".* They'll tend to justify their shortcomings by saying, *"I just don't have an ability at this,"* They'll look at others & justify others successes by saying, *"They were born like that"* or *"They've always been good at that, if I was born like them, I would be as good".*

Meanwhile, those with a *'growth mindset'* will tend to refer to their abilities & skills as *trained*. They'll say things like, *"I'm good at this because I worked at it"* or just like Michelangelo said: *"If people knew how hard I worked to get my mastery, it wouldn't seem so wonderful at all."* They'll tend to respond to failure, not by blaming their lack of gifts, but by saying things like *"If I work harder at this, I'll get better results next time".*

When you begin to move from a *'fixed mindset'* to a *'growth mindset'* by understanding how truly controllable our skill & abilities are, you'll remove this learning speed killer & you'll learn - almost anything - faster.

Simply put, those who feel a greater sense of personal control of their learning, thrive.

Have the courage to step into control, develop a *'growth mindset'*, remove this obstacle & begin to learn faster.

3 | SLOW FEEDBACK SPEED

> *"You don't learn to walk by following rules. You learn by doing, and by falling over"*
>
> - *RICHARD BRANSON*

As we first discussed back in section 1, the speed in which our mind connects an *action* with a *result* to form a *feedback loop* has a massive impact on our learning speed.

FEEDBACK SPEED

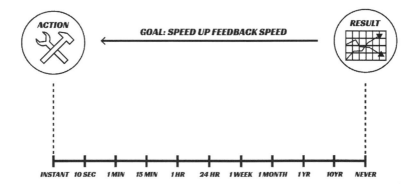

Which makes *slow feedback speed* a big killer of learning speed in itself. The good part is this is yet another obstacle you can remove to accelerate your learning speed.

The way you remove this obstacle is by putting in tracking measures that allow you to quickly link *action* & *result*.

Think about the young child that touches a hot pan *(action)* & *instantly (speed of feedback)* gets the physical pain of getting a finger burned *(result)*.

Or think about the basketball player seeing how his footing impacts his ability to effectively shoot hoops.

Whenever he tests a new footing position (new *action*) & shoots the ball, he *instantly (speed of feedback)* gets back a new *result* as interpreted from the movement of the ball.

Both are examples of *'near-instant'* feedback speed.

And while some topics or skills have quick feedback speed built into them, others don't.

That's when you have to create your own *tracking measures* to support your mind to learn faster.

Remember, the goal is to move away from 'never' feedback (as you can see on the right side of the visual) & move towards 'instant' feedback (as you can see on the left side).

The faster your *feedback speed* is, the faster you'll learn.

EXERCISE: INCREASING FEEDBACK SPEED
Take a topic or skill you're developing (or looking to develop in the future) & brainstorm ways you can increase your *feedback speed* within it.

Take 3 minutes right now & brainstorm ways you could add tracking measures, such as ongoing surveys, feedback forms, rankings, scoring or video reviews, to increase feedback speed, remove this obstacle & learn anything you choose faster. Then, continue.

4 | DISTRACTION

> *"Success at anything will always come down to this: focus & effort. And we control both"*
>
> - *THE ROCK*

We all know that focus is a critical part of success - a topic we've covered quite a bit so far - yet few people realize that one of the fastest & most effective ways to increase focus is by consciously removing distractions.

Distractions are a big killer of learning speed because they bring you out of focus, bring you out of flow & break you out of the powerful forward momentum you may be in.

Yet, this is a tougher challenge than ever. As today...

| We live in a distracted world

Particular studies, conducted in 2013, showed the average attention span of a human being is just 8 seconds. That's 1 second *less* than the attention span of a goldfish.

A large part of society - especially in more technologically advanced countries - gets distracted dozens of times every hour. Phone calls. Constant notification. Hundreds of emails. More advertisement than ever before.

And while in itself these aren't problems, they quickly become problems when we allow them to distract us from focusing on our learning, skill development & productivity.

Other studies show when you're distracted, you temporarily lose IQ points.

Now, of course, we know that IQ doesn't matter much outside of success in the education system, however, it's fascinating to find that simply being distracted can cause such an effect on our mental processing power & intellect.

The study concluded that when you're multitasking (a lack of focus), it's like you just lost 10% of your IQ.

And if 10% doesn't sound like a lot, that same study shows when someone is stoned (on drugs; baked out of their mind) they lose only 5% of their IQ.

Yes, when you're distracted - specifically, multitasking - you're essentially stoned. On drugs. Actually, it's like you're stoned twice; that's the impact of distraction.

While this a great start to data that shows the effects of distracted, it is, once again, data that we don't really need as the above is obvious & logical. Distraction - & lack of focus - lowers performance. And in the context of learning & skill development, it kills your *learning speed*.

As to how you can remove distraction, much of this we've already covered in previous sections, specifically in the chapter about *strategic allocation* & the subchapter about *immersion*. However, beyond that, know that...

| Focus is a trainable skill

Like developing any skill, at first, sustaining focus over a longer period of time is hard. If the longest you've ever done something with complete focus is 20 minutes & you're stretching yourself to be fully focused for 1 hour, your mind is going to get uncomfortable as you're entering new, uncharted territory.

However, just like any habit, it gets easier over time. It becomes easy for you to just sit down, lock in on an objective & get it done (fully focused; no distractions). It gets easier as you train this ability; the ability to focus.

When you do, you'll become not just less distracted in your work, but also in your learning & skill development, which will reduce the effect of this obstacle.

5 | LACK OF CLEAR STRATEGY

"Failing to plan is planning to fail"

- *ALAN LAKEIN*

A recurring theme of this book is *intention*. It's because the world's highest achievers - across all fields, topics, skills, professions & industries - tend to approach learning, skill development, opportunities, interactions & decisions with greater *intention* than others. They're more *intentional*.

They don't hope for good luck or good fortune, rather they create their own luck through strategy & intention.

They don't hope things will just work out, rather, they *intentionally* skew the odds of success in their favour.

It's very hard to *guarantee* (meaning; 100% chance of success, 0% chance of failure) success at anything. There are just too many variables we can't control.

And it's why I implore you to take great caution of anyone - or anything - that *guarantees* you an outcome.

With that said, we can *always* skew the odds of success at anything in our favour.

If you picture the future as simply an infinite number of possibilities streams, then education, learning, skill development & self-mastery are the processes that increase the odds of a more positive future being formed.

It's all about increasing the odds of the positive (good) possibility streams turning into reality while reducing the odds of the negative (bad) possibility streams happening.

For example, the wisdom of *'look right, look left, stop, look & listen'* applied before crossing a road increases the odds of a future in which your body is fully-functional while avoiding this guidance increases the odds of a future in which you're in a wheelchair after being hit by a car.

That guidance doesn't guarantee you won't get hit by a car, but it *massively* skews the odds of success in your favour.

When we lack *intention* in our actions, we leave our future in the control of luck, good fortune or '50:50' odds, which slows down our learning, skill development & achievement.

However, when we are *intentional* about our actions, it allows us to strategically skew the odds of faster learning, skill development, mastery or success in our favour.

And a huge part of this is *strategic planning*; the process of figuring out what you want (ambitions) & planning the steps you're going to take to get there (actions). Doing this - strategizing - naturally raises your level of *intentionality*.

And it why those who go into their learning or skill training with a plan (strategy) for improvement tend to learn faster.

This prioritization of strategic planning removes confusion (the bad type of *'confusion'*) & accelerates learning, while a lack of planning & strategy kills your learning speed.

Before going into a learning situation, take time to plan.

What is your intention to learn from this class? What is your motive? What obstacles could come up & how could I deal with them now - in advance - so they don't come up?

How can I get myself in a great pre-learning state?

How can I apply all the acceleration & optimization tools in this section to learn & progress more effectively?

What steps do I need to take? And, in which order?

These are the questions you should be thinking though as part of your planning before entering a learning situation.

Just like a great chess player is a few steps ahead & moves each piece to skew his odds of victory in his or her favour, you too can maximize your learning, skill development & success by raising your level of *intentionality*.

Don't let this learning speed killer, a lack of strategy - or any other one we've discussed - limit your learning.

These 5 obstacles we've discussed in this chapter can derail people in a big way, but with this new awareness, you can avoid that. And instead - by avoiding these obstacles - you can truly seize your fullest learning potential.

The goal is to set ourselves up for the greatest levels of skill, success, happiness, health, love, joy & fulfillment in our lives. And that happens one step at a time. Each & every concept, methodology, strategy, tactic, practice & habit skews our odds of success in our favour.

4.

INTEGRATION:
BECOME EXTRAORDINARY

"What is easy to do is also easy not to do"

JIM ROHN

Learning should never stop with awareness or understanding. Rather, it should always continue through to the ultimate phase of learning, integration. Because it's only once you implement & effectively integrate new learnings into your life - when that new information becomes a way of life - that's when people really follow through, do what others put off for 'later' or 'tomorrow' & turn their dreams into reality. That's the type of learning that can truly change the course of somebody's life.

15 | POWER OF INTEGRATION: THE ULTIMATE LEARNING STEP

"Action is the foundational key to all success"

- PABLO PICASSO

This is the shortest, yet perhaps, most important section in this entire book.

Not because it's the most informational, most content-rich or even the best-written section, rather because it's the section in which we talk about the *implementation* & *integration* of everything we've covered so far (as well as everything you already know but aren't implementing).

It's the section in which we get out of the clouds of philosophy, mindset & higher-level thinking & ground everything in deep practicality.

This is the section in which we get our hands dirty, made new decisions & strategize about how you can implement everything from the last 3 sections to achieve great results.

If you've been passively reading up until now, this is a chance to pause, reflect & make some new decisions about your learning, skill development & life going forward.

And this is the section I believe a lot of books, lectures, training programs, events & teachings are lacking.

Because while good ideas, philosophies & understandings

are great, without implementation (action) they fail to create any bottom-line results.

And without *integration* - the *consistent, ongoing* implementation of that which we have learned - dreams remain dreams. *Action is the foundational key to success.*

At the end of the day, if results were based on what we *know* (the intellectual information, knowledge & wisdom we possess) our lives would be very different than they are.

For example, most people know - *intellectually* - how to get fit. They may not know everything, but they know a lot.

They know they need to exercise regularly. To eat well. To stay active. To avoid foods (or drinks) that are unhealthy. To get quality sleep. However, while there are literally millions (if not billions) of people that intellectually know these basics, they aren't fit & healthy.

Obesity rates are through the roof. Two out of every three Americans are considered overweight or obese.

Clearly, intellectually knowing something - without doing anything about it - isn't enough to get results.

In that same way, most people know how to build great, strong friendships, relationships, & family relations.

They know that they should be honest, be trustworthy, do what they say without breaking their word, have presence in their interactions & have a deep care for others.

Intellectually, a huge portion of people on the planet know this, yet, so many people burn bridges with people around them & aren't consider to have great relationships in life.

The simple reason that explains these scenarios is that we don't achieve results based on what we intellectually know, but rather on what we actually do.

Without *action*, dreams remain dreams. However, with action, energy & effort, now dreams can turn into reality.

However, beyond this, even *implementation* isn't enough. It's not enough to do something *once*. Rather, the key is...

INTEGRATION: BEYOND IMPLEMENTATION

"Action is the real measure of intelligence"

- *NAPOLEON HILL*

Success is not the result of what you do once. Success is not a 1-time thing. It's not created through 1 big breakthrough, 1 grand action or 1 big moment.

Rather, it's the result of doing the right things *consistently*.

It's that accumulation of little things coming together that create amazing results.

"It's the little details that are vital. Little things make big things happen" - John Wooden

It's about consistency. It's about day-in, day-out focus.

"Success isn't owned. It's leased, and rent is due every day" - J. J. Watt

Just like you don't get ripped by going to the gym once, you don't become extraordinary by doing something once.

It takes more than *implementation*; it requires *integration*.

Integration, simply put, is the *consistent* implementation of what you know. It's about *consistently* doing the right things & making them the norm - a way of life - for you.

However, there is a massive disconnect (caused largely by the education system) between learning & doing.

People believe that because they've learned something (intellectually understood it) they know it. They don't.

True knowledge of something is the application of that information. And you don't ever really know something unless you've acted on (implemented) that information.

And the ultimate level of learning is not *awareness* (being aware of something). It's not *understanding* (a deep intellectual understanding of something). It's not even *implementation* (doing something once). The ultimate level is *integration* (consistent implementation).

2 GOALS FOR LEARNING & LIFE

"Without continual growth and progress, such words as improvement, achievement, and success have no meaning"

- *BENJAMIN FRANKLIN*

I believe we have 2 goals & objectives for learning & life:

1. **Expand Awareness** (to learn as much as we can)
2. **Expand Results** (to integrate what we learn)

The first is to learn as much as we possibly can. To become as aware as we possibly can. To gather as much knowledge, experience & expertise as we can throughout our life.

The second is to do the best we can with what we know. To best put what we know (awareness) into practice & to be consistent & congruent with what we believe, know & say.

This is the also one of the biggest reasons why some people are so popular, loved & trusted, while others aren't. Those who are *congruent* - what they believe & say is aligned with what they actually do - tend to have this great appeal.

However, it's important to understand that both of these 2 goals for learning & living are critical & work together.

Firstly, ignorance is *not* bliss. Ignorance limits potential. By *not* expanding your awareness, you're limiting your ability to live an extraordinary life filled with options, opportunities & possibilities.

However, at the same time, holding a toolbox full of state-of-the-art tools (awareness, information, knowledge & wisdom) but not using those tools to actually achieve what you want isn't effective either. Both parts are crucial.

It's why, going forward - every day, every week, every month & every year - 1) continue to *expand awareness* & 2) integrate *(expand results)* as best as you possibly can.

Don't let a lack of effort limit you. As *Michael Jordan* said:

"The game has its ups and downs, but you can never lose focus of your individual goals and you can't let yourself be beat because of lack of effort"

Every day, make this your big-picture to-do list:

1) **Learn** (expand awareness)
2) **Integrate** (expand results)
3) **Learn** (expand awareness)

4) **Integrate** (expand results)
5) **Learn** (expand awareness)
6) **Integrate** (expand results)

You get the point. However, it doesn't come automatically. Like success in general, these 2 things don't just happen. Rather, it requires work. It requires effort to execute these.

First, you must continue to learn. As we discussed all the way back in chapter 1, the world's highest achieving people are those who tend to continue their education forever. For them, it doesn't stop after they finish school, rather it's an ongoing, never-ending process of *'expanding awareness'*.

You've got to continually immerse yourself in new learning. Research topics. Research new fields. Read books. Watch trainings. Attend events. Spend time with people who know what you may not. Simply put, *never stop learning*.

Secondly, get adamant about *integrating* what you learn. Whenever you learn anything, ask yourself:

'How can I implement this?'

It's like the teachability index concept we covered before. You must be both, willing to learn, & willing to make changes in your life by *integrating* what you learn.

Nearly anything is possible, but it requires *awareness* & it requires *work*. It doesn't just happen; it's a process.

16 | CREATING LASTING CHANGE: INFORMATION INTO RESULTS

"Change is the end result of all true learning"

- *J.P. MORGAN*

We all have things that we want to change (improve at) in the topics we learn, the skill we train & the life we lead.

Change, as we've discussed, is a part of life; it's a constant.

However, how do you consciously create change in your life? And, how do, not just create change, but, make that change stick? How do you make it last?

Every year we watch people make New Year's Resolutions, only to break them a few days later & return back to old habits. Despite good intentions, their change doesn't stick.

We watch people commit to never drink alcohol again or to never smoke another cigarette in their life. Or commit to wake up early, exercise regularly or eat better. They have the intent to change, but only a small percentage of those intentions actually stick & last over time.

So, how do we create, not just change, but lasting change?

And, specific to learning & skill development, how do you make your intentions stick & your changes last, so you can progress, improve & become extraordinary?

In this second-last chapter, we're going to demystify & understand how change actually works, what steps it goes through, as well as, how you can stack the odds in your favour to make your change last.

If you really want to get the most out of your learning & skill development, this is a critical understanding we must have. And it's what will help you better implement (& *integrate*) everything we've covered in this book so far.

4 STEPS TO LASTING CHANGE

"There is nothing permanent except change"

- *HERACLITUS*

All *lasting change* goes through the same 4 steps:

STEP 1 | AWARENESS

It starts with awareness. It's impossible to consciously create lasting change at something if you're not aware of the problem (or the better option available to you).

It's the reason that 'admitting you have a problem' (awareness) is the first step in the 12 steps to overcome alcoholism, the first step in the 5 steps to overcome addiction, as well as in most other step-by-step programs.

And even if you don't have a problem - for example, you're improving (changing) something which is already good - the first step is still *awareness* as you need to know (be aware of) some type of new option, opportunity or possibility available to you. If you don't know a better way exists you can't consciously create lasting change.

| Awareness is always the first step to anything

It all starts with new *awareness*. Which is yet another reason why *'expanding awareness'* is goal 1 in the 2 goals of learning & life we discussed in the last chapter.

It's because *awareness* opens up more potential. The more aware you are of what's not working (problem, issues, challenges) & of new options, possibilities & opportunities in your life, the greater the potential to improve & thrive.

And when it comes to implementing what you've learned in this book - or any other one - know that this book has already given you a huge amount of new *awareness* of what you can change & improve to learn faster, train like the best & become extraordinary at anything. However...

| Awareness creates the potential for change, but doesn't, in itself, create change.

For change to really happen, the other steps are required...

STEP 2 | COMMITMENT

Commitment; a desire or decision to change something.

Just because someone is aware of a new possibility (new *awareness*) doesn't mean that they have the desire or motive to change (in other words, they lack *commitment*)

For example, someone may be aware that they are an alcoholic (*awareness*) but may have no desire to actually change this (*commitment* - a lack of it).

To consciously make any sort of positive change in your life, you must *decide* to make it. You must have some sort of purpose, passion or motive that drives you to change.

And specifically in this context, this is an opportunity for you to really think back over the last 3 sections of this book & decide about the changes you're committed to making.

Are you committed to finding what you're passionate about? Committed to levelling-up your discipline? Ready to decide & commit to approach each learning situation with greater innovation; a seeking of constant growth?

Are you committed to changing how you approach failure, feedback or responsibility in your life?

Are you committed to testing the 9-step learning process?

Are you committed to implementing greater immersion, intentional difficulty & effective rest & recovery into your learning & skill development? To become more teachable? To develop your 'growth mindset'? Be more intentional?

As you can see, there's a lot you can change - improve - as a result of the *awareness* you may have gained over the last 3 sections. However, to progress & make that change real, you must go beyond step 1 (*awareness*) to step 2 (*commitment*). You have to decide to change it.

Which brings us to the third step that each & every change anyone has ever made goes through...

STEP 3 | ACTION

You must take some type of new *action* to make an actual change. It's obvious. It's simple. But, it's a critical part of these 4 steps to *lasting change*. Before you can do anything consistently - form a habit - you must first do it once.

As we talked about, results aren't created as the result of what we *know*, rather as a result of what we do (*action*).

To make a change, you must go beyond *awareness*, go beyond *commitment* & step into *action*; actually doing it.

And, it's this step that creates *change*.

When you've turned that commitment to go to gym into an action. You were committed to the gym & did what you said you would do - you actually went - *change* occurred.

However, while these 3 steps may create *change*, they don't create *lasting change*. For that, the last step is required...

STEP 4 | INTEGRATION

Integration is about turning a change into a habit - & recurring action - in your life.

It's about turning a 1-time action into a way of life; a new, consistent way of operating.

It's that moment when a former smoker no longer calls themselves a 'smoker' because that's not part of their identity or routine anymore. It's the moment when an alcoholic stops seeing themselves as an 'alcoholic'.

The moment when a change becomes your new 'norm' is when *integration* happens & *lasting change* is created.

It's the moment when running in the morning is no longer the hard thing to do - something outside of your normal routine (way of operating) - but rather is something that you do automatically with little resistance. The point where it's become a habit (a way of life) is when it's *integrated*.

Integration is the critical step. It's about turning that which you have implemented - done once - into something that you continue to do as part of your new way of living.

And this is where the importance of the change cycle & consciously forming habits comes in...

THE CHANGE CYCLE & BUILDING HABITS

"The first step towards getting somewhere is to decide you're not going to stay where you are"

- *J.P. MORGAN*

Beyond the 4 steps, all change goes through a *cycle of difficulty*. Meaning, a change shifts difficulty over time.

At first, any change you make is actually easy. Very easy in fact. Think about the first few days of the year & how easy it is for people to fulfil their New Year's Resolutions.

Day 1 (January 1st) is usually a walk in the park; it's easy. And usually has a very high completion rate. *But why?*

It's because of the *excitement* that comes from making a new change. Day 1 of making a decision to, run every day, go to the gym, quit smoking, ride your bike to work or pretty much anything else, is usually easy because the *excitement* of making that decision is still very present.

That's where the cycle starts. The first day tends to be the easiest. The following few, slightly harder, but still easy.

And then the cycle tends to go downhill fast.

Day 5, 12 or 17 of making a decision to change something isn't so easy anymore. There's more resistance & it takes a lot more willpower & discipline to actually follow through.

Why? Simply put, the *excitement* of making that decision has long worn off. That buzz from the New Year (or whenever day 1 was) has long faded away.

However, beyond the hardship of day 11, 14 or 18, over time, the cycle moves back up & change gets easier.

Day 45 tends to be easier than day 15. Day 51 is easier than day 18. And, day 71 is usually easier than day 12.

The reason is we - human beings - are creatures of *habit*.

And over time, a change becomes more habitualized (a strong habit in our life). *Integration* starts to kick in making a change easier. Making it the new norm.

And as a change turns into habit - part of how we operate 'normally' - the resistance begins to fade away.

Our mind stops seeing it as hard but rather views it as 'normal'. It views it as the *default* way of operating.

Think about it. Brushing your teeth or showering probably aren't very difficult thing to do every day. Chances are, you have little-to-no resistance to make those changes happen consistently. Why? It's because they are *a way of life.*

In fact, it would probably take more motivation & discipline to *not* brush your teeth - or shower - for a few days, than it will to do those habitualized actions.

These changes have been *integrated* into your life. You've done them so long that they are strong habits in your life.

And if something is aligned with your 'way of life' - your normal way of operating - it stops being a challenge.

When you see yourselves as someone who doesn't run every day, yet you set the commitment to run, there's resistance because this behaviour is outside your norms of living. It's not a habit yet. However, if you've run every single day for the last 2 years, now *not* running is actually harder, while doing the run in the morning is easier.

Why? It's because, after 2 years of day-in, day-out running, it's become a strong habit. It's become *a way of life.* It's so strong that you can't even imagine a day without running. It's deeply *integrated* - the 4th step to change - in your life.

Hence, after a certain period of time, the cycle will change & go back in the other direction; towards greater & greater ease. As the change you're making becomes more habitual, it becomes easier & easier, until it's near effortless to do.

When it comes to forming habits, research shows it takes 66 days to form one. Although other research says it takes 30 days & other studies show it takes as long as 90 days.

The reason these numbers differ so widely is because of the change itself, as well as the environment & context around the person making that change.

Rule of thumb: it takes 30 - 90 days to form a habit.

However, just like anything else, the process of forming new habits in your life (*integrating* change) can also be improved, optimized & accelerated. Here's how...

1. **Timing.** Studies show that doing the behaviour you want to habitualize at the *same time of the day every day* will help you turn it into a habit faster.

2. **Consistency.** If you're consistent - you don't miss days - the habit will form faster.

3. **Reinforcement.** If you reinforce your actions well, they will also form habits faster.

   Which is another reason why 'celebration' is a powerful part of the 9-step learning process. Celebrate. Reward yourself. Give yourself a pat on the back. Tell yourself *'you're awesome'*. It doesn't have to be big, however by powerfully reinforcing the action, you can form a habit more efficiently.

4. **Track progress.** This builds upon the previous point about reinforcement. If you're tracking - just like in the feedback speed concept - your mind can better link *action* to *result*, which further reinforces the behaviour, turning it into a habit faster.

5. **Counting The Days.** This an incredible strategy when you're beginning a new change.

   1 day completed. 5 days down. 10 downs without a cigarette. 20 days without a drink. 30 days of daily exercises. 45 days of daily journaling. By counting the day, you're further reinforcing your actions, making them easier to continue to do.

However, while this is effective at first, it's also something that, beyond a certain point, loses its effectiveness & can actually hurt you.

This is because if something is truly *a way of life* - a long-term, lasting change in your life - you don't need to count the days anymore as there's nothing you're counting too - or away - from.

If anything, at a certain point, counting the days actually makes it harder for things to become deeply habitual parts of our lives, as counting days assumes you're doing something for a certain period of time, rather than something everlasting.

So if you want to make any type of change, start by counting the days, but at a certain point, stop, & recommit to make it a way of life. A consistent ongoing change. Then it will become even more deeply integrated (step 4) in your life.

In summary, at first, a change is easy as it's driven by the *excitement* of doing something new. It's a little like when you buy something new. At first, the excitement drives you to take extreme levels of care & caution for that new thing you now own. But, over time, this excitement fades away.

And, as that excitement fades, it gets harder to continue. Which is the point where many people quit the change they want to make & go back to the way things were.

Don't be one of those people; be like a high achiever & follow through, knowing it will get easier. Knowing that the change cycle will swing back & that change (new action) will become easier over time.

We know this based on extensive research, as well as from the understanding of how habits are built & operate.

Which is why after this hard point, the change cycle shifts & change becomes increasingly easy to the point where most resistance is gone & the change has been *a way of life* (the norm; a deeply *integrated* part of your life).

Think about change as a tree. It starts as a seed. And, wind (external resistance) will have a hard time knocking over a seed as it's a seed (it's covered by a coat of excitement).

However, as your seed turns into something - as your tree begins to grow & is no longer protected by the ground - now the wind will have a better chance of knocking it over.

The wind represents the resistance. It represents your old ways of being attempting to pull you back. It represents your survival instincts (your reptilian brain) that are attempting to protect you. It represents your old urges, attachments, habits & ways of operating.

During this early stage when the tree is visible, but still very small, is when the wind is most likely to knock it over. The excitement has faded away, however, your new change (your new habit) is still weak. It's still new. It's not habit.

Which is why most people won't quit on day 1 or day 2 of a new change, but will most often quit during that period between day 5 & day 30. Although this too varies depending on the change you're making.

However, over time, as your tree grows bigger & it's rooted deeper into the ground, now the odds of the wind blowing that tree over go down dramatically.

Think of habits as the roots of the tree. If you've done something every day for 10 years, the roots of that action are very deep & it's harder to change. It's also harder for resistance such as peer pressure, a bad day or a stressful situation to knock that tree over as the roots are so strong.

It's the reason it would be infinitely harder (near impossible) to convince someone who's been a vegetarian for 4 years to eat meat, while it's far more likely someone who's been a vegetarian for 4 days will quit & eat meat.

The wind is like the pressure that we talked about in the last section & pressure can mess with the change cycle.

For example, if day 1 of a new change, it's raining outside, while day 7 it's a beautiful sunny day, this external pressure will change the difficulty & alter the change cycle.

Fortunately, this pressure (the wind) will have little effect on you if your tree (your roots) are very strong. If you've run every single day for 3 years, rain won't stop you. A snowstorm (massive pressure) might, but rain won't.

It's why we must work on our habits (the deep integration of what we do) to strengthen the roots & make change *last*.

IMPLEMENTATION & INTEGRATION SPEED

"A true champion can adapt to anything"

- *FLOYD MAYWEATHER, JR*

The last - yet, also important - thing we must consider when implementing, integrating & creating lasting change in our lives is our speed at which we go through the steps.

Some people learn something, but don't do anything with that new information (*expanded awareness*) until 5 years later. While others are like implementation machines; they learn something & 10 minutes later implement it.

We must strive to accelerate our, not just learning speed, but *implementation & integration speed*; to accelerate the process from step 1 (awareness) to step 2 (commitment) to step 3 (action) to step 4 (integration).

And we accelerate the speed of the whole by accelerating the speed of the parts. We must filter our thoughts when learning through questions like:

How can I take this information (awareness) & make new decisions I want to live by (commitment)? How can I increase the speed between awareness & commitment?

How can I take quick action on my decisions; quickly move from decision (commitment) to action (step 3)?

How can I use the 'accelerated habit-building techniques' discussed in this chapter & speed up the process from action (step 3) to integration (step 4)?

By accelerating each part individually, you'll accelerate the *implementation & integration speed* of the whole process.

And for obvious reasons, those who take new awareness & put it into practice *fast* tend to outperform those who gain awareness, but rarely - & slowly - apply it. And know that...

| Success loves speed

Speed creates incremental advantages that, combined, lead to a huge advantages. And, speed boosts momentum.

Remember: the ultimate level of learning isn't awareness but implementation (& better yet, integration). And, even when creating change, it's beneficial that we look to improve, optimize, heighten & accelerate the process.

IT'S TIME TO DECIDE

"The secret of getting ahead is getting started"

- MARK TWAIN

Don't read passively. Now's an opportunity for you to pause, reflect & boost your implementation speed.

EXERCISE: MAKING NEW DECISIONS
It's time to implement. There's no point of waiting until you finish reading to think about action. It's time for implementation to become an ongoing filter of thinking.

Of everything we're covered in this book, what are the 3 biggest things you want to implement quickly?

Take 2 minutes right now & write down the 3 decisions - 3 changes - you want to make as soon as possible.

Why 3? Why not 100? It's because...

| Change requires focus

One of the other challenges with New Years Resolutions (& their shockingly low success rates) is that people decide to, in 1 day, eat better, go to the gym every day, reconnect with their extended family, be a better partner, grow their business, learn 2 new languages, train their guitar skills at least 20 minutes per day, walk their dog every day, read 1 book per week & meditate daily.

They've never done any 1 of these things consistently, yet somehow they let the hype of New Year's let them believe they're going to make all these changes at the same time.

The issue is that they're attempting to juggle 10 different balls, which too often, causes all of them to drop & fail.

They fail to notice *change requires focus.* It requires energy, focus & effort to change 1 behaviour (let alone 10).

Just like we talked about at the beginning of section 2 when we discussed about time allocation, too often people scatter themselves too much to make any change last.

And that's often what we do when making decision to change. We attempt to change everything all at once. Instead, we must be more focused. Change a few things (or better, focus on 1 big thing that will create a ripple effect across everything else in your life). Then, move on.

As those changes become increasingly habitual (less resistance), begin to make new decisions (new changes).

However, find those prioritizes & work on them first. And best, find the 'domino's' in your life that once you figure out will have an effect on everything else in your life.

Either way, it's time for us to step up into new, higher levels of implementation (& *integration*) of that which we learn. It times for us to value, not just knowledge, but action, as action is what will create the life we want.

17 | BECOME EXTRAORDINARY: RECAP & ACTION-PLAN

"I think it is possible for ordinary people to choose to be extraordinary"

- *ELON MUSK*

I congratulate you for getting here. The fact you're reading these words shows me a lot about you.

Most of all, it shows you're a *'finisher'*. You're not someone who starts something, quits & moves onto something new the next shiny object.

You're not a quitter, but a *finisher*; someone who finishes that which they start.

Which is also an incredible tell - indicator - of success. It's those who have built up a habit of completing that which they have started that tends to outperform & outachieve others. Hence, congratulations on this as well.

And now - thanks to your commitment to read, explore & learn from this book - you have powerful insights you can use to learn anything faster, train your skills just like the world's best & a path to follow to become extraordinary at whatever you choose to do.

You have the understandings & tools you need to become extraordinary. Or, in other words...

YOU HAVE THE RULES OF THE GAME

"The key to growth is the introduction of higher dimensions of consciousness into our awareness"

- *LAO TZU*

The purpose of this book was simple.

And that purpose was *not* to tell you what to do.

What someone should do depends so much on someone's ambitions, preferences & circumstances, that giving individual guidance in a book is near-impossible.

Rather, the purpose was to give you the rules of the game.

In the words of Albert Einstein,

"You have to learn the rules of the game. And then you have to play better than anyone else"

The purpose of this book was to give you the rules of the game in the areas of learning, skill development, mastery & extraordinary levels of performance.

To give you all the critical psychological, philosophical & practical understandings you need to deeply understand what makes people extraordinary at what they do.

And, think of this book like a map. It maps out how you can become truly extraordinary at what you do, but it doesn't tell you what to do as that type of instruction is dependent on where you currently are in your life, where you want to get to, what drives you & what makes you tick.

And it's your job to plug your current reality, ambitions & preferences into this map you've been provided to better, more effective trek towards the life you want.

People don't achieve more because of natural born gifts, 'innate talents,' superior genetics or good luck; they achieve more because they know the rules of the game & play that game better than everyone else.

It's pretty hard to do well & 'win' (achieve what you want) if you don't know the rules of the game & you're just trekking blindly without any clue about the game you're playing.

What you now have - if you've been paying attention - is the rules of the game for faster learning, skill development & extraordinary levels of skill. You have the rules for achieving mastery at what you & become one of the best in the world at what you do (if what's what you want).

Which puts you ahead of 99% of people on this planet who don't have the rules yet, or have an incomplete set of rules.

While everybody's ambitions may be different. And even the topics & skills they want to become extraordinary at may be wildly different, the rules to become extraordinary stay - in most parts - the same.

It's because the rules you now have are the universal success principles that work across all topics, skills, professions & industries & will continue to work over time.

And that's what this book was written to give you. The rules of the game. To give you clarity. You give confidence.

To give you an action-plan you can use to become extraordinary at anything you choose.

A RECAP: A PATH TO EXTRAORDINARY

"There is only one corner of the universe you can be certain of improving, and that's your own self"

- *ALDOUS HUXLEY*

If you're here - reading these words - you'll probably agree, it's been a wild journey we've been on together in this book.

A long - but worthwhile - journey of exploration, discovery, demystification, intention, strategy & alignment.

We've covered a lot. I guess that's just what you get when you attempt to compress 5 years of research, study & testing into 1 book. However, let's reminisce a little bit.

I want you to deeply understand the stuff in this book (not just know it), recall it effectively & be most likely to integrate it into your life (hence this recap).

As you first opened this book, it probably built up some curiosity, expectation or even excitement inside you.

As human beings, we tend to go into a new opportunity with a sense of curiosity & expectation about what we could possibly emerge with on the other side.

You may have even though to yourself, *'learn faster, train like the best, become extraordinary at anything; that's pretty ambitious - sounds like a big ask for a book'.*

However, you took the leap. You took action. You trusted that this book would help you discover some things that you may not have previously known. You were teachable. Curiosity. Willing. Committed. I congratulate you for that.

And as you first entered this new world we've laid out here, you started with your entry into it. You started with...

THE INTRODUCTION

For starters, we talked about the power & importance of skill. We talked about the amazing correlation between skill & success, as well as how the world's highest achievers are also, not coincidentally, the world's most skilled people.

We talked about how skill is the greatest power & how it leads to new, higher levels of income, impact, reach, confidence, self-belief & power in our lives.

We talked about how learning is a gift. That the capacity to learn is something we're born with & should be grateful for. However, *the ability to learn effectively* (optimally) isn't a gift & is something we must work at to develop. It's a skill in itself. And, it's the ultimate skill - the meta-skill - in life.

| The skill of 'learning' is the ultimate skill

If you become a great learner, you can become skilled at anything you choose to become great at.

We then laid the groundwork for getting maximum value out of this book & continued onto...

SECTION 1 | UNDERSTANDING

We started by making sure we were on the same page.

We know that the world's highest achievers think differently & we started discussing those thinking patterns (mindset) of the world's highest achievers.

We talked about how *achievement is a science*. And that success (or, mastery) isn't as mystical as we may have been misled to believe. We emerged knowing that...

| If anyone has ever achieved anything you want to achieve it means you can achieve it too

We also talked about how we are an *accumulative species*. We - humanity - thrive, in big part, because we're able to work together & build on the discoveries, understandings & findings of others. It's what makes us so extraordinary.

After that, the focus was on giving you back control over your future (specifically, your capacity to learn anything).

We walked through many of the misconceptions people have been misled to believe about learning, skill development & extraordinary achievement.

And how factors such as innate talent, natural born gifts, IQ, genetics, DNA, experience or success in the education system have little-to-no correlation to real-world success.

It's time for all to step up into greater personal power & control over our destiny. In the words of Abraham Lincoln:

"The best way to predict your future is to create it"

It's time for us to live life how we design it, not how others want to design it for us. We must step into this power.

We then deconstructed learning to fully understand how it works (something most people don't know). You learned about distinctions & how it's the accumulation of little distinctions coming together that makes someone progress from a beginner, to an amateur, to professional, to a master to someone who's world-class at what they do.

You learned about the power of nuances, feedback loops, how your mind processes information (mental bandwidth), chunking, skill isolation & integration, as well as how everything comes together to make you extraordinary.

SECTION 2 | FOUNDATIONS

We talked about how everybody is, technically, 'skilled' (good at something), yet it's how they've allocated their time during their life that makes the difference.

We also discussed *specialization* & how the world has given us greater opportunity than ever before to spend our time doing that which we love.

Then, we covered the 3 foundations of mastery:

1. **Passion:** The Fuel Of Pursuit
2. **Discipline:** The Driving Force Of Work
3. **Innovation:** The Seeking Of Growth

The 3 keys that all masters share (without exception).

I implore you to memorize these 3 keys. Hang them on your fridge, above your desk & on your bathroom mirror. These 3 are so critical & form the foundation of all skill development. In fact, you even heard stories of how the world's highest achievers apply these 3 keys to thrive.

Then we talked about failure, feedback & responsibility.

Another powerful trio. This time, based on the powerful mindset shifts you can make that will make a massive positive shift in your life. So, challenge yourself.

From this point forward, commit to fall in love with failure, embrace feedback - seek it - & take full responsibility knowing that when something is your fault, that's a good thing as it gives you the power to shape it how you please.

And we finished by walking through the 9-step learning process; a strategy 9-step plan to learn anything faster.

During this section we laid powerful foundations you can begin to use to, not only learn faster, but also live a better quality of life; one filled with new, higher levels of achievement, happiness, joy, confidence & fulfilment.

However, we weren't done. We continued onto...

SECTION 3 | ACCELERATION

Anything can be improved, optimized, heightened & accelerated & there is always a better, faster, most effective way to do anything in our lives.

We first covered 3 strategies for faster & better learning:

1. **Memory Triggers**
2. **Emotional Learning**
3. **Learn To Teach**

And then walked through 5 powerful strategies for faster & better skill development (modelled of the world's best):

1. **Pre-Learning State**
2. **Coaching & Mentoring**
3. **Immersion**
4. **Train Hard To Ease Execution**
5. **Rest & Recovery**

And wrapped up with the 5 learning speed killers. We discussing how you can remove each one of these obstacles to further accelerate your growth & progress.

It's my belief that human potential is near boundless. And research & evidence continues to support this; that human potential really is near boundless & that nearly anything is possible with the right thinking, strategy & action.

And when we approach our life with this thinking, it opens up floods of new possibilities & opportunities for us.

And this all brings us to where we are right now...

SECTION 4 | INTEGRATION

The shortest, yet perhaps, most important section because it's the section you get to make some new decisions.

We talked about how implementation (or better yet, *integration*) is so critical & is the ultimate level of learning.

And, you learned what really makes change *last*.

And with that, I want to say...

If you loved this book, don't thank me. While I may be the one curating this, putting it all together & sharing it, this book is largely built on the back of the research, study & analysis of the world's highest achievers.

It's inspired by those people who already trekked the way to extraordinary levels of skill. I'm simply the analyst & messenger who took their life stories, life principles, beliefs & actions, & turned them into a book that shares it all with you in simple, step-by-step, way that allows you to achieve whatever it is that you desire.

However, if you hated this book, I want to apologize for misrepresenting & ineffectively deconstructing the proven principles & field-tested research that works over & over again. Please blame *me* for the lack of clarity, detail or practicality; not the research, study or intent behind it.

Either way, I hope this book has given you greater awareness of what's possible. That it has helped lift your level of ambition; to really believe that anything is possible.

However, more than that, I hope this book has allowed you to see this unlimited potential we have, not as an optimistic, delusional belief, but rather as a practical, strategic, evidence-backed, understanding of progress, improvement, innovation & life as we know it.

WHAT HAPPENS NOW: BUSYNESS OF LIFE

"It is not enough to be busy. So are the ants. The question is: What are we busy about?"

-   HENRY DAVID THOREAU

I must warn you: unless you're reading this book in a forest or at the top of a mountain, the moment you finish it & put it down, the world is going to jump back at you.

The busyness will return. Often, almost immediately.

And life will want to drag you into what's urgent & must be done right now. Things will attempt to distract you. Or, bring you back to where you were before reading this book.

And as days, weeks, months & years go on, there will be countless low priority tasks for you to complete. Countless squeezy chairs that need to be greased up, countless new movies (or shows) that you 'must-watch' & countless other distractions that will want to pull you away from learning your topic, cultivating your skills & honing your craft.

Low priorities will beg you to give them some attention, but you must remember the greatest upside comes from focusing on what's truly important in your life.

It's why I remind you that which you already know: don't let them. Don't let low priorities sabotage your upside.

Don't let 'busy work' prevent you from fulfilling the dreams that will bring you the most happiness, joy & fulfilment.

Instead, be focused. Get clear on what you want & set yourself up to win. Be present. Be committed. Take awareness & turn it into *integration* (a way of life).

Don't put your ambition to become extraordinary (or, even more extraordinary than you are today) off until 'the perfect time' as the perfect time rarely exists.

It's rarely convenient to change your life & make tweaks that will help you live the life you want to live.

Hence, do it anyway. Don't wait for the right time, instead, make the time right. Be focused. Think at a higher level. And, just get started. Step by step. Knowing it's the little things accumulated together that make you extraordinary & allow you to lead an extraordinary life.

LET ME LEAVE YOU WITH THIS...

> *"The future belongs to those who believe in the beauty of their dreams"*
>
> *-   ELEANOR ROOSEVELT*

One does not become extraordinary overnight; success is the result of day-in, day-out, action & implementation.

Success isn't something you do once & move onto something else; it's a process. It's a journey.

And so is becoming extraordinary. One does not become extraordinary by doing something once & moving onto the next thing. Being extraordinary - & reaping all the upside that comes along with it - is the result of passion, discipline, intention, ongoing innovation & the day-in, day-out doing of the things others are not willing to do.

It's not easy. And it's why so few become truly masterful at what they do. Most settle. They settle for comfort, conformity & safety. And there's nothing wrong with that (if that's what they want), but if there is a desire inside you - a deep down drive for something more - than it's your mission to pursue that. To never quit. To never back down. But rather, to strive for greatness with tenacity & focus.

The path to success isn't a mystery. It's been figured out. But knowing something & actually doing it, are - as you know - are 2 wildly different things.

| To be in the top 10%, you have to do things differently than the 90%

Or, in the words of Mark Twain:

"Whenever you find yourself on the side of the majority, it is time to pause and reflect."

The world's highest achievers do things differently. And they're willing to do the things others aren't. They commit & follow through until they achieve that they were after.

Some may say they're too obsessed, or they're crazy to be that dedicated to something, but to those high achievers, it's not crazy at all. It's the only way they would ever want it. It's like a calling. A purpose. That's what really creates success, joy, fulfilment & extraordinary achievement.

It's not easy, but it's worth it. And it comes down to the implementation & willingness to go on the journey.

It has been a great privilege to share everything in this book with you. Nothing makes me happier.

Now, I implore you to take action. To make some new decisions about how you can take what you learned here & apply (integrate) it all into your life.

This is me calling you out to step into your true greatness.

Approach life with intention, strategy & willingness.

Be willing to do what others are not willing to do. Do that which you know will give what you want long-term.

And learn topics, train skills & overall, live life, in such a way that you, when you're old, you're not filled with regret for what you 'could've,' 'should've' or 'would've' done, but rather, you can look back with joy & ecstasy for the life that you've lived, the topics you've learned, the skills you've developed, the extraordinary abilities you've cultivated & the amazing life you have led. Live like that; live that way...

This book is dedicated to the people who have supported me most, for the longest, on my journey.

To my dad, who ignited my entrepreneurial spirit and inspired me to chase my dreams, just like he chases his.

To my mum, who has always been there to care for me, love me and support me, fully and unconditionally, even when it wasn't easy or convenient to do so.

To my brother, who fills my life with more enjoyment, fun, and energy that he would ever know.

You all support me, challenge me and inspire me every day. I'm grateful for every moment we get to spend together.

ABOUT THE AUTHOR

Bogdan believes that human potential is near boundless & that almost anything is possible with the right thinking, strategy & action. It's why he has dedicated his life to leveling the education playing field *(re-shaping how we all learn)* & demystifying the understandings that one needs to achieve their ambitions. He does this by taking complex, yet powerful, concepts & simplifying them for anyone to implement to achieve their dreams.

He focuses on the science of achievement, consistently challenging the status quo & deconstructing what *really* creates achievement & fulfillment. He believes in focusing on that which is proven & will continue to produce results, for anyone *(irrelevant of gender, race or upbringing)* over the long term. Bogdan approaches achievement with an *optimization mindset*, looking for ways anyone can get the greatest long-term results, the fastest, with least resistance.

He does that through his books, programs & in-person work with audiences, customers & clients worldwide.

Bogdan Juncewicz is the author of multiple books & international speaker who has spoken on stages across 3 different continents, teaching thousands & thousands of people worldwide. Including multi-millionaires, TEDx speakers, musicians, teachers, Lyme disease survivors, entrepreneurs, gym owners, Reiki masters, and more.

As well as founder & CEO of 2 businesses, which serve fans, readers, customers & clients spanning 4 continents.

He has more than 5 years of real-world, regular 100-hour work weeks, experience, studying & teaching topics, such as accelerated learning, skill development, motivation, productivity & accelerated achievement. His teachings are grounded in years of study in the fields of neuroscience, psychology & human behavior.

Bogdan made a choice to drop out of high school at age 14 to start his own businesses & figure out what makes people achieve extraordinary results. And he's frickin' glad he did.

After dropping out, age 14, he became an achievement coach, coaching his first clients, and now, clients pay him upwards of $2995 for 1-to-1 coaching and consulting.

He's also the host of *The Accelerated Achievement Show* & the man behind the content & marketing of other top influencers, businesses & brands teaching wellness, self improvement, business, finance & more.

Author. International Speaker. CEO. High School Dropout.

You can learn more about his mission & work over at **BogdanJuncewicz.com**

Throughout history, we have been told that certain things just aren't possible. That they can't be done. That they are, in fact, impossible.

Roger Bannister & the 4-minute mile. The Wright Brothers & flight. Henry Ford & the car. Alexander Graham Bell & the phone. Thomas Edison & the light bulb. Apple & the personal computer. Martin Luther King Jr. & The Civil Rights Movement.

All of these things - & countless others - at one time in history were considered impossible.

Yet, somehow, with the right drive, strategy & action, we - human beings - achieved them. We beat the odds & achieved the seemingly impossible.

Human potential is near boundless & almost anything we can think about, we can achieve. Based on what we know about success, it's almost never easy, but, it's, almost always, worth it.

Deep down we know this. We know that we have great power to do nearly anything we could ever think about. We know that human potential is near boundless. But sometimes, we, ourselves, fear this great power inside ourselves. We fear how much power we have & what would happen if something goes wrong. We can fear - it's an important human instinct that has it's time & place - but, we mustn't let fear stop us chasing what we want.

It's time for us to pursue the future even more courageously, armed with new understandings, strategies & capabilities. We must continue to step into the light of possibility & pursue that which we really want to bring into our lives.

Made in the USA
Columbia, SC
09 March 2019